Hypnotic Induction

The age-old notion of 'hypnotic induction' receives a fresh look from notable scholars from Canada, England, Sweden, and the USA in this book. These scholars represent a breadth of theoretical perspectives: cognitive-behavioral, Ericksonian, psychoanalytic, and trance-state. It is well known that a wide range of hypnotic induction protocols is used to prepare individuals to enhance their receptivity to test or clinical suggestions. However, despite its popularity of use, it appears that little is known about its relevancy and boundary conditions either for testing for hypnotisability or for enhancing clinical efficacy. In this volume, the authors reflect on issues surrounding its definitions, relevancy, possible components, and approaches; they also suggest considerations and strategies for optimizing inductions. This book will be of benefit to both newcomers to the field and seasoned researchers and clinicians alike – it can stimulate new thinking and research about this important, but often taken for granted, notion of hypnotic induction.

This book was originally published as a special issue of the *American Journal of Clinical Hypnosis.*

V. K. Kumar is Professor of Psychology at West Chester University of Pennsylvania, USA. He is a Fellow of the APA Society of Psychological Hypnosis.

Stephen R. Lankton is Editor-In-Chief of the *American Journal of Clinical Hypnosis*. He is a Fellow of the American Society of Clinical Hypnosis.

Hypnotic Induction

Perspectives, Strategies and Concerns

Edited by

V. K. Kumar and Stephen R. Lankton

Routledge
Taylor & Francis Group
LONDON AND NEW YORK

First published 2018 by Routledge

2 Park Square, Milton Park, Abingdon, Oxfordshire OX14 4RN
52 Vanderbilt Avenue, New York, NY 10017

Routledge is an imprint of the Taylor & Francis Group, an informa business

First issued in paperback 2019

British Library Cataloguing in Publication Data
A catalogue record for this book is available from the British Library

ISBN 13: 978-1-138-10456-3 (hbk)
ISBN 13: 978-0-367-32174-1 (pbk)

Typeset in Times New Roman
by RefineCatch Limited, Bungay, Suffolk

Publisher's Note
The publisher accepts responsibility for any inconsistencies that may have arisen during the conversion of this book from journal articles to book chapters, namely the possible inclusion of journal terminology.

Contents

Citation Information

The following chapters were originally published in the *American Journal of Clinical Hypnosis*, volume 59, issue 2 (2016). When citing this material, please use the original page numbering for each article, as follows:

Guest Editorial
The Paradox of Induction
V. K. Kumar
American Journal of Clinical Hypnosis, volume 59, issue 2 (2016), pp. 123–127

Chapter 1
Hypnotic Induction: Enhancing Trance or Mostly Myth?
David B. Reid
American Journal of Clinical Hypnosis, volume 59, issue 2 (2016), pp. 128–137

Chapter 2
What Can a Hypnotic Induction Do?
Erik Woody and Pamela Sadler
American Journal of Clinical Hypnosis, volume 59, issue 2 (2016), pp. 138–154

Chapter 3
Nuances and Uncertainties Regarding Hypnotic Inductions: Toward a Theoretically Informed Praxis
Devin B. Terhune and Etzel Cardeña
American Journal of Clinical Hypnosis, volume 59, issue 2 (2016), pp. 155–174

Chapter 4
Conscious/Unconscious Dissociation Induction: Increasing Hypnotic Performance With "Resistant" Clients
Stephen Lankton
American Journal of Clinical Hypnosis, volume 59, issue 2 (2016), pp. 175–185

Chapter 5

Perspectives on Pathways to Induction: Confronting Unexpected Challenges
Richard P. Kluft
American Journal of Clinical Hypnosis, volume 59, issue 2 (2016), pp. 186–203

Chapter 6

Induction Technique: Beyond Simple Response to Suggestion
Arreed Barabasz and Marianne Barabasz
American Journal of Clinical Hypnosis, volume 59, issue 2 (2016), pp. 204–213

Chapter 7

A Comparison of Hypnotic Induction, Task Motivation, and a "Cold Start" Control Group on Hypnotizability
Stephen Krystek and V. K. Kumar
American Journal of Clinical Hypnosis, volume 59, issue 2 (2016), pp. 214–230

The following chapter was originally published in the *American Journal of Clinical Hypnosis*, volume 59, issue 4 (2016). When citing this material, please use the original page numbering for each article, as follows:

Chapter 8

The Hypnotic Induction in the Broad Scheme of Hypnosis: A Sociocognitive Perspective
Steven Jay Lynn, Reed Maxwell and Joseph P. Green
American Journal of Clinical Hypnosis, volume 59, issue 4 (2016), pp. 363–384

Notes on Contributors

Arreed Barabasz, Professor of Counseling Psychology, Washington State University, is the editor of *The International Journal of Clinical and Experimental Hypnosis*. He has won numerous awards including the *Distinguished Contributions to Scientific Hypnosis Award* from the APA Society of Psychological Hypnosis.

Marianne Barabasz is Professor of Counseling Psychology, Washington State University. She is a recipient of the *Distinguished Contributions to Professional Hypnosis Award* from the APA Society of Psychological Hypnosis.

Etzel Cardeña holds the endowed Thorsen Chair at Lund University, Sweden, which includes hypnosis in its remit. His areas of inquiry include the neurophenomenology of hypnotic experience, personality correlates of hypnotizability, hypnosis for traumatic conditions, and cultural aspects of hypnosis.

Joseph P. Green is Professor of Psychology at The Ohio State University in Lima, OH, USA. He has published over 65 articles and chapters focusing on myths about hypnosis, attitudes and expectancies, and integrating hypnosis into treatments for smoking.

Richard P. Kluft, MD, PhD, is Clinical Professor of Psychiatry at Temple University School of Medicine and teaches at the Psychoanalytic Center of Philadelphia. A Fellow of both ASCH and SCEH, in his other life, he is a novelist.

Stephen Krystek is a Measurement Analyst at the National Board of Medical Examiners, USA.

V. K. Kumar, Professor of Psychology, West Chester University of Pennsylvania, is a Fellow of APA and the Society of Clinical and Experimental Hypnosis. He is a former President of the APA Society for Humanistic Psychology.

Stephen R. Lankton, an ASCH Fellow and Editor-in-Chief of the *American Journal of Clinical Hypnosis*, received two *Lifetime Achievement Awards*, trained therapists worldwide since 1979, and published 18 clinical books. He was fortunate to have studied for several years with Milton Erickson.

Steven Jay Lynn, Distinguished Professor of Psychology (SUNY), has published more than 380 books and articles in the areas of hypnosis, dissociation, memory, trauma, and psychopathology. He is a former president of the hypnosis division of the American Psychological Association.

Reed Maxwell, PhD, Postdoctoral Associate of Psychology in Psychiatry with the Personality Disorders Institute at New York Presbyterian-Weill Cornell Medical College in New York, NY.

David B. Reid is a Licensed Clinical Psychologist who works in a private practice in Fishersville, Virginia, USA.

Pamela Sadler is Professor of Psychology at Wilfrid Laurier University, Ontario, Canada, and a registered Clinical Psychologist. Her research on individual differences in hypnosis reflects a broader interest in the dynamics of social interaction and its positive and negative outcomes.

Devin B. Terhune is a Senior Lecturer in Psychology at Goldsmiths, University of London, UK. He is a Fellow of the Society for Clinical and Experimental Hypnosis and an Associate Editor of *Consciousness and Cognition.*

Erik Woody is Professor Emeritus of Psychology at the University of Waterloo, Ontario, Canada, where he served for several years as the Director of Clinical Training.

INTRODUCTION

The Paradox of Induction

V. K. Kumar

Foremost, I express my appreciation to Stephen Lankton, Editor-in-Chief of the *American Journal of Clinical Hypnosis* (*AJCH*) for inviting me to serve as guest editor for this special issue on induction. I also take this opportunity to express my appreciation to everyone who contributed to the special issue and worked with us under severe time constraints.

My interest in induction goes back to my training days when I took careful notes of all the clever words and phrases workshop leaders used in "inducing" hypnosis. Indeed, many of my fellow workshop participants did the same, and it is not uncommon to see workshop attendees looking for the precise magical combination of words to induce their clients into a trance to obtain involuntary responses.

An adage says "the pen is mightier than the sword," despite the historic and current state of the world, which suggests otherwise. However, health care professionals engaged in the business of producing change recognize the importance of appropriately phrased messages to establish rapport and produce motivational sets and expectancies for their clients to help accept the idea of making efforts to change. We use words, phrases, and images to do the same prior to, during, and after a hypnotic stage of treatment to establish rapport and produce motivational sets and expectancies for our clients.

The use of the term "induction" to demark the preliminary steps to establish hypnosis makes intuitive sense; we as therapists recognize the need to warm up and ease clients into suggestions so that hypnotic responses occur. However, matters are not so simple—the two words "induction" and "trance" have been debated for years, both for their definitions and need. These terms are often taken for granted as relevant and important to hypnosis. For example, Lankton (2015) found the American Psychological Association (APA) Division 30's definition of induction, "a procedure designed to induce hypnosis," as "tautological" (p. 368). He further reflected, "Does induce mean 'add to client's experience' or alter it, or deny it, (help) shift states, or does it not even involve the client's experience at all?" (p. 368). Similarly, trance, often understood as a "special state," is characterized by altered states of consciousness, attention, absorption, and suspension of critical thinking that facilitates the production of suggested responses involuntarily or sub- or un-consciously. A persistent issue is whether or not induction is a necessary and/or sufficient condition for trance states to occur. And, if we call the actions taken prior to establishing a trance state "induction," then what are its requisite components?

In general, experimental evidence for the impact of induction on enhancing responsiveness to suggestions is weak. It appears that induction is neither necessary nor sufficient to enhance responsiveness to suggestions. It has been argued that induction does not produce a special state; rather, it helps create a positive set and expectancies to respond in particular ways (Barber & De Moor, 1972; Kirsch, 1985). The demand characteristics of being in a "hypnosis" session itself may suffice to produce a "hypnotic" response. While inductions are intended to make participants responsive to test suggestions, it may be argued that responding to suggestions themselves may have further inducing (deepening) or "de-inducing" properties via successful or failed responding. Further, the effects of induction are not uniform across types of individuals or types of suggestions. Indeed, items' pass rates vary on standardized assessment instruments despite the use of inductions. *Ordinarily*, it is not easy to determine if responses are 'hypnotic," i.e., experienced classically as effortless and involuntary (Weitzenhoffer, 1974). This is because such reported subjective experiences might themselves be colored by demand characteristics and cultural expectations.

Inductions take many forms—they may involve asking participants to close their eyes, take deep breaths, relax (any number of scenarios are used), become more focused, let things happen, count (e.g., from 20 to 1) as a way of deepening, go up or down an escalator, experience feelings of being in a trance state, etc. Inductions even involve repetitive suggestion of the aforementioned sort. They may be long or short, tailored to individuals or even generally scripted, and with or without elaborate imagery.

Some investigators have argued that there are different types of trances (Barber, 1981) and different types of responders to hypnosis (Barber, 2000; Barrett, 1990, 1996; Forbes & Pekala, 1996; Terhune & Cardeña, 2010, this issue). What is interesting is that even when all participants receive the same induction, practitioners get different types of responders. These types of results suggest that no matter what one does, people respond according to their abilities and interpretations of the situation, induction instructions, and test or clinical suggestions. The results of induction seem to depend upon multiple factors: participants' abilities, motivations, expectancies, and the therapists' skills in establishing a relationship and conveying suggestions. Further, the various responder types (e.g., amnesia-prone, dissociaters, inward attention, or the relaxation types; Barber, 2000; Barrett, 1990, 1996; Forbes & Pekala, 1996; Terhune & Cardeña,

2010) are possibly not tidy, discrete categories. Identification of such putative types requires prior assessment and cumbersome scoring procedures; it is well documented that clinicians are reluctant to incorporate assessment procedures in their practice. The clinical use of such typologies must await further developments (Kumar, 2010).

We need more empirical research on induction including its value, its methodologies (direct, indirect, passive, active-alert, physical activity), and its role in achieving trance depth. What type of induction is helpful and when? How does one establish when an adequate trance depth has been achieved to produce the response that could be called truly hypnotic and therapeutic? Does it matter whether or not responses to suggestions fit the definition of the classic suggestion effect in order to be clinically effective? Is all communication basically hypnotic, particularly when the session is defined as hypnosis? In this special issue, we have internationally reputable scholars from Canada, England, Sweden, and the United States reflecting upon induction from different perspectives.

David Reid questions "the legitimacy of the term 'hypnotic induction' and its derivatives" and considers the possibility that such terms may inadvertently help perpetuate myths and misconceptions of hypnosis. He also examines the implications of the language of hypnosis, for example, "Can you really *hypnotize* someone?" "How can you tell if someone is in *hypnosis?* [italics in original]" He argues if the purpose of induction is to facilitate, elicit, or evoke a response, then the word induction (to cause) may not be quite the right word.

Erik Woody and Pamela Sadler consider why induction may or may not be a relevant topic. They argue that genuine hypnotic responding is not a result of imagination but is a result of change in the sense of agency, the classic suggestion effect; thus, they argue for separating the "hypnotic" response from other types of responses. They present a "work sample" perspective on induction as a procedure to set the initial stage or the context for the participant to know as to what skills and strategies are required to perform the "to be suggested" tasks. Their perspective includes Michael Nash's notion of induction as a preamble, but it also includes everything that happens up to when the first test or clinical suggestion is given. They discuss possible ways induction can help hypnosis in terms of the cues they offer to how responses are to be enacted, the nature of interpersonal interactions to be expected, provide meta-suggestions, and allow for a clear transition for new behaviors to emerge.

Terhune and Cardeña lament the practice of induction is based on dated concepts and "uninformed by recent developments in theory and research." They stress that "uncertainties abound" with respect to what constitutes an optimal induction, what are its essential elements, and its necessity. They examine research on suggestibility, spontaneous phenomenology, neuropsychology, and cognition and "call attention to the relatively impoverished state of knowledge" with respect to induction. They also discuss the notion of optimizing inductions for various types of suggestions and responders.

Stephen Lankton discusses Erickson's non-authoritarian naturalistic induction in contrast to a ritualistic approach. Natural induction requires "Speaking the client's own experiential language" (Erickson, 1958, as cited by Lankton, this issue), accepting the situation, and utilizing it to facilitate "reassociation of experiences." It integrates induction and therapy. Erickson's approach often involved storytelling, confusion techniques, encouraging dissociation between the unconscious and the conscious mind, and varying voice tones to reinforce the dissociation so as to discourage linear, conscious type thinking that contained learned experiences that served as source of resistance to suggestions for therapeutic experiences. Lankton provides the language for encouraging such dissociation (conscious/unconscious dissociation suggestion) and elaborates on his states of consciousness model and its usefulness in induction and therapy.

Richard Kluft argues that the process of induction may be "more complex and nuanced" than the way it is typically presented in workshop settings. He is concerned that induction is taught similarly to professionals from different disciplines, and that such oversimplification may produce failures for the clients and for the therapists who may, as a result, prematurely give up the practice of hypnosis. He calls for congruence between a therapist's practice modality and the nature of induction used. He reflects on the important question, "When does a hypnotic induction actually begin?" He discusses the importance of expectancies, events prior to diagnosis (e.g., whether the patient had experienced trauma or not), therapeutic alliance and the real relationship, and elements of transference in creating induction strategies that may be more effective than the use of formulaic approaches.

Arreed Barabasz and Marianne Barabasz make a case for the use of induction. They differentiate between a simple response and a veracious hypnotic response and convey the idea that a response is not due to hypnosis if the participant is not hypnotized. They argue that merely generating expectancies is insufficient during an induction; rather, certain things need to be attended to in order to obtain a veridical hypnotic response. They identify three phases of induction and give specific suggestions on what to do (and what not do) during each phase.

Stephen Krystek and I present an experimental study that compared trance induction, task-motivational instruction, and a "cold-start" control group that was simply told "we will begin the hypnosis procedure now." We found no significant differences among the three groups on the Barber's Creative test of imagination and Fields Inventory Scale of Hypnotic Depth. Our findings are predictable from sociocultural perspectives of cultural expectancies.

Both academics and clinicians will find a plethora of useful materials in these articles. Hopefully, they will stimulate a broad discussion and research on this age-old concept of induction and its boundary conditions for appropriate use for subsequent issues of *AJCH*. Some might argue that the progress in hypnosis has been slow, but consider how long it took for an abacus to turn into an electronic computing device or a landline phone to turn into a wireless smart phone.

References

Barber, T. X. (1981). Innovations and limitations in Erikson's hypnosis. *Contemporary Psychology*, *26*, 825–827.

Barber, T. X. (2000). A deeper understanding of hypnosis: Its secrets, its nature, its essence. *American Journal of Clinical Hypnosis*, *42*, 208–272. doi:10.1080/00029157.2000.10734361

Barber, T. X., & De Moor, W. (1972). A theory of hypnotic induction procedures. *American Journal of Clinical Hypnosis*, *15*, 112–135. doi:10.1080/00029157.1972.10402228

Barrett, D. (1990). Deep trance subjects: A schema of two distinct subgroups. In R. G. Kunzendorf (Ed.), *Mental imagery* (pp. 101–112). New York, NY: Plenum Press.

Barrett, D. (1996). Fantasizers and dissociaters: Two types of high hypnotizables, two different imagery styles. In R. G. Kunzendorf, N. P. Spanos, & B. Wallace (Eds.), *Hypnosis and imagination*. Amityville, NY: Baywood.

Erickson, M. (1958). Naturalistic techniques of hypnosis. *American Journal of Clinical Hypnosis*, *1*(1), 3–8.

Forbes, E. J., & Pekala, R. J. (1996). Types of hypnotically (un)susceptible individuals as a function of phenomenological experience: A partial replication. *Australian Journal of Clinical and Experimental Hypnosis*, *24*, 92–109.

Kirsch, I. (1985). Response expectancy as a determinant of experience and behavior. *American Psychologist*, *40*, 1189–1202. doi:10.1037/0003-066X.40.11.1189

Kumar, V. K. (2010). Reflections on the varieties of hypnotizables: A commentary on Terhune and Cardeña. *Consciousness and Cognition*, *19*(4), 1151–1153. doi:10.1016/j.concog.2010.04.006

Lankton, S. (2015). A SoC model of hypnosis and induction. *American Journal of Clinical Hypnosis*, *57*, 367–377. doi:10.1080/00029157.2015.1011461

Terhune, D. B., & Cardeña, E. (2010). Differential patterns of spontaneous experiential response to a hypnotic induction: A latent profile analysis. *Consciousness and Cognition*, *19*, 1140–1150. doi:10.1016/j.concog.2010.03.006

Weitzenhoffer, A. M. (1974). When is an "instruction" an "instruction?" *International Journal of Clinical and Experimental Hypnosis*, *22*, 258–269. doi:10.1080/00207147408413005

Hypnotic Induction: Enhancing Trance or Mostly Myth?

David B. Reid

Hypnosis has often, and primarily, been portrayed as a mystical means that controls and exploits vulnerable and defenseless people. Sources accused of perpetuating hypnosis myths and misconceptions have included numerous media productions and stage demonstrations at state fairs and festivals. Ironically, one largely unexamined potential culprit disseminating misinformation about hypnosis is the field of clinical hypnosis itself. This article not only questions the legitimacy of the term "hypnotic induction" and its derivatives but also explores the potential impact these terms have on the perpetuation of hypnosis myths and misconceptions. Through an examination of a selective history of hypnotic induction, the customary language of hypnosis, and information promoted by professional hypnosis societies, some of the contributing terminology is identified. Alternative terms that more appropriately embody the manifestation of trance are offered and discussed.

Hull (1933/2002) studied *it*, Erickson individualized *it* (Erickson, 1958; Erickson, Rossi, & Rossi, 1976), others quantified *it* (Shor & Orne, 1962; Weitzenhoffer & Hilgard, 1959, 1962), and professional hypnosis societies offer training opportunities for mastering *it* (American Society of Clinical Hypnosis [ASCH], 2016; Society for Clinical and Experimental Hypnosis [SCEH], 2016). *It* is the subject of this special issue of the *American Journal of Clinical Hypnosis* (*AJCH*). *It* is hypnotic induction.

Since 1950, the terms "induction" and/or "induce" have appeared in the titles of 76 articles published in the *AJCH* and 84 articles published in the *International Journal of Clinical and Experimental Hypnosis*. Obviously, this term has been, and continues to be, embraced and promoted as an essential component of hypnosis. Furthermore, pragmatic techniques intended to bring this term to life have been taught at regional and national workshops sponsored by clinical hypnosis societies for several decades. Specifically, there is the eye-roll technique (Spiegel & Spiegel, 1978), hand and arm levitation induction (Erickson, 1958), eye fixation technique (Spiegel & Spiegel, 1978; Weitzenhoffer, 2000), Chiasson's induction (Chiasson, 1973), conscious/unconscious dissociation induction (Lankton & Lankton, 1983/2008), progressive relaxation induction (Kirsch, Lynn, & Rhue, 1993), and alert hypnosis induction (Wark, 2006, 2015), to name only a few.

Interestingly, with the exception of the eye-fixation and eye-roll technique espoused by Spiegel and Spiegel (1978), there has been minimal empirical investigation of seemingly essential techniques for "producing" trance. Nevertheless, the *Standards of Training in Clinical Hypnosis* (Hammond & Elkins, 2005), published and advocated by ASCH, proposes a minimum amount of time to be dedicated to induction techniques, including didactic seminars and "in-vivo" supervised practice opportunities, for attendees of their Basic Workshop (60 and 240 minutes, respectively) and their Intermediate Workshop (60 and 180 minutes, respectively).

So apparently there you have it: Hypnotic induction techniques, mastered through practice and supervised experiences, and the subject matter of hundreds of peer-reviewed publications over the years, is apparently essential for hypnosis. Indeed, after the establishment of rapport, hypnotic induction has generally been considered the second in a series of necessary steps when using hypnosis (Hammond & Elkins, 2005). This is what I was taught, what I taught others, and what I practiced for many years. Then I read Laurence Sugarman's guest editorial introducing the January 2015 special issue of the *AJCH* dedicated to the nature and domain of hypnosis. Sugarman's words gave me pause, and his invitation to respond to articles published in that special issue prompted the writing of this article nearly 1 year later.

With the closed journal resting on my lap, I contemplated and questioned all that I understood about hypnosis, and more importantly, all that I *did* (or *thought I did*) when assisting others using hypnosis. I considered the concept of "hypnotic induction" and wondered: Does the term "hypnotic induction" truly characterize what we do during hypnosis? Does this term inadvertently perpetuate myths and misconceptions about hypnosis? And if so, should we adopt an alternative term that more accurately conceptualizes the apparent process that facilitates trance? Or, perhaps, should we abandon the term entirely, along with any notion that we as therapists or supposed "facilitators" of trance *do* anything *to* anyone during hypnosis?

I believe answers to these questions warrant a critical examination of the following: (1) hypnosis myths and misconceptions, (2) a selective review of the history of hypnotic inductions, (3) the language of hypnosis (emphasized by italics henceforth), and (4) education/training provided by professional clinical hypnosis societies and organizations.

Hypnosis Myths and Misconceptions

Fifty years have passed since Kroger (1963) opined that the general public feared losing control during hypnosis (e.g., "I will reveal secrets"; "I will do things against my will"). Despite persistent efforts of clinical hypnosis societies (e.g., ASCH, SCEH), professional psychological organizations (e.g., APA Division 30, Psychological Hypnosis), and trained clinicians promoting the health and behavioral benefits of clinical hypnosis, this therapeutic intervention remains misunderstood, poorly accepted, and underutilized (Lynn, Rhue, & Kirsch, 2010; Thomson, 2003). In a survey of 272 adults evaluating public opinion about hypnosis, Johnson and Hauck (1999) found that 55% of those surveyed believed that the therapist controlled hypnosis, and 50% maintained that during hypnosis a person could be made to do things they would not ordinarily do.

Negative attitudes concerning hypnosis have been promulgated by multiple sources including silver screen productions (i.e., *The Manchurian Candidate, Silence of the Lambs*), children's cartoons (i.e., *Scooby Doo, Robin Hood, Jungle Book*), and sensational hypnosis stage shows where seemingly entranced volunteers involuntarily quack like ducks (Pratt, Wood, & Alman, 1988). At the very least, hypnosis has been portrayed as controlling and exploitive of defenseless, vulnerable people. Or worse, perceived as a nefarious key that unlocks a nebulous portal to the human mind, permitting satanic and unholy possession (Barrett, 2006).

A Selective History of Hypnotic Induction

In one form or another, hypnosis has been practiced throughout recorded history and traced back 4,000 years to the ancient Egyptian priest and pyramid architect, Imhotep (Osler, 2004). Inscriptions on walls of sleep and dream temples dating to Imhotep's time tell of supposed cures by Egyptian priests who *induced* trance-like states that cast out "bad spirits," offering relief to the suffering (Osler, 2004). It was also the Egyptians who introduced magnets and magnetized objects to produce therapeutic "sleep states" 2,000 years before Mesmer filled his first tub with water, iron filings, and powdered glass (Bonwick, 1878; Edmondston, 1986).

John Joseph Gasner, a German priest and exorcist, gained notoriety for his alleged cures of patients suffering from epileptic convulsions (Laurence & Perry, 1988). Relying on techniques compelling the devil to manifest his presence though hypnotic phenomena, Gasner *expelled* the evil deity through a patient's extremities (Sheehan & Perry, 1976).

Best known for his writings and promotion of *animal magnetism*, some sources suggest that Mesmer likely plagiarized the writings of William Maxwell for his own self-promotion (Francher, 1990; Pattie, 1994). Mesmer eventually abandoned his theory concerning magnetic fluid (i.e., artificial tide) and maintained that "mesmeric" passes of his hands over a patient's body was sufficient for *producing* cures.

Consistent with his reputation of being a flamboyant showman, Mesmer reportedly "mesmerized" a tree outside his offices, permitting the underprivileged to touch the "entranced" tree and benefit from his *transferred curative energy* (Hammond,

2013, emphasis added). Eventually, Mesmer constructed oak tubs, or baquets, resembling shallow, modern-day hot tubs that served as conduits for healing. While sitting in a tub of "mesmerized water, powdered glass, and iron filings," patients were "magnetized" by Mesmer, or one of his assistants (Hammond, 2013, emphasis added).

During these sessions, Mesmer observed that some individuals were either unresponsive, seemed to enter into a deep sleep, or were minimally responsive, presumably due to personality traits or hereditary factors (Bowers, 1983; Morgan, Hilgard, & Davert, 1970). In essence, according to Mesmer, the facilitator was given credit for any positive treatment outcomes, while limited or no benefits were attributed to the patient.

Mesmer's work was eventually discredited in 1784. King Louis XVI appointed a "blue ribbon" commission from the Faculty of Medicine to investigate animal magnetism. This commission, chaired by Benjamin Franklin, concluded that Mesmer's methods were ineffective, and any cures or benefits could be attributed to the *power of the magnetizer's will* and the imagination of the subject (Franklin et al., 1784/1965, 2002). In their report, the Commissioners described patients' responses to animal magnetism techniques: "All *submit to the magnetizer*; even though they may appear to be asleep, his voice, a look, a signal *pulls them out of it*" (Franklin et al., 1784/1965, 2002, p. 335, emphasis added).

The Marquis de Puysegur, a student of Mesmer, focused his attention on "artificial somnambulism," a relaxed, hypnotic, sleep-like state (Ellenberger, 1970; Laurence & Perry, 1988). Adhering to the magnetic theory of his mentor, the Marquis utilized light physical touch and passes over the head and stomach and a light stroke over the eyes to facilitate eye closure (Edmondston, 1986). He also emphasized the importance of "rapport" between the hypnotist (magnetist) and subject and maintained that *the will of the doctor* was the catalyst for creating observed hypnotic phenomena (Hammond, 2013). Unfortunately, at the time of de Puysegur and well into the next century, hypnosis became increasingly associated with paranormal, mystical and spiritualistic phenomena.

James Braid (1795–1860), a Scottish surgeon of high repute practiced "auto-" or "self-hypnosis" and discovered the natural psychophysiological mechanism underlying the genuine effects of what he referred to as "neurypnology" and eventually "hypnosis" (Braid, 1843). Using self-hypnosis, Braid demonstrated that the experience and benefits had nothing whatsoever to do with the "gaze," "charisma," or "magnetism" of the operator or any magnetic agency whatsoever. Hammond (2013) described Braid's work as "a major contribution in the progression of hypnosis away from the use of mesmeric passes and magnetic fluid theory, and toward an emphasis on relaxation, [and] the use of *induction techniques* resembling modern methods" (p. 184, emphasis added). Braid (1845) maintained that hypnosis "is most readily *induced by causing the patient* to fix his thoughts and sight on an object, and suppress his respiration" (p. 627, emphasis added).

Sigmund Freud's brief, but reportedly potent, association with the prominent French neurologist, Jean-Martin Charcot (who inaccurately concluded that hypnosis was a form of hysteria) influenced his conceptualization of different levels of consciousness and the capacity of people to access the unconscious mind. Freud used hypnosis from 1887–1892 and was reportedly criticized by his peers for being "only a hypnotist" (Hammond, 2013, p. 187). He eventually abandoned hypnosis for several reasons, including concerns that he "could not succeed in *bringing more than a fraction of his patients into a hypnotic state*" (Hammond, 2013, p. 187, emphasis added).

The Language of Hypnosis

"Can you really *hypnotize* someone?"
"How can you tell if someone is *in hypnosis*?"
"That song is so *hypnotic*."
"Do you want to *do hypnosis* or *be hypnotic*?"
"I'm not a *hypnotist*, I'm a *hypnotherapist*."
"I don't *hypnotize people*, I help them *hypnotize themselves*."

Based on these comments, uttered during a Basic Workshop by attendees and faculty at the most recent annual ASCH conference, hypnosis can be separately and/or simultaneously referred to as a process (*hypnotize*), a state of being or consciousness (*in hypnosis*), externally influenced (*hypnotic*), and an identity (*hypnotist/hypnotherapist*). From my unintended eavesdropping, it seems the term "hypnosis" is either a versatile one that defies congruence, or as Hope and Sugarman (2015) opined, "without a clear distinction and context … [the term hypnosis] becomes nearly meaningless" (p. 212). Hope and Sugarman also posited that "hypnosis is merely a skill set that perpetuates and influences trance" (2015, p. 212). I wholeheartedly agree.

In an effort to mitigate theoretical bias regarding the domain of hypnosis, the American Psychological Association, Division 30 (Society of Clinical Hypnosis), offered what is arguably a more concise definition of hypnosis than those previously forwarded by the Hypnosis Definition Committee (HDC):

> A state of consciousness involving focused attention and reduced peripheral awareness characterized by an enhanced capacity for response to suggestion. (Elkins, Barabasz, Council, & Spiegel, 2015, p. 6)

The HDC's efforts provide a step in the right direction when it comes to establishing a common ground for disparate theoretical orientations. At the same time, I concur with Stephen Lankton's (2015) reaction to their revised definition: "it seems that we are still using the same card deck of terminology and just arranging the cards in a different order" (p. 367). And while Lankton's metaphorical "card deck" specifically refers to the 2003 HDC definition of hypnosis (Green, Barabasz, Barrett, & Montgomery, 2003), I contend that his "deck of terminology" extends beyond this single reference and readily applies to the first time the term "induction" was associated with hypnosis. In essence, we have been playing with the same "deck" for a very long time. Sadly, my attempt to unearth an original source pairing the terms induction and hypnosis were unsuccessful.

With regards to the issue of hypnotic induction, the HDC offered the following definition:

> A procedure designed to *induce* hypnosis. (Elkins et al., 2015, p. 6, emphasis added).

In his editorial, Lankton (2015) criticized the HDC's depiction of "hypnotic induction" as being, "thin and lacking in a type of insight … [and perhaps] merely tautological" (pp. 367–368). Lankton stops short of suggesting a dismissal of the term altogether. Though how could he, since "induction" and its derivatives routinely appear in peer-reviewed hypnosis literature, textbooks (including two of my own), and training programs sponsored by clinical hypnosis societies and organizations?

While perusing several dictionaries, I was able to discern that the origination of the word "induction" derives from the Latin term "inducere," meaning "lead into" (Oxford Dictionary). The following definitions were also retrieved:

Induction:	the formal act or process of placing someone into a new job, position, government office, etc.; the act of causing or bringing on or about (Induction, n.d.b).
Induction:	the act of inducing, bringing about, or causing (Induction, n.d.a).
Induction:	the process or action of bringing about or giving rise to something (Induction, n.d.c).
Induce:	to lead or move, as to a course of action, by influence or persuasion (Induce, n.d.b).
Induce:	to lead or move by persuasion or influence, as to some action or state of mind (Induce, n.d.a).
Induce:	to cause (someone or something) to do something; to cause (something) to happen or exist (Induce, n.d.c).

Perceiving these definitions as disparate to the domain of hypnosis, I revisited the above referenced dictionaries in search of more applicable alternatives and retrieved the following:

Elicit:	to get (a response, information) from someone; to call forth or draw out (as information or a response) (Elicit, n.d.b).
Elicit:	to draw or bring out or forth; educe; evoke (Elicit, n.d.a).
Evoke:	to bring (a memory, feeling, image, etc.) into the mind; to call forth or up (Evoke, n.d.).
Facilitate:	to make easier; to help bring about (Facilitate, n.d.b).
Facilitate:	to make easier or less difficult; help forward (an action, a process, etc.) (Facilitate, n.d.a).

Given these alternative definitions, clinicians, researchers, and instructors of hypnosis should consider if hypnosis involves something that is "done *to* someone," or "brings about/forth *from* someone." If hypnosis characterizes the former, then "induction" is the correct and applicable term, rendering the thesis espoused in this article untenable. If, however, we ascribe hypnosis to a process or skill set that *influences* (see Hope & Sugarman, 2015; Lankton, 2015) the generation of a response/reaction *from* someone, then "induction" is not what we do, and terms such as "elicit," "evoke," and/or "facilitate" may be more appropriate.

Professional Clinical Hypnosis Societies and Induction Education

The ASCH website (2016) maintained: "In hypnosis, the patient is *not under the control* of the hypnotist" and that "hypnosis is *not something imposed* on people, but something they *do for themselves* (emphasis added). ASCH also opined that, "A hypnotist simply serves as a *facilitator* to guide them" (emphasis added). SCEH (2016) defined hypnosis as "a state of focused attention and receptivity which can be an extremely useful tool for individuals wishing to master certain abilities and accomplish specific tasks." SCEH further offered that, "Hypnosis is considered to be a normal and adaptive altered state of consciousness that occurs spontaneously for many individuals throughout life."

ASCH and SCEH, through their published statements, distance themselves from the notion of hypnosis being initiated, controlled, or manipulated by another yet continue to embrace and employ the term "induction." As mentioned above, ASCH's standards of learning guidelines recommend at least 9 hours of didactic and experiential training through basic and intermediate workshops dedicated to learning and ideally mastering "induction techniques." It, therefore, stands to reason that professional hypnosis societies would be motivated to embrace, or at least consider, terms like elicit, evoke, and facilitate if, indeed, hypnosis is appreciated as a process or skill set that promotes the generation of a response/reaction *from* someone. To do otherwise, it seems, unwittingly promotes the very myths and misconceptions that are born of the notion that hypnosis is controlled and manipulated by the hypnotist (i.e., magnetizer, inducer).

Conclusions

Mark Twain said, "The difference between the almost right word and the right word is really a large matter—'tis the difference between the lightning-bug and the lightning." Whether hieroglyphs on walls of ancient Egyptian temples, a report on animal magnetism undersigned by Benjamin Franklin, experimental findings discovered in Hull's laboratory, or unequaled insights into the human mind and behavior espoused by Milton Erickson, it is words that tell the stories. It is also words, that when unquestioned and unexamined, can be readily adopted as sacrosanct and perpetuate myths and misconceptions, like those highlighted throughout this article pertaining to hypnotic induction.

More to the point of this present article, and building on the impetus and momentum initiated by Hope and Sugarman's (2015) orienting hypnosis hypothesis, I propose the following conversation starters, specific to hypnotic induction: Have induction techniques been empirically validated as an essential component of hypnosis? Can hypnosis be beneficial/therapeutic without the utilization of formal "induction" techniques? Are hypnotic induction techniques nothing more than contemporary bells and whistles akin to Mesmer's baquet and mesmerized trees, intended to promote the power of the hypnotist at the expense of the true source of trance production: the patient? Does the term "induction" potentiate myths and misconceptions about hypnosis since it implies *doing something to another*? If so, should alternative terms that more accurately epitomize experiences associated with hypnosis be employed? Finally, should professional hypnosis societies distance themselves from the term "induction" and modify their current standards of training?

I contend that "induction" is "the almost the right word." I also appreciate that others should weigh in on this matter before I toss the proverbial baby out with the baquet water.

References

American Society of Clinical Hypnosis (ASCH). (2016). *Definition of hypnosis*. Retrieved from http://www.asch.net/Public/GeneralInfoonHypnosis/DefinitionofHypnosis.aspx

Barrett, D. (2006). Hypnosis in film and television. *American Journal of Clinical Hypnosis*, *49*, 13–30. doi:10.1080/00029157.2006.10401549

Bonwick, J. (1878). *Egyptian belief and modern thought*. London, UK: C. Keegan Paul.

Bowers, K. (1983). *Hypnosis for the seriously curious*. New York, NY: W. W. Norton.

Braid, J. (1843). *Neurypnology: Or the rationale of nervous sleep considered in relation with animal magnetism*. London: J. Churchill.

Braid, J. (1845). On hypnotism. *The Lancet*, *1*, 627–628. doi:10.1016/S0140-6736(02)65024-X

Chiasson, S. W. (1973). Chiasson's method. *Syllabus on hypnosis and a handbook of therapeutic suggestions*. The American Society of Clinical Hypnosis, Chelsea, MA: Education and Research Foundation.

Edmondston, W. E. (1986). *The induction of hypnosis*. New York, NY: John Wiley & Sons.

Elicit. (n.d.a). In *Dictionary.com*. Retrieved from http://www.dictionary.com/browse/elicit?s=t

Elicit. (n.d.b). In *Merriam-Webster's Online Dictionary*. Retrieved from http://www.merriam-webster.com/dictionary/elicit

Elkins, G. R., Barabasz, A. F., Council, J. R., & Spiegel, D. (2015). Advancing research and practice: The revised APA division 30 definition of hypnosis. *International Journal of Clinical and Experimental Hypnosis*, *57*, 378–385. doi:10.1080/00029157.2015.1011465

Ellenberger, H. F. (1970). *The discovery of the unconscious*. New York, NY: Basic Books.

Erickson, M. (1958). Naturalistic techniques of hypnosis. *American Journal of Clinical Hypnosis*, *1*, 3–8. doi:10.1080/00029157.1958.10401766

Erickson, M., Rossi, E., & Rossi, S. (1976). *Hypnotic realities: The induction of clinical hypnosis and forms of indirect suggestion*. New York, NY: Irvington.

Evoke. (n.d.). In *Merriam-Webster's Online Dictionary*. Retrieved from http://www.merriam-webster.com/dictionary/evoke

Facilitate. (n.d.a). In *Dictionary.com*. Retrieved from http://www.dictionary.com/browse/facilitate?s=t

Facilitate. (n.d.b). In *Merriam-Webster's Online Dictionary*. Retrieved from http://www.merriam-webster.com/dictionary/facilitate

Francher, R. F. (1990). *Pioneers of psychology* (2nd ed.). New York, NY: W. W. Norton.

Franklin, B., De Bory, G., Lavoisier, A. L., Bailly, J. S., Majault, S., D'Arcet, J., & LeRoy, J. B. (1784/1965). Secret report on mesmerism, or animal magnetism. In R. E. Shor & M. T. Orne (Eds.), *The nature of hypnosis: Selected basic readings*. New York, NY: Hold, Rinehart, & Winston.

Franklin, B., Majault, S., Le Roy, J. B., Sallin, B. J. S., D'arcet, J., De Bory, G., … Lavoisier, A. (2002). Report of the commissioners charge by the king with the examination of animal magnetism.

International Journal of Clinical and Experimental Hypnosis, *50*, 332–363. doi:10.1080/00207140208410109 (Original work published 1784)

Green, J. P., Barabasz, A. F., Barrett, D., & Montgomery, G. H. (2003). Forging ahead: The 2003 APA division 30 definition of hypnosis. *International Journal of Clinical and Experimental Hypnosis*, *53*, 259–264. doi:10.1080/00207140590961321

Hammond, D. C. (2013). A review of the history of hypnosis through the late 19th century. *American Journal of Clinical Hypnosis*, *56*, 174–191. doi:10.1080/00029157.2013.826172

Hammond, D. C., & Elkins, G. R. (2005). *Standards of training in clinical hypnosis*. Bloomingdale, IL: American Society of Clinical Hypnosis (ASCH)—Education and Research Foundation.

Hope, A. E., & Sugarman, L. I. (2015). Orienting hypnosis. *American Journal of Clinical Hypnosis*, *57*, 212–229. doi:10.1080/00029157.2014.976787

Hull, C. (2002). *Hypnosis and suggestibility: An experimental approach*. Williston, VT: Crown House Publishing. (Original work published 1933)

Induce. (n.d.a). In *Dictionary.com*. Retrieved from http://www.dictionary.com/browse/induce?s=t

Induce. (n.d.b). In *Thefreedictionary.com*. Retrieved from http://www.thefreedictionary.com/induce

Induce. (n.d.c). In *Merriam-Webster's Online Dictionary*. Retrieved from http://www.merriam-webster.com/dictionary/induce

Induction. (n.d.a). In *Dictionary.com*. Retrieved from http://www.dictionary.com/browse/induction?s=t

Induction. (n.d.b). In *Merriam-Webster's Online Dictionary*. Retrieved from http://www.merriam-webster.com/dictionary/induction

Induction. (n.d.c). In *Oxford Dictionaries Online*. Retrieved from http://www.oxforddictionaries.com/us/definition/american_english/induction

Johnson, M. E., & Hauck, C. (1999). Beliefs and opinions about hypnosis held by the general public: A systematic evaluation. *American Journal of Clinical Hypnosis*, *42*, 10–20. doi:10.1080/00029157.1999.10404241

Kirsch, I., Lynn, S., & Rhue, J. (1993). Introduction to clinical hypnosis. In J. Rhue, S. Lynn, & I. Kirsch (Eds.), *Handbook of clinical hypnosis* (pp. 3–22). Washington, DC: American Psychological Association.

Kroger, W. S. (1963). An analysis of valid and invalid objections to hypnotherapy. *American Journal of Clinical Hypnosis*, *6*, 12–131. doi:10.1080/00029157.1963.10402331

Lankton, S. (2015). A SoC model of hypnosis and induction. *American Journal of Clinical Hypnosis*, *57*, 367–377. doi:10.1080/00029157.2015.1011461

Lankton, S., & Lankton, C. (2008). *The answer within: A clinical framework of Ericksonian hypnotherapy* (pp. 141–147). Bethel, CT: Crown House Publishers, Inc. (Original work published 1983)

Laurence, J.-R., & Perry, C. (1988). *Hypnosis, will, and memory: A psycho-legal history*. New York, NY: Guildford Press.

Lynn, S. J., Rhue, J. W., & Kirsch, I. (2010). *Handbook of clinical hypnosis* (2nd ed.). Washington, DC: American Psychological Association.

Morgan, A. H., Hilgard, E. R., & Davert, E. C. (1970). The heritability of hypnotic susceptibility in twins. *Behavior Genetics*, *1*, 213–224. doi:10.1007/BF01074653

Osler, W. (2004). *The evolution of modern medicine*. Whitefish, MT: Kessinger Publishing.

Pattie, F. A. (1994). *Mesmer and animal magnetism*. Hamilton, NY: Edmonstron Publishing.

Pratt, G. J., Wood, D. P., & Alman, B. M. (1988). *A clinical hypnosis primer*. New York, NY: John Wiley & Sons.

Sheehan, P. W., & Perry, C. W. (1976). *Methodologies of hypnosis*. Hillsdale, NJ: Lawrence Erlbaum Associates, Inc.

Shor, R., & Orne, E. (1962). *Harvard group scale of hypnotic susceptibility, form A*. Palo Alto, CA: Consulting Psychologists Press.

Society for Clinical and Experimental Hypnosis (SCEH). (2016). *What is hypnosis?* Retrieved from: http://www.sceh.us/what-is-hypnosis.

Spiegel, H., & Spiegel, D. (1978). *Trance and treatment: Clinical uses of hypnosis*. New York, NY: Basic.

Sugarman, L. I. (2015). Mapping the domain of hypnosis. *American Journal of Clinical Hypnosis*, *57*, 209–211. doi:10.1080/00029157.2015.985565

Thomson, L. (2003). A project to change the attitudes, beliefs and practices of health professionals concerning hypnosis. *American Journal of Clinical Hypnosis*, *46*, 31–44. doi:10.1080/00029157.2003.10403563

Wark, D. M. (2006). Alert hypnosis: A review and case report. *American Journal of Clinical Hypnosis*, *48*, 291–300. doi:10.1080/00029157.2006.10401536

Wark, D. M. (2015). Traditional and alert hypnotic phenomena: Development through anteriorization. *American Journal of Clinical Hypnosis*, *57*, 254–266. doi:10.1080/00029157.2014.976784

Weitzenhoffer, A. (2000). *The practice of hypnotism* (2nd ed.). New York, NY: Wiley.

Weitzenhoffer, A., & Hilgard, E. (1959). *Stanford hypnotic susceptibility scale, forms A and B*. Palo Alto, CA: Consulting Psychologists Press.

Weitzenhoffer, A., & Hilgard, E. (1962). *Stanford hypnotic susceptibility scale, form C*. Palo Alto, CA: Consulting Psychologists Press.

What Can a Hypnotic Induction Do?

Erik Woody

Pamela Sadler

In contrast to how recent definitions of hypnosis describe the induction, a work-sample perspective is advocated that characterizes the induction as an initial, stage-setting phase encompassing everything in a hypnotic session up to the first hypnotic suggestion of particular relevance to the therapeutic or research goals at hand. Four major ways are then discussed in which the induction could affect subsequent hypnotic responses: It may provide information about how subsequent behaviors are to be enacted; it may provide cues about the nature of the interpersonal interaction to be expected in hypnosis; it may provide meta-suggestions, defined as suggestive statements intended to enhance responses to subsequent hypnotic suggestions; and it may provide a clear transition to help allow new behaviors and experiences to emerge. Several ideas for future research are advanced, such as mapping hypnosis style onto the interpersonal circumplex, evaluating whether attentional-state changes measured at the end of the induction actually mediate subsequent hypnotic responsiveness, and systematically examining the impact of ritual-like aspects of inductions.

There are some reasons to anticipate that the hypnotic induction should not be a particularly interesting or promising topic. First, although the hypnosis literature offers a wide variety of types of induction, the available evidence tends to indicate that the type of induction used may have only negligible effects on subsequent responsiveness to suggestions (e.g., Lynn, Neufeld, & Maré, 1993; Skiba, 1983). Second, there do not seem to be any necessary properties of a hypnotic induction, aside from the participant's impression that it is plausible. For example, although many inductions involve instructions for muscle relaxation and slow, deep breathing (e.g., Shor & Orne, 1962), people can become hypnotized via strong physical exertion as well, such as riding a stationary bicycle (Bányai & Hilgard, 1976). Third, the available evidence tends to indicate that use of a hypnotic induction, compared to no induction at all, has surprisingly modest effects on subsequent responsiveness to suggestions, increasing it by no more than 10%–20% (Braffman & Kirsch, 1999; Lynn & Kirsch, 2006).

Given these considerations, it is perhaps not surprising that some important recent perspectives on hypnosis have strongly de-emphasized the induction. To quote Nash (2005, p. 270): "What we have in the past called 'an induction' is nothing more than the first suggestion after the nominal preamble." With such a conception, the induction virtually disappears as a distinct, legitimate topic. Indeed, in defining hypnosis, Nash (2005, p. 269) remarked:

> There is no need to mention an induction because, as Ernest Hilgard stated many times, an induction *is* a suggestion. The only thing that needs to happen after the preamble for the procedure to qualify as a hypnotic procedure is ... to administer the first suggestion.

However, there are also some reasons to believe that the hypnotic induction might be, on the contrary, a particularly interesting and promising topic. First, it is a crucial component of the sociocultural script of hypnosis—that is, a major aspect of the mystique of hypnosis in our culture. For example, to a roomful of students anticipating the experience of hypnosis, the induction is the expected portal. Moreover, traditional inductions have ritual-like qualities (such as slowly counting to "deepen" hypnosis) that may have interesting psychological properties, as we discuss later.

Second, in therapeutic applications, individualizing the induction has an important role in tailoring the approach to hypnosis to fit the characteristics of the particular individual, taking into account the person's personality, understanding, and interpretation of experiences and thus fostering treatment acceptance and success. J. Barber (1991) has engagingly called these individualized adjustments in the approach to hypnosis the "locksmith model." For example, with a person showing a high need for personal control, hypnosis may be introduced in an open-ended way, wherein a variety of experiences, even opposite ones (e.g., "your fingers may feel hot or cold") are suggested as valid.

Third, recent neurophysiological research shows that the hypnotic induction, rather than being an empty ritual, may have important effects on brain functioning. In particular, neuroimaging reveals changes in the state of activation of various brain systems (e.g., Maquet et al., 1999; Rainville et al., 1999; Rainville, Hofbauer, Bushnell, Duncan, & Price, 2002), including attentional control systems (e.g., Deeley et al., 2012; McGeown, Mazzoni, Venneri, & Kirsch, 2009). Likewise, Electroencephalography studies reveal intriguing state changes in functional connectivity (Cardeña, Jonsson, Terhune, & Marcusson-Clavertz, 2013; Fingelkurts, Fingelkurts, Kallio, & Revonsuo, 2007; Jamieson & Burgess, 2014; Terhune, Cardeña, & Lindgren, 2011). Important effects of the hypnotic induction can also be demonstrated through self-report measures of phenomenology (e.g., Pekala & Kumar, 2002; Pekala et al., 2010a, 2010b); in addition, it is interesting that subjective self-reports during hypnosis can show very high correlations with measures of underlying neurophysiological states (e.g., Szechtman, Woody,

Bowers, & Nahmias, 1998). This range of work has helped to move the field beyond the previous critical paralysis over whether the concept of a hypnotic state is problematically circular—that is, only inferred after the fact from behavioral responses to suggestions (e.g., Kirsch & Lynn, 1995).

Definitional Issues

But what exactly is a hypnotic induction? This turns out to be a somewhat tricky issue. A reasonable place to start is to look at definitions of hypnosis with particular attention to the nature and role ascribed to the induction. Let us consider the two most recent definitions advanced by the American Psychological Association Division 30, one in 2003 and the other in 2014.

Here is the relevant part of the 2003 definition (Green, Barabasz, Barrett, & Montgomery, 2005):

> Hypnosis typically involves an introduction to the procedure during which the subject is told that suggestions for imaginative experiences will be presented. The hypnotic induction is an extended initial suggestion for using one's imagination, and may contain further elaborations of the introduction. (p. 262)

Conspicuously de-emphasized is the role of the induction in producing a hypnotic state (i.e., a change in the person's state of consciousness). Instead, according to this definition, the induction is simply a suggestion. Moreover, according to this definition, the nature of the suggestion provided in the induction is for the person to use his or her imagination.

Unfortunately, as we have pointed out previously (Woody & Sadler, 2005), this characterization of the hypnotic induction is empirically false. First, the introduction and induction of the most commonly used hypnosis scales do not ever use the words "imaginative" or "imagination," or synonyms of them; thus, this is not what participants are actually told. Second, there is a very substantial body of research evidence showing that imagination is not the main mechanism underlying hypnosis (e.g., Zamansky, 1977; Zamansky & Clark, 1986). For example, Hargadon, Bowers, and Woody (1995) showed experimentally that counter-pain imagery actually had no role at all in hypnotic analgesia. In a neuroimaging study of participants in hypnosis, Szechtman et al. (1998) demonstrated that responses when participants are asked to imagine are readily differentiated from genuine hypnotic phenomena like hallucinations, a result that has been replicated for a wide range of hypnotic phenomena, including motor responses (Blakemore, Oakley, & Frith, 2003) and pain and analgesia (Derbyshire, Whalley, Stenger, & Oakley, 2004; Raij, Numminen, Närvänen, Hittunen, & Hari, 2005). Third, the terms "imaginative experiences" and "using one's imagination" are inaccurate descriptions of the phenomenology of hypnosis. In genuine hypnotic phenomena, the person's experience is not that he or she is imagining things, but that there is an alteration of the sense of agency, a feeling of involuntariness called the "classic suggestion effect" (Weitzenhoffer, 1974, 1980). In short, because of its incorrect emphasis on the role of using one's imagination in hypnosis, the 2003 definition does not offer a workable characterization of the induction.

The 2014 definition (Elkins, Barabasz, Council, & Spiegel, 2015) is a considerable departure from the 2003 one. Here are the 2014 definitions of hypnosis and the hypnotic induction:

> *Hypnosis*: "A state of consciousness involving focused attention and reduced peripheral awareness characterized by an enhanced capacity for response to suggestion." (p. 282)
>
> *Hypnotic induction*: "A procedure designed to induce hypnosis." (p. 283)

According to this conception, hypnosis is a state of consciousness, and the induction is defined as a procedure for producing this state.

Because the 2014 definition provides no other information about what a hypnotic induction is, what it specifies about the state of consciousness to be attained is crucial. Unfortunately, the definition's characterization of the hypnotic state seems far too inclusive. For example, checking one's smartphone would appear to qualify as hypnosis: there is focused attention, reduced peripheral awareness, and an enhanced response to suggestion (which advertisers are willing to spend many millions of dollars to exploit). In other words, the definition does not distinguish the hypnotic state from a myriad of other transitory states of consciousness. Perhaps more importantly, the definition does not specify what kinds of response to suggestion are relevant to hypnosis. For instance, if a person says, "Wow, I suggest you look out the window," and another person does it, this would be an example of a response to suggestion, but it does not meet the minimal acceptable definition of a hypnotic response, because there would be no alteration of the sense of agency involved (i.e., no "classic suggestion effect"). Indeed, although the 2014 definition is quite different in many ways from the 2003 definition, it has the same core flaw: namely, it evades dealing with the classic suggestion effect.

In summary, the 2014 definition of hypnosis does not distinguish the hypnotic state from many other transitory states of consciousness, and a crucial part of this shortcoming is that it does not differentiate hypnotic responsiveness from the many other unrelated kinds of response to suggestion (Tasso & Pérez, 2008). Hence, it is not as helpful as we might have hoped in defining what the state-producing procedure, namely an induction, really is. We need a different approach.

A Pragmatic Conceptualization of the Hypnotic Induction

The approach to the hypnotic induction that we will adopt here stems from the work-sample perspective on measurements taken by Woody and Barnier (2008) in discussing standardized hypnosis scales. They conceptualized the hypnotic induction, including possible introductory remarks by the hypnotist, as a crucial initial phase for creating the appropriate context, or setting the stage, for hypnosis. From a work-sample perspective, such stage-setting is important because the context is often a potent determinant of how a person approaches a relatively unfamiliar situation (e.g., which skills and strategies may be relevant), what kinds of behaviors the person will enact, and how the person understands or interprets these behaviors.

Following this perspective, here we conceptualize the hypnotic induction as including everything that happens from the beginning of the hypnosis session up to the first hypnotic suggestion of particular relevance to the therapeutic or research matter at hand (i.e., a suggestion of potential therapeutic benefit, or a suggestion the response to which will be scored for the purposes of the research). It encompasses what Nash (2005) called the "preamble," which often intergrades imperceptibly into more frankly inductive procedures, and it may include a variety of suggestive statements. For example, consider a session that starts with the hypnotist saying, "I believe hypnosis can help you; let's try it." This statement is already suggestive (however, it is not a hypnotic suggestion, because an altered sense of agency in response is neither appropriate nor intended).

Given this pragmatic conceptualization of the induction, our focus is on the following question: What effects might this introductory or preparatory phase of a hypnotic session have on subsequent hypnotic responses, and why might these effects be important? In other words, what are the things that a hypnotic induction, inclusively defined, could possibly do? We now turn to considering four major possibilities.

Providing Cues About How Suggested Behaviors are to be Enacted

When faced with an unfamiliar task, such as hypnosis, the individual has to determine which of multiple possible ways for approaching the task to adopt. Moreover, the choice of how to approach the task can have very substantial impact on the nature and meaning of the person's ensuing behavior.

A couple of anecdotal examples may help to illustrate these points. Some years ago, the first author's son told him he had just participated in a psychology experiment, in which he was asked to look at stimuli on a computer screen and told to "name the actual color as quickly as possible"—in other words, it was a Stroop experiment. When I asked him how it went, he replied: "At first it was quite difficult. But I figured out that if I blurred my eyes and looked only at the corner of the screen, it was much easier. Then I was really fast." He was proud of this discovery and quite unaware that it lay well outside the parameters of interest to the experimenters. (By the way, in the debriefing, the experimenter did not ask him how he had approached the task.)

This kind of problem has the potential to be particularly relevant to hypnosis. Consider that the expected or desired behaviors in response to the items on a standardized hypnosis scale, for instance, are almost always obvious, but it is up to the participant to figure out what appropriate passing responses would consist of (Woody, Bowers, & Oakman, 1992). Some years ago, a student who had taken part in several hypnosis experiments as a high hypnotizable participant at a Canadian university (not either of ours) was troubled enough about this issue to seek out a meeting with the faculty researcher overseeing these studies. The student told the researcher that although he enjoyed participating in these studies, he felt honor-bound to admit that he was not actually responsive to hypnosis and had simply been acting out what he perceived to be the expected responses. To the student's surprise, the researcher responded, "Don't worry; that's all right. You're what we call a 'behavioral high.'"

From our point of view, a "behavioral high" does not fit within the appropriately defined domain of hypnosis, because it does not involve the classic suggestion effect (i.e., an alteration in the sense of agency). However, even for modes of response that fall more clearly within the domain of hypnosis, there are multiple alternatives that a person may take. Hypnosis researchers from a wide variety of perspectives have characterized hypnotically responsive participants as creative problem solvers making use of a diversity of approaches for enacting hypnotic suggestions (e.g., T. X. Barber, 1999; Galea, Woody, Szechtman, & Pierrynowski, 2010; Lynn & Sivec, 1992; McConkey & Barnier, 2004; McConkey, Glisky, & Kihlstrom, 1989; Winkel, Younger, Tomcik, Borckardt, & Nash, 2006). Unfortunately, this diversity of approaches may often be hidden in studies because of a relatively narrow focus on whether the suggested behavior occurred or not, with little attention to the particular pathways that individuals took to produce that end-response.

What, then, determines which approach a person takes to enacting hypnotic suggestions? One important possibility is that people come to hypnosis with a variety of individual-difference profiles (e.g., Terhune & Cardeña, 2010; Woody, Barnier, & McConkey, 2005), with each person presumably being more likely to adopt an approach that fits his or her own individual skills and attitudes. However, surely another possible determinant is situational cues, including those provided, both explicitly and implicitly, by the induction.

As a straightforward illustration, let's consider Nash's (2005) minimal, "fully adequate" preamble, which would be followed immediately by the hypnotic suggestions:

> I am going to ask you to imagine some changes in the way you think and feel. Is that OK? Let's see what happens. (p. 269).

Given what we know about context effects (e.g., Kirsch & Council, 1992), this link of hypnosis to imagination might increase the correlation of subsequent responsiveness to other, imagery-like individual differences. More importantly, it may explicitly cue the person about the types of individual-difference resources that may be relevant to responding hypnotically, and thus affect what underlying abilities and strategies are recruited (i.e., it is just using one's imagination, which individuals may think they are good or not so good at). Imagination is a volitionally controlled mental activity (as contrasted, say, with daydreaming); thus, adopting this mode of responding may limit the extent to which people experience the classic suggestion effect. (Indeed, Comey and Kirsch [1999] found that removing the goal-directed imagery from the Carleton University Responsiveness to Suggestion Scale actually increased subjective, as well as objective, responsiveness to suggestion.) In addition, some possible effects of such introductory statements on the person may be subtly hypnotist mediated. Rosenthal (1963) showed that experimenters presented with different hypotheses subtly biased the conduct of the experiment toward eliciting the phenomena the experimenter had been led to expect. Similarly, to the extent hypnotists themselves believe the cues offered in the induction, they may subtly pull for modes of response that fit these expectations. Indeed, in this way it is even possible that different hypnosis laboratories may be studying somewhat different phenomena—e.g., purely behavioral response versus imagination versus dissociative phenomena.

In summary, the rationales and cues, both purposeful and inadvertent, that are presented in the induction may not be so innocuous as is often presumed and may push people in various directions with regard to the ways they go about enacting subsequent suggestions.

Providing Cues About the Nature of the Interpersonal Interaction in Hypnosis

For many years, Kihlstrom has advanced a definition of hypnosis that puts front and center an aspect that is almost entirely absent from the APA Division 30 definitions. Here is the relevant part of a recent statement of this definition (Kihlstrom, 2013):

> Hypnosis is a *social interaction* [emphasis added] in which one person, designated the subject, responds to suggestions offered by another person, designated the hypnotist. (p. 365)

Similarly, Kihlstrom (2008) has noted that "the phenomena of hypnosis reflect alterations in consciousness that take place *in the context of a social interaction* [emphasis added]" (p. 21). Other writers have also drawn attention to the importance of the interpersonal interaction that takes place as a major aspect of hypnosis (e.g., Bonshtein, 2012; Diamond, 1987; Haley, 1958).

As we will review in a moment, hypnotists may differ considerably in the interpersonal style they adopt in hypnosis. Hence, another potentially important aspect of the hypnotic induction is that it provides crucial initial cues about what the style of interpersonal interaction will be like in hypnosis—in other words, what the person should expect about the working relationship with the hypnotist.

The best known work on differences in interpersonal style among hypnotists is the research by Bányai and her colleagues (e.g., Bányai, 1991; Banyai, Gősi-Greguss, Vágó, Varga, & Horváth, 1990). They argued that through interpersonal cues, hypnotists signal to people "what what kind of relationship patterns they should mobilize (recollect or fantasize) along which they can organize their interactional expectations or experiences in connection with the actual hypnosis" (Varga, Bányai, Józsa, & Gősi-Greguss, 2008, p. 23). This work has mainly focused on distinguishing between two different hypnosis styles: a "maternal" style, posited to be "based on love;" and a "paternal" style, posited to be "based on fear" (Varga et al., 2008, p. 15). Varga and colleagues (2008) attempted to measure some other possible hypnosis styles, such as a "sibling style" (p. 26), but these proved somewhat difficult to code reliably from written transcripts of sessions (possibly because of the absence of nonverbal and paralinguistic cues). As might be expected, hypnosis style has a wide variety of effects on the hypnotized individual's phenomenological experiences, although the subjective experience of an altered state of consciousness does not seem to be exclusively related to either style.

The descriptions of the maternal style of hypnosis are characterized by what appear to be cues for affiliation (e.g., smiling and proximity), whereas the descriptions of the paternal style of hypnosis are characterized by what appear to be cues for dominance (e.g., inhibiting the other person's independent initiatives). Hence, we would propose that work on interpersonal styles in hypnosis might profitably be reconceptualized in terms of the interpersonal circumplex (IPC; Kiesler, 1996; Leary, 1957), an empirically supported model that has level of affiliation (from friendly to hostile) as its horizontal dimension and level of dominance (from dominant to submissive) as its vertical dimension—see Figure 1. In this model, a wide spectrum of different interpersonal styles is represented as a circular structure; in the figure, for example, eight different styles are represented as octants. This IPC model has been found to characterize differences in interpersonal style across a very wide range of types of interactions, including different psychotherapeutic schools (Andrews, 1989; Thomas, Hopwood, Woody, Ethier, & Sadler, 2014); hence there is good reason to think that it would apply to the interpersonal aspects of hypnosis as well. In addition, interpersonal theory, on which the IPC is based, offers a very rich framework for understanding how interpersonal styles mesh or clash, how they frame partners' expectations for each other, and how they affect exchanges between partners and interaction outcomes—a set of phenomena called *complementarity* in interpersonal theory (Sadler, Ethier, & Woody, 2011). This framework also makes important distinctions between various levels at which partners affect each other—for example, matching of overall (mean) levels of affiliation between partners is a different phenomenon from matching of moment-to-moment variations of affiliation.

Although our experience of seeing hypnotists doing their work is somewhat limited, we have witnessed huge variation in hypnotists' interpersonal styles. For example, some years ago at the convention of the Society for Clinical and Experimental Hypnosis, a Russian hypnotist gave a presentation that included videos of his work with budding pianists. He was a very large and imposing figure, and already in the induction he loomed over the seated person like a bear. He delivered the suggestion in a commanding, deep voice: "You are Rachmaninoff" (a renowned pianist), and then asked, "Who are you?" After each mumbled response from the hypnotized person, the hypnotist repeated the suggestion more loudly, until it seemed thunderous, and the person finally responded clearly, "I am Rachmaninoff." Referring to Figure 1, this hypnotist was

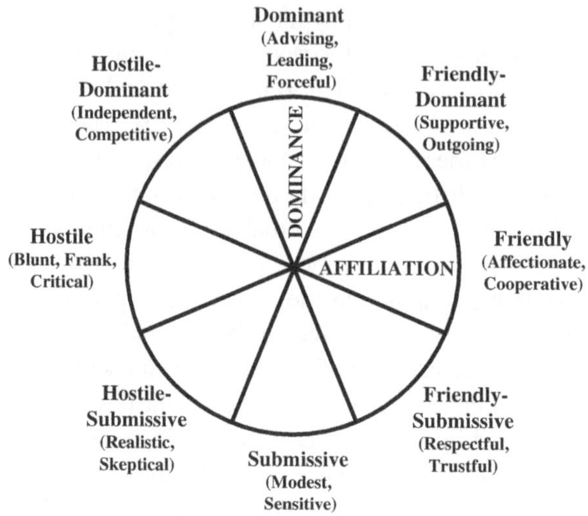

FIGURE 1 Interpersonal Circumplex (IPC). *Note.* Descriptors in parentheses are derived from Andrews's (1989) characterizations of the corresponding psychotherapeutic styles.

demonstrating a hostile-dominant interpersonal style. Although this style of hypnosis may be unusual in North America, there is some reason to believe it could have strong effects (Woody & Szechtman, 2003). A contrasting example would be Joseph Barber's work with a pain patient, as seen in an excellent BBC documentary on hypnosis made some years ago (Barnes, 1982). Barber's approach to the person is quite warm and gentle, and he very artfully, repeatedly emphasizes the person's autonomy in responding to hypnosis. Referring to Figure 1, this approach to hypnosis appears to involve a friendly–submissive interpersonal style.

As an illustration of how an IPC perspective might contribute to further understanding in hypnosis, consider the somewhat fraught topic of indirect suggestions. These have been characterized in two quite different ways (e.g., Lankton & Matthews, 2010). One perspective is that they help to produce a "permissive atmosphere" that encourages clients in "cocreating the outcomes that emerge from the ongoing interaction" (Lankton & Matthews, 2010, p. 226). Such indirect suggestions would fit a relatively submissive style by the hypnotist, fostering self-direction in the client. However, indirect suggestions have also often been characterized as a strategy by which the "client's conscious limitations and criticism can be bypassed" (Lankton & Matthews, 2010, p. 213)—in other words, as a way for the hypnotist to direct a client who might otherwise resist. Such indirect suggestions would fit a relatively dominant interpersonal style by the hypnotist. In short, without clarification of the interpersonal style in which indirect suggestions are embedded, there may be considerable misunderstanding about what they entail.

In conclusion, a lot more work needs to be done on the possible effects of these interpersonal style differences in hypnosis, but they may be an important aspect of hypnosis that, at least in part, is set in motion during the induction.

Providing Meta-Suggestions

The induction also provides an opportunity to give what may be termed *meta-suggestions*—that is, suggestions that may affect, and are intended to enhance, the person's response to subsequent hypnotic suggestions. In particular, suggestive statements in the induction about a shift in mental state are likely intended as meta-suggestions, the immediate responses to which are not of prime interest in themselves, but which instead may have subsequent influence on responses to the suggestions given later in the hypnotic session.

For example, consider the typical hypnotic induction used in standardized hypnosis scales for hypnosis research around the world (e.g., Shor & Orne, 1962; Weitzenhoffer & Hilgard, 1959). This induction tells the participant that hypnosis involves an unusually narrow state of attention; it gives instructions to help produce such a shift, such as focusing on a single spot and listening only to the hypnotist's voice; and it suggests repeatedly that the person is entering a different mental state, with frequent allusions to "sleep" as an analogous, already familiar state-shift. The purpose of all this material in the induction is not primarily to evoke the suggested state-change, which indeed is not even scored in standardized hypnosis scales. Instead, it serves as a set of meta-suggestions, intended to enhance responsiveness to subsequent hypnotic suggestions.

This perspective on the hypnotic induction raises some interesting issues for further investigation. In particular, too little is known about what the attention-altering effects of such a hypnotic induction actually are. Can it be shown in the lab, with appropriate probes and measures of attention, that the induction (compared to a control condition) leads to a genuine narrowing of participants' attentional processing? In addition, can it be demonstrated that any such change in attentional state actually mediates the induction's effect on subsequent responsiveness to hypnotic suggestions? In other words, does the induction yield greater hypnotic responsiveness through the putative mediator of state-like changes in attention, or, alternatively, are such state changes just concomitants of hypnosis, lacking a causal role in subsequent response to hypnotic suggestions?

Neurophysiological (e.g., functional magnetic resonance imaging, *fMRI*) indicators could readily be integrated into this needed line of research. Demonstrations that an induction affects brain functioning are, by themselves, of uncertain relevance, because many likely inessential phenomena stemming from the induction, such as relaxation and spontaneous mental imagery, would alter the measured pattern of brain activity but possibly have little relevance for subsequent hypnotic responsiveness (Mazzoni, Venneri, McGeown, & Kirsch, 2013; Rainville et al., 2002). Indeed, some neuroimaging work suggests that effects on brain functioning of an induction, such as hypnotic depth, could be quite distinct from mechanisms underlying responsiveness to hypnotic suggestions (McGeown, Mazzoni, Vannucci, & Venneri, 2015). Figure 2 provides a structural-modeling schematic laying out the major questions that remain to be answered: (1) Do objective measures of attention and neurophysiological indices actually cohere as the indicators of a common underlying latent construct of attentional shift, represented in the figure as an oval? (2) Do attentional shifts actually mediate the effect of an induction on subsequent hypnotic responsiveness, represented in the figure by the combination of paths *a* and *b*; or does the induction mainly have a direct (unmediated) effect on subsequent hypnotic responsiveness, represented by path *c*? Unfortunately, the 2014 APA Division 30 definition of hypnosis (Elkins et al., 2015) simply assumed, prematurely, that we already have the answers to these crucial questions.

There are several other intriguing questions that could be addressed about the possible meta-suggestive effects of hypnotic inductions. In particular, what are the effects of other, less traditional types of meta-suggestions? Traditional hypnotic inductions suggest the narrowing and restriction of attention, but what might be the effects of meta-suggestions for the broadening of attention (e.g., "You can now attend to everything around you, even the subtlest things, much more clearly than usual.") or the intensification of attention (e.g., "You can now tune into all the processes in your mind much more clearly than usual.")? Or rather than meta-suggestions for imagination, how about something like this: "There are no longer any of the usual images in your mind. Instead, you sense things as they are, without

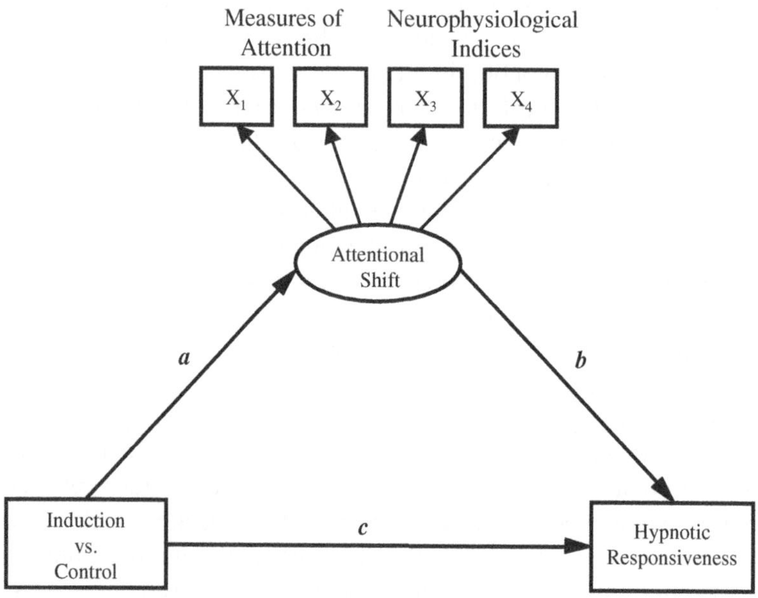

FIGURE 2 Mediation model of attention-altering effects of a hypnotic induction.

any mental pictures." How might these alternative meta-suggestions affect subsequent overt and phenomenological responses to hypnotic suggestions?

Finally, what is the possible role of the ritual-like aspects of traditional hypnotic inductions? A good example would be slowly counting through increasing integers to deepen hypnosis (followed eventually by the opposite ritual of slowly counting through the same numbers in the reverse direction for the de-induction). Ritualization, which involves features like strict adherence to a script, a carefully preset order, and mandatory repetitions, is important in many cultural contexts, such as religion, and may have important effects on the control of behavior and its self-perception. Boyer and Lienard (2006) argued that the effect of ritualization is to alter how the person parses the action-flow, shifting the focus of attention toward low-level units of behavior (i.e., the details of performance) and away from goal-related higher units. Such goal-demotion may be relevant for the classic suggestion effect, in which the person does not have the usual experience of self-mediated agency. Hence, an interesting direction for further investigation might be to intensify ritualization in the hypnotic induction to ascertain its effects on subsequent behavioral and phenomenological responses to suggestions. This increased ritualization could be obtained by using an unfamiliar, arbitrarily specific, somewhat complex script with a strictly prescribed order and, possibly, prescribed numbers of repetitions.

Providing a Clear Transition

Among other possible effects of a hypnotic induction, there is one that seems particularly worth mentioning: The induction provides a potentially important transition from everyday circumstances to help allow different behaviors, experiences, and self-evaluations to emerge. In a research setting, the induction serves as a clear demarcation that gives the person permission in the ensuing hypnosis to experience things that might seem problematic or even inappropriate in everyday life. For example, outside of hypnosis, "I was hallucinating" is not normally a valid explanation or excuse. In a therapeutic context, the hypnotic induction can foster a shift away from unproductive expectations and stultifying interpersonal patterns that may have arisen, possibly inadvertently, in previous, non-hypnotic sessions.

To some extent, simply labeling a session clearly with the word "hypnosis" can provide the cue needed to afford such a transition (Woody, Bowers, & Oakman, 1992). An anecdote may help to illustrate this point. Some years ago, for his graduate course on hypnosis, Ken Bowers had scheduled a live demonstration of the administration of the Stanford Hypnotic Suggestibility Scale, Form C. He had invited a person who, because of his very high hypnotizability, responded interestingly to every item, and who enjoyed giving such demonstrations. However, it soon became clear that on this occasion the person was not going to show up. In a pinch, Ken approached a graduate student who happened to be in the corridor and asked if she would please help him out and stand in for the missing individual. He told her she could just play along, not concern herself about hypnosis per se, and act however seemed to make sense to her, because the point of the session was to demonstrate the administration of the scale, not the nature of real hypnotic responsiveness. In other words, as far as this person was concerned, the session had not been labeled as genuine hypnosis. During the demonstration, Ken was impressed with her acting; for instance, she responded very convincingly to the personal questions supposedly coming over a loudspeaker. However, she turned out to have unusually high hypnotizability, and her responses were genuine, not acted. It was only during the subsequent discussion that she found out, for instance, that the questions she had clearly heard were not heard by anyone else. Rather than being amused by such experiences, as the other individual would have been, she found them to be quite disturbing; for instance, she worried whether she might be prone to spontaneously hallucinate like this at other times, without even realizing it. Inadvertently, for her the hypnosis session had not been demarcated as something clearly separate from everyday experience, as it would have been for the other equally responsive person.

In short, the hypnotic induction may serve as an important transition that signifies, in the words of Monty Python, "And now for something completely different!"

Conclusions

Optimizing the usefulness of hypnotic inductions may require more systematic analysis of the various kinds of effects they could possibly have. In particular, we have argued that the induction may provide important cues about the expected modes of enacting suggestions and the expected nature of the interpersonal interchange in hypnosis. In addition, the induction may provide meta-suggestions that could enhance subsequent response to hypnotic suggestions, and it may also provide a clear transition to help allow new modes of behavior and new experiences to emerge in hypnosis. Hopefully, these ideas will serve as a framework for further empirical study to evaluate the extent to which the variations in inductions we have discussed actually produce the hypothesized effects.

In past research, the specifics of hypnotic inductions may have seemed relatively unimportant because standardized hypnosis scales, as well as much of the research conducted with them, has focused on pass-versus-fail behavioral performance with little attention to variations in underlying mechanisms and phenomenology. Detecting potentially important effects of differences in inductions may require expanded, more detailed measures of the responses to hypnotic suggestions, including the strategies that people adopt in hypnosis and their subjective experiences about what they are doing.

In contrast to the last half-century of hypnosis research, which has generally assumed that hypnotizability is a reasonably unitary underlying trait, there has recently been burgeoning interest in heterogeneity among those highly responsive to hypnosis (e.g., Terhune & Cardeña, 2010; Woody et al., 2005). In work attempting to differentiate among different types of high hypnotizable individuals, it may be important to be careful not to word the induction in ways that might inadvertently discourage some possible modes of response (e.g., promoting an imagery-based mode in people who might otherwise rely on a dissociation-based mode).

However, careful optimization of the hypnotic induction could hold the greatest potential benefit for those individuals who tend to fall in the moderate to low range of hypnotizability. Indeed, these people, too, might show some degree of heterogeneity. For clinical applications, we particularly want to know how variations in the induction might enhance the responses of people who would otherwise show only modest responsiveness. This understanding could serve as a valuable empirical foundation for the tailoring of the induction to the individual client.

Funding

This research was supported by the Social Sciences and Humanities Research Council of Canada in the form of a grant (435-2014-1784) awarded to Pamela Sadler and Erik Woody.

References

Andrews, J. D. W. (1989). Integrating visions of reality: Interpersonal diagnosis and the existential vision. *American Psychologist*, *44*, 803–817. doi:10.1037/0003-066X.44.5.803

Bányai, É. I. (1991). Toward a social-psychobiological model of hypnosis. In S. J. Lynn & J. W. Rhue (Eds.), *Theories of hypnosis: Current models and perspectives* (pp. 564–598). New York, NY: Guilford.

Bányai, É. I., Gősi-Greguss, A. C., Vágó, P., Varga, K., & Horváth, R. (1990). Interactional approach to the understanding of hypnosis: Theoretical background and main findings. In R. Van Dyck, P. Spinhoven, A. Van Der Does, Y. Van Rood, & W. De Moor (Eds.), *Hypnosis: Current theory, research and practice* (pp. 52–69). Amsterdam, Netherlands: Free University Press.

Bányai, É. I., & Hilgard, E. R. (1976). A comparison of active-alert hypnotic induction with traditional relaxation induction. *Journal of Abnormal Psychology*, *85*, 218–224. doi:10.1037/0021-843X.85.2.218

Barber, J. (1991). The locksmith model: Accessing hypnotic responsiveness. In S. J. Lynn & J. W. Rhue (Eds.), *Theories of hypnosis: Current models and perspectives* (pp. 240–274). New York, NY: Guilford.

Barber, T. X. (1999). Hypnosis: A mature view. *Contemporary Hypnosis*, *16*, 123–127. doi:10.1002/(ISSN) 1557-0711

Barnes, M. (Producer & Writer). (1982). *Hypnosis: Can your mind control pain?* [Motion picture]. London, UK: BBC.

Blakemore, S.-J., Oakley, D. A., & Frith, C. D. (2003). Delusions of control in the normal brain. *Neuropsychologia*, *41*, 1058–1067. doi:10.1016/S0028-3932(02)00313-5

Bonshtein, U. (2012). Relational hypnosis. *International Journal of Clinical and Experimental Hypnosis*, *60*(4), 397–415. doi:10.1080/00207144.2012.700613

Boyer, P., & Lienard, P. (2006). Why ritualized behavior? Precaution systems and action parsing in developmental, pathological and cultural rituals. *Behavioral and Brain Sciences*, *29*(6), 595–613.

Braffman, W., & Kirsch, I. (1999). Imaginative suggestibility and hypnotizability: An empirical analysis. *Journal of Personality and Social Psychology*, *77*, 578–587. doi:10.1037/0022-3514.77.3.578

Cardeña, E., Jonsson, P., Terhune, D. B., & Marcusson-Clavertz, D. (2013). The neurophenomenology of neutral hypnosis. *Cortex*, *49*, 375–385. doi:10.1016/j.cortex.2012.04.001

Comey, G., & Kirsch, I. (1999). Intentional and spontaneous imagery in hypnosis: The phenomenology of hypnotic responding. *International Journal of Clinical and Experimental Hypnosis*, *474*, 65–85.

Deeley, Q., Oakley, D. A., Toone, B., Giampietro, V., Brammer, M. J., Williams, S. C. R., & Halligan, P. W. (2012). Modulating the default mode network using hypnosis. *International Journal of Clinical and Experimental Hypnosis*, *60*, 206–228. doi:10.1080/00207144.2012.648070

Derbyshire, S. W. G., Whalley, M. G., Stenger, V. A., & Oakley, D. A. (2004). Cerebral activation during hypnotically induced and imagined pain. *NeuroImage*, *23*, 392–401. doi:10.1016/j.neuroimage.2004.04.033

Diamond, M. J. (1987). The interactional basis of hypnotic experience: On the relational dimensions of hypnosis. *International Journal of Clinical and Experimental Hypnosis*, *35*, 95–115. doi:10.1080/00207148708416046

Elkins, G. A., Barabasz, A. F., Council, J. R., & Spiegel, D. (2015). Advancing research and practice: The revised APA Division 30 definition of hypnosis. *American Journal of Clinical Hypnosis*, *57*, 378–385. doi:10.1080/00029157.2015.1011465

Fingelkurts, A. A., Fingelkurts, A. A., Kallio, S., & Revonsuo, A. (2007). Cortex functional connectivity as a neurophysiological correlate of hypnosis: An EEG case study. *Neuropsychologia*, *45*, 1452–1462. doi:10.1016/j.neuropsychologia.2006.11.018

Galea, V., Woody, E. Z., Szechtman, H., & Pierrynowski, M. R. (2010). Motion in response to the hypnotic suggestion of arm rigidity: A window on underlying mechanisms. *International Journal of Clinical and Experimental Hypnosis*, *58*(3), 251–268. doi:10.1080/00207141003760561

Green, J. P., Barabasz, A. F., Barrett, D., & Montgomery, G. H. (2005). Forging ahead: The 2003 APA Division 30 definition of hypnosis. *International Journal of Clinical and Experimental Hypnosis*, *53*, 259–264. doi:10.1080/00207140590961321

Haley, J. (1958). An interactional explanation of hypnosis. *American Journal of Clinical Hypnosis*, *1*, 41–57. doi:10.1080/00029157.1958.10734336

Hargadon, R., Bowers, K. S., & Woody, E. Z. (1995). Does counter-pain imagery mediate hypnotic analgesia? *Journal of Abnormal Psychology*, *104*, 508–516. doi:10.1037/0021-843X.104.3.508

Jamieson, G. A., & Burgess, A. P. (2014). Hypnotic induction is followed by state-like changes in the organization of EEG functional connectivity in the theta and beta frequency bands in high-hypnotically susceptible individuals. *Frontiers in Human Neuroscience*, 8:528. doi:10.3389/fnhum.2014.00528

Kiesler, D. J. (1996). *Contemporary interpersonal theory and research: Personality, psychopathology, and psychotherapy*. Hoboken, NJ: Wiley.

Kihlstrom, J. F. (2008). The domain of hypnosis, revisited. In M. R. Nash & A. J. Barnier (Eds.), *The Oxford handbook of hypnosis* (pp. 21–52). Oxford, UK: Oxford University Press.

Kihlstrom, J. F. (2013). Neuro-hypnotism: Prospects for hypnosis and neuroscience. *Cortex*, *49*, 365–374. doi:10.1016/j.cortex.2012.05.016

Kirsch, I., & Council, J. R. (1992). Situational and personality correlates of hypnotic responsiveness. In E. Fromm & M. Nash (Eds.), *Contemporary hypnosis research* (pp. 267–291). New York, NY: Guilford.

Kirsch, I., & Lynn, S. J. (1995). The altered state of hypnosis: Changes in the theoretical landscape. *American Psychologist*, *50*, 846–858. doi:10.1037/0003-066X.50.10.846

Lankton, S. R., & Matthews, W. J. (2010). An Ericksonian model of clinical hypnosis. In S. J. Lynn, J. W. Rhue, & I. Kirsch (Eds.), *Handbook of clinical hypnosis* (2nd ed., pp. 209–237). Washington, DC: American Psychological Association.

Leary, T. (1957). *Interpersonal diagnosis of personality: A functional theory and methodology for personality evaluation*. New York, NY: Ronald Press.

Lynn, S. J., & Kirsch, I. (2006). *Essentials of clinical hypnosis: An evidence-based approach*. Washington, DC: American Psychological Association.

Lynn, S. J., Neufeld, V., & Maré, C. (1993). Direct versus indirect suggestions: A conceptual and methodological review. *International Journal of Clinical and Experimental Hypnosis*, *41*, 124–152. doi:10.1080/00207149308414543

Lynn, S. J., & Sivec, H. (1992). The hypnotizable subject as creative problem solving agent. In E. Fromm & M. Nash (Eds.), *Contemporary hypnosis research* (pp. 292–333). New York, NY: Guilford.

Maquet, P., Faymonville, E., Degueldre, C., Delfiore, G., Franck, G., Luxen, A., & Lamy, M. (1999). Functional neuroanatomy of hypnotic state. *Biological Psychiatry*, *45*, 327–333. doi:10.1016/S0006-3223(97)00546-5

Mazzoni, G., Venneri, A., McGeown, W. J., & Kirsch, I. (2013). Neuroimaging resolution of the altered state hypothesis. *Cortex*, *49*, 400–410. doi:10.1016/j.cortex.2012.08.005

McConkey, K. M., & Barnier, A. J. (2004). The highly hypnotizable person: Unity and diversity in behaviour and experience. In M. Heap, R. Brown, & D. Oakley (Eds.), *High hypnotisability: Theoretical, experimental and clinical issues* (pp. 61–84). London, UK: Brunner-Routledge.

McConkey, K. M., Glisky, M. L., & Kihlstrom, J. F. (1989). Individual differences among hypnotic virtuosos: A case comparison. *Australian Journal of Clinical and Experimental Hypnosis*, *17*, 131–140.

McGeown, W. J., Mazzoni, G., Vannucci, M., & Venneri, A. (2015). Structural and functional correlates of hypnotic depth and suggestibility. *Psychiatry Research: Neuroimaging*, *231*, 151–159. doi:10.1016/j.pscychresns.2014.11.015

McGeown, W. J., Mazzoni, G., Venneri, A., & Kirsch, I. (2009). Hypnotic induction decreases anterior default mode activity. *Consciousness and Cognition*, *18*, 848–855. doi:10.1016/j.concog.2009.09.001

Nash, M. R. (2005). The importance of being earnest when crafting definitions: Science and scientism are not the same thing. *International Journal of Clinical and Experimental Hypnosis*, *53*(3), 265–280. doi:10.1080/00207140590961934

Pekala, R. J., & Kumar, V. K. (2002). Operationalizing "trance" I: Rationale and research using a psychophenomenological approach. *American Journal of Clinical Hypnosis*, *43*, 107–135. doi:10.1080/00029157.2000.10404265

Pekala, R. J., Kumar, V. K., Maurer, R., Elliott-Carter, N., Moon, E., & Mullen, K. (2010a). Suggestibility, expectancy, trance state effects, and hypnotic depth: I. Implications for understanding hypnotism. *American Journal of Clinical Hypnosis*, *52*, 271–286.

Pekala, R. J., Kumar, V. K., Maurer, R., Elliott-Carter, N., Moon, E., & Mullen, K. (2010b). Suggestibility, expectancy, trance state effects, and hypnotic depth: II. Assessment via the PCI-HAP. *American Journal of Clinical Hypnosis*, *52*, 287–314.

Raij, T. T., Numminen, J., Närvänen, S., Hittunen, J., & Hari, R. (2005). Brain correlates of subjective reality of physically and psychologically induced pain. *Proceedings of the National Academy of Sciences*, *102*, 2147–2151. doi:10.1073/pnas.0409542102

Rainville, P., Hofbauer, R. K., Bushnell, M. C., Duncan, G. H., & Price, D. (2002). Hypnosis modulates activity in brain structures involved in the regulation of consciousness. *Journal of Cognitive Neuroscience*, *14*, 887–901. doi:10.1162/089892902760191117

Rainville, P., Hofbauer, R. K., Paus, T., Duncan, G. H., Bushnell, M. C., & Price, D. D. (1999). Cerebral mechanisms of hypnotic induction and suggestion. *Journal of Cognitive Neuroscience*, *11*, 110–125. doi:10.1162/089892999563175

Rosenthal, R. (1963). On the social psychology of the psychological experiment: The experimenter's hypothesis as unintended determinant of experimental results. *American Scientist*, *51*(2), 268–283.

Sadler, P., Ethier, N., & Woody, E. (2011). Interpersonal complementarity. In L. M. Horowitz & S. N. Strack (Eds.), *Handbook of interpersonal psychology: Theory, research, assessment, and therapeutic interventions* (pp. 123–142). New York, NY: Wiley.

Shor, R. E., & Orne, E. C. (1962). *The Harvard group scale of hypnotic susceptibility, form A*. Palo Alto, CA: Consulting Psychologists Press.

Skiba, A. H. (1983). *The comparative efficacy of traditional hypnotic and rapid induction analgesia*. Unpublished manuscript, Hofstra University, Hempstead, NY.

Szechtman, H., Woody, E., Bowers, K. S., & Nahmias, C. (1998). Where the imaginal appears real: A PET study of auditory hallucinations. *Proceedings of the National Academy of Sciences*, *95*, 1956–1960. doi:10.1073/pnas.95.4.1956

Tasso, A. F., & Pérez, N. A. (2008). Parsing everyday suggestibility: What does it tell us about hypnosis? In M. R. Nash & A. J. Barnier (Eds.), *The Oxford handbook of hypnosis* (pp. 283–309). Oxford, UK: Oxford University Press.

Terhune, D. B., & Cardeña, E. (2010). Differential patterns of spontaneous phenomenological response to a hypnotic induction: A latent profile analysis. *Consciousness and Cognition*, *19*, 1140–1150. doi:10.1016/j.concog.2010.03.006

Terhune, D. B., Cardeña, E., & Lindgren, M. (2011). Differential frontal-parietal phase synchrony during hypnosis as a function of hypnotic suggestibility. *Psychophysiology*, *48*, 1444–1447. doi:10.1111/j.1469-8986.2011.01211.x

Thomas, K. M., Hopwood, C. J., Woody, E., Ethier, N., & Sadler, P. (2014). Momentary assessment of interpersonal process in psychotherapy. *Journal of Counseling Psychology*, *61*(1), 1–14. doi:10.1037/a0034277

Varga, K., Bányai, É. I., Józsa, E., & Gősi-Greguss, A. C. (2008). Interactional phenomena of maternal and paternal hypnosis styles. *Contemporary Hypnosis*, *25*(1), 14–28. doi:10.1002/ch.347

Weitzenhoffer, A. M. (1974). When is an "instruction" an instruction? *International Journal of Clinical and Experimental Hypnosis*, *22*, 258–269. doi:10.1080/00207147408413005

Weitzenhoffer, A. M. (1980). Hypnotic susceptibility revisited. *American Journal of Clinical Hypnosis*, *22*, 130–146. doi:10.1080/00029157.1980.10403217

Weitzenhoffer, A. M., & Hilgard, E. R. (1959). *Stanford hypnotic susceptibility scale, forms A and B*. Palo Alto, CA: Consulting Psychologists Press.

Winkel, J. D., Younger, J. W., Tomcik, N., Borckardt, J. J., & Nash, M. R. (2006). Anatomy of a hypnotic response: Self-report estimates, actual behavior, and physiological response to the hypnotic suggestion of arm rigidity. *International Journal of Clinical and Experimental Hypnosis*, *54*, 186–205. doi:10.1080/00207140500528430

Woody, E., & Sadler, P. (2005). Some polite applause for the 2003 APA Division 30 definition of hypnosis. *American Journal of Clinical Hypnosis*, *48*, 99–106. doi:10.1080/00029157.2005.10401502

Woody, E., & Szechtman, H. (2003). How can brain activity and hypnosis inform each other? *International Journal of Clinical and Experimental Hypnosis*, *51*, 232–255. doi:10.1076/iceh.51.3.232.15521

Woody, E. Z., & Barnier, A. J. (2008). Hypnosis scales for the twenty-first century: What do we need and how should we use them? In M. R. Nash & A. J. Barnier (Eds.), *The Oxford handbook of hypnosis* (pp. 255–281). Oxford, UK: Oxford University Press.

Woody, E. Z., Barnier, A. J., & McConkey, K. M. (2005). Multiple hypnotizabilities: Differentiating the building blocks of hypnotic response. *Psychological Assessment*, *17*, 200–211. doi:10.1037/1040-3590.17.2.200

Woody, E. Z., Bowers, K. S., & Oakman, J. M. (1992). A conceptual analysis of hypnotic responsiveness: Experience, individual differences, and context. In E. Fromm & M. Nash (Eds.), *Contemporary hypnosis research* (pp. 3–33). New York, NY: Guilford.

Zamansky, H. S. (1977). Suggestion and countersuggestion in hypnotic behavior. *Journal of Abnormal Psychology*, *86*, 346–351. doi:10.1037/0021-843X.86.4.346

Zamansky, H. S., & Clark, L. E. (1986). Cognitive competition and hypnotic behavior: Whither absorption? *International Journal of Clinical and Experimental Hypnosis*, *34*, 205–214. doi:10.1080/00207148608406986

Nuances and Uncertainties Regarding Hypnotic Inductions: Toward a Theoretically Informed Praxis

Devin B. Terhune

Etzel Cardeña

Although most definitions of hypnosis consider inductions as the initial stage in a hypnosis protocol, knowledge of inductions remains poor and uninformed by recent developments in theory and research. It is frequently argued that inductions play a critical role in hypnotic responding or, by contrast, are largely interchangeable and unimportant. Drawing on the literature on suggestibility, spontaneous phenomenology, neurophysiology, and cognition, this article argues that the value of inductions, as well as the *potential* value of inductions, is more nuanced and uncertain. Certain components of standard inductions appear to be efficacious in enhancing suggestibility, whereas others do not have any clear benefits. The impact of inductions on suggestibility seems to vary across suggestions and modes of assessment with the sources of this variability being unknown. Considering these effects, and the broader impact of inductions on spontaneous conscious states and cognition, through the lens of heterogeneity in high hypnotic suggestibility and componential models of hypnotic suggestibility may offer novel research avenues in this area. The article concludes by arguing for the practical and theory-driven optimization of inductions.

Most definitions of hypnosis consider inductions as the initial stage in a hypnosis protocol (Elkins, Barabasz, Council, & Spiegel, 2015; Nash, 2005). Hypnotic inductions may follow introductory remarks about hypnosis and typically consist of instructions and suggestions intended to make the participant receptive to subsequent suggestions for changes in experience and behavior. Although inductions vary considerably, most are implemented with the *goal* of promoting an attentional state in which one is absorbed in the words and actions of the therapist or experimenter but inattentive to environmental stimuli and extraneous concerns (Barber, 1984). However, despite their widespread use and some early systematic research (Barber, 1969; Hilgard, 1965), knowledge of inductions remains relatively poor and uninformed by recent developments in theory and research. As is unfortunately the case with other features of hypnosis, some clinicians and researchers overstate the case, declaring either that some specific inductions are especially effective (Bandler & Grinder, 1975) or, contrariwise, that inductions are unimportant and/or that all inductions have relatively similar effects (Spanos, 1986). In contrast, we believe that the value of inductions, as well as the *potential* value of inductions, is more nuanced and uncertain and warrants greater empirical attention. In what follows, we summarize research on the impact of inductions, drawing on the literature on suggestibility, spontaneous phenomenology, neurophysiology, and cognition. We further consider a number of these effects through the lens of heterogeneity in high hypnotic suggestibility. Rather than arguing for or against the impact of inductions on suggestibility, we maintain that uncertainties abound. We aim to call attention to the relatively impoverished state of knowledge regarding inductions and their component features and argue for renewed attention to the *optimization* of inductions.

Inductions and Their Components

Most hypnosis protocols, and all measures of hypnotic suggestibility, involve some type of induction. In the *indirect* or *informal* approach championed in the Milton Erickson clinical perspective, there may not be any obvious induction; in contrast, formal inductions involve suggestions to relax and/or imagine something, fixate on a target or look upward, manipulate the person's body, confuse, or even shock the person with a sudden movement or word, and so on (Hammond, 1988; Weitzenhoffer, 2000). Inductions vary depending on the scale used or the aims, theoretical orientation, and practical considerations of the clinician or experimenter administering the induction. For example, Barber (1969) devised the *Barber Suggestibility Scale* with alternatives for prefacing specific suggestions with a typical hypnotic induction, task motivational instructions, or no instruction at all. The structure of inductions varies considerably in clinical contexts, whereas most empirical studies use variations of the inductions included in standardized scales of hypnotic suggestibility (Woody & Barnier, 2008). However, the most widely used hypnotic suggestibility scales are decades old and consequently do not take into consideration recent theoretical advances. Moreover, the inductions included in these scales are often grafts of various historical ideas about hypnosis that have been shown to be false (e.g., implied associations between hypnosis and sleep) (Hilgard, 1982) and are, at times, cumbersome, poorly phrased, and too long (e.g., Shor & Orne, 1962).

Standardized inductions used in research are often comprised of four components: (a) *procedure identification*: identifying the procedure as hypnosis and informing someone that they will enter a state of hypnosis; (b) *receptive set*: instructions and suggestions to put the participant in an appropriate or receptive experiential set; (c) *relaxation*:

instructions, exercises, and suggestions intended to promote relaxation; and (d) *absorption set*: instructions and suggestions to promote absorption in the words and actions of the experimenter and the corresponding suggested or spontaneous inner experiences while diminishing attention to environmental stimuli and extraneous concerns. Although these components are present in the vast majority of inductions used in hypnosis research, an obvious question is whether they represent *essential* or *functional* elements of an induction.

The research carried out to investigate this question indicates that not all of these components are efficacious. There is evidence that the first is important: the word *hypnosis* embedded within an induction elicits greater suggestibility than an induction without it (Gandhi & Oakley, 2005). The probable reason is that this word produces for many people in Western culture the expectation that the procedure will bring about unusual changes, which may elicit the appropriate response from the participant according to her/his capacity (Cardeña, 2014b; Wagstaff, 2014). In contrast, in other sociocultural contexts in which *hypnosis* does not have the same cultural baggage, using the term will probably have no, or even negative, effects (Cardeña & Krippner, 2010). However, the use of the word alone is potentially insufficient and may require some type of induction to have a greater effect. For instance, Barber (1969) found that participants felt more hypnotized if the word *hypnosis* was accompanied by relaxation suggestions.

The second common component of inductions would fall to a large degree under *Response Set Theory* (Kirsch & Lynn, 1998; Lynn, Kirsch, & Hallquist, 2008), which states that providing the context for expectations of behavioral and subjective changes may elicit such responses. Although there is considerable evidence for an association between response expectancies and hypnotic suggestibility (Benham, Woody, Wilson, & Nash, 2006; Lynn et al., 2008), there are very few studies that bear on the influence of different types of verbalizations intended to change the person's set (e.g., "Remain open to whatever you experience" versus "You can analyze your behavior") on hypnotic responding. One example is a study in which, after a relaxation induction, suggestions encouraging reduced critical thinking or absorption were more efficacious in increasing suggestibility than additional relaxation suggestions (Brown, Antonova, Langley, & Oakley, 2001). There is also some, albeit mixed, evidence that manipulating environmental stimulation to enhance expectancies for response to suggestion increases suggestibility (Benham, Bowers, Nash, & Muenchen, 1998; Lifshitz, Howells, & Raz, 2012; Wickless & Kirsch, 1989). An example of this might be surreptitiously manipulating the lighting in the room after informing participants that those very responsive to hypnosis might experience changes in the lighting (Wickless & Kirsch, 1989).

The available evidence indicates that the third component (relaxation) is incidental and unnecessary. Research has shown that inductions involving physical exercise and/or verbalizations for mental alertness are as effective as relaxation-based inductions (Bányai & Hilgard, 1976; Cardeña, Alarcon, Capafons, & Bayot, 1998; Malott, 1984;

Mitchell & Lundy, 1986). Other research suggests that relaxation inductions may not reliably enhance suggestibility (Brown et al., 2001). In contrast, the fourth component, absorption, seems to enhance suggestibility, although not as much as reducing critical thinking (Brown et al., 2001) or as using facilitative sensory stimulation (Wickless & Kirsch, 1989). Thus, research suggests that certain components of standardized inductions (using the word hypnosis, fostering absorption, and reducing critical thinking) enhance suggestibility, whereas others (relaxation) are incidental and unnecessary (see also Hilgard, 1982). However, the scant research on the influence of these different components on suggestibility has largely treated them in isolation, and thus an outstanding question is whether, and to what extent, they have additive or interacting effects on suggestibility.

Another important question is whether different inductions are beneficial for certain types of subsequent suggestions or for individuals with particular abilities. Thus, for instance, it may be that relaxation inductions will facilitate later suggestions to imagine oneself lying on a beach because they decrease afferent somatosensory stimulation, whereas arousing inductions may be more beneficial for suggestions to increase one's sense of bodily vigor and energy (cf. Cardeña, 2005). Similarly, inductions that implicitly or explicitly encourage specific strategies for hypnotic responding may be differentially effective depending on the individual's preferred or habitual strategy, cognitive set, and the respective suggestion (Sheehan & McConkey, 1982). Such contextual influences have not been properly explored, although they are consistent with the observation that the preceding suggestion seems to influence the underlying ability or strategy one uses when responding to a suggestion (Woody, Barnier, & McConkey, 2005) and the reliable finding that highly suggestible individuals display pronounced inter-individual variability in the types of suggestions to which they respond (McConkey & Barnier, 2004; Terhune, 2015).

Inductions and Suggestibility

Some researchers maintain that anything can function as an induction, from an extended relaxation-based induction to the ringing of a bell, and that the components of inductions are relatively unimportant (Spanos, 1986). According to such accounts, what is important is the contextual cue that one is about to undergo a hypnotic procedure and the elicitation of any associated response (Lynn et al., 2008). This position is largely based on data showing that a hypnotic induction elicits only a modest increase in suggestibility (Braffman & Kirsch, 1999; Hilgard & Tart, 1966). In our opinion, discussions about the impact of inductions on suggestibility have stopped prematurely in the wake of such data, failing to properly consider other equally rich data that complicate interpretation.

There are a number of concerns with generalizing solely on the basis of behavioral hypnotic suggestibility scales. First, it is unclear to what extent hypnotic suggestibility scales accurately index the *classic suggestion effect*, namely, the perceived involuntariness of responses to suggestions (Weitzenhoffer, 1980; for alternative interpretation, see K. S. Bowers, 1981; Hilgard, 1981). For example, research measuring involuntariness during response to suggestions in a standardized scale showed that as many as 20% of responses are executed in a *completely* voluntary manner (P. Bowers, Laurence, & Hart, 1988). Thus, hypnotic suggestibility scales probably index a mixture of involuntary and compliant responses that cannot be reliably distinguished solely on the basis of behavioral indices (see also Balthazard & Woody, 1992; Barnes, Lynn, & Pekala, 2009; Kirsch, Silva, Comey, & Reed, 1995). Second, only minimal attention has been devoted to experiential responses to hypnotic suggestions in the wake of an induction. Although behavioral and experiential scales are moderately to strongly associated (Kirsch, Council, & Wickless, 1990; Kirsch, Milling, & Burgess, 1998), they are not redundant (P. Bowers et al., 1988; Ruch, Morgan, & Hilgard, 1974), and experiential scales may offer valuable information absent from studies that rely solely on behavioral measures (Bates & Brigham, 1990; Cardeña & Terhune, 2014; Cardeña, Terhune, Loof, & Buratti, 2009; Council, Kirsch, & Hafner, 1986; Spanos, Arango, & Degroot, 1993). Third, statements regarding the impact of inductions have typically neglected behavioral and experiential data drawn from experimental research involving different inductions and/or more complex suggestions and methods for assessing responsiveness to suggestion.

Different inductions have been compared only very rarely, despite the importance of such knowledge. Spanos and colleagues (1986) found no differences in different behavioral and experiential measures of suggestibility between the *Carleton University Responsiveness to Suggestion Scale* (CURSS) induction (Spanos et al., 1983)—which, in contrast with most other standardized inductions, emphasizes that responsiveness depends entirely on the willingness to cooperate, and that the participant retains full control—and the *Stanford Hypnotic Susceptibility Scale: Form C* (Weitzenhoffer & Hilgard, 1962) induction, which includes a standard relaxation-based induction. However, in a later study, the CURSS induction produced a greater number of participants of low hypnotic suggestibility than two other inductions, the Harvard Group Scale of Hypnotic Susceptibility: Form A (HGSHS:A) and the Group Scale of Hypnotic Ability (GSHA) (an abbreviated version of the matching the length of the CURSS), and reports of feeling less deeply hypnotized, more rational, and so on (Barnes et al., 2009).

With regard to informal Ericksonian approaches, indirect inductions have not been shown to be more effective in enhancing suggestibility than direct ones (Lynn, Neufeld, & Mare, 1993); in fact, the latter have been found to elicit greater spontaneous changes in consciousness (Robin, Kumar, & Pekala, 2005). Page and Handley (1991) also found no difference in behavioral or experiential suggestibility between a standard relaxation-based induction and a Chiasson induction, in which one stares at her/his outstretched hand; nor did Page and colleagues find that adding a visual and auditory device to enhance gaze fixation produced a greater effect than a standard eye fixation induction (Page, Handley, & Carey, 2002). Similarly, an induction that includes visual fixation, although widespread, does not seem to have a greater effect than one without it (Weitzenhofer & Sakata, 1970). The length of the induction does not appear to be critical either, as rapid inductions appear to be similarly effective and may actually be viewed more favorably than traditional inductions (Martinez-Tendero, Capafons, Weber, & Cardeña, 2001), although at least one study observed noticeably greater, albeit non-significantly so, behavioral and experiential hypnotic suggestibility for a 10-minute than a 1-minute induction (Klinger, 1970). Furthermore, individuals feel more deeply hypnotized after some minutes have elapsed than immediately after an induction, which would speak against a very rapid induction (Cardeña, Jonsson, Terhune, & Marcusson-Clavertz, 2013). There is also some evidence that formal inductions may also be less important in clinical contexts (Straus, 1980). On the whole, these studies reveal relatively few—and minor—differences in the impact of different inductions on suggestibility.

Research on complex suggestions in experimental settings using more advanced methods introduces greater nuance into the impact of an induction on suggestibility. It has been shown, for instance, that non-hypnotic suggestions are comparably effective to posthypnotic suggestions in disrupting the Stroop interference effect (Raz, Kirsch, Pollard, & Nitkin-Kaner, 2006). This aligns with some of the studies reviewed above stating that an induction may have only minimal impact. In contrast, research on delusions in which participants judged the magnitude of their response continuously using a dial found that hypnotic suggestions elicited more *rapid* responses than suggestions that were preceded by a puzzle task rather than an induction, even though the two methods were associated with roughly equivalent *frequencies* of response to the suggestions (McConkey, Szeps, & Barnier, 2001). Another study on induced delusions similarly found that the same suggestion for a mirror-self misidentification delusion was eight times more effective when preceded by an induction (Connors, Barnier, Coltheart, Cox, & Langdon, 2012). These data suggest that the impact of an induction on suggestibility is far less clear-cut than suggested by some authors. In particular, these results raise the question whether an induction is more effective for particular suggestions. They also suggest the possibilities that the impact of an induction may be more salient for particular *features* of an individual's response to a suggestion and/or that certain measurement methods may be better at detecting the efficacy of an induction (e.g., McConkey et al., 2001).

Other questions regarding the impact of inductions on suggestibility remain largely unexplored. Inductions may include explicit or implicit suggestions regarding the strategies to use when responding to suggestions, which may impact suggestibility (Woody & Barnier, 2008). For example, Comey and Kirsch (1999) found that *omitting* instructions for goal-directed fantasy in an induction was associated with increased responsiveness to some suggestions. There is also evidence that responsiveness to different suggestions recruits different underlying mechanisms (Woody et al., 2005). In particular, this research implies that hypnotic suggestibility may be comprised of a core ability *and* ancillary componential abilities that differentially influence responsiveness to specific suggestions (e.g., ideomotor versus hallucination suggestions). Thus, different inductions or different components of inductions may have a different impact on ensuing suggestions. Previous research found that non-hypnotic suggestibility was more strongly associated with easy (ideomotor) suggestions than difficult (cognitive-perceptual) suggestions (Woody, Drugovic, & Oakman, 1997). If this association holds, responsiveness to cognitive-perceptual suggestions should be influenced by an induction to a greater extent than ideomotor suggestions.

Induction Response Variability

An indisputable fact about hypnosis is that individuals display marked variability in their responsiveness to suggestions. Conceptualizing an induction as the first suggestion in a hypnosis procedure (Nash, 2005) implies that individuals may vary in their response to the induction. Although an understudied question, research indicates that inductions do not elicit uniform changes in suggestibility across participants. For example, Tart and Hilgard (1966) identified subgroups of participants who were either highly suggestible at baseline *and* following an induction or low in suggestibility at baseline *but* highly suggestible following an induction (see also Hilgard & Tart, 1966). Braffman and Kirsch (1999) similarly found that an induction increased behavioral and experiential suggestibility in ~45% of participants but decreased them in ~28% of participants. Although the relative lack of observable change in suggestibility following an induction in some highly suggestible individuals may be due to ceiling effects (Kirsch et al., 2011), these data still highlight the considerable variability in response to an induction.

These data might be reconciled with typological models of high hypnotic suggestibility, according to which there may be two or three discrete subtypes of respondents (Barber, 1999; Carlson & Putnam, 1989). These accounts maintain that one of these subtypes is characterized by pronounced dissociative tendencies, and there is growing evidence in favor of this typology (Terhune & Cardeña, 2015). Barber (1999), in particular, predicted that high dissociative highly suggestible individuals would be more responsive to an induction than highly suggestible individuals low in dissociation. This prediction has not yet been directly tested to our knowledge, but preliminary, indirect evidence comes from studies showing that individuals with pronounced dissociative symptoms (i.e., those with dissociative, post-traumatic, or functional neurological disorders) display elevated hypnotic suggestibility (Bryant, Guthrie, & Moulds, 2001; Roelofs et al., 2002; Spiegel, Hunt, & Dondershine, 1988; but see Litwin & Cardeña, 2001), but do not seem to differ from controls in non-hypnotic suggestibility

(Brown, Schrag, Krishnamoorthy, & Trimble, 2008). This leads to the prediction that dissociative tendencies will be associated with an individual's increase in suggestibility following an induction. These potentially rich inter-individual differences are lost in the use of aggregate data to contrast baseline and hypnotic suggestibility and should be considered more thoroughly in future research on the impact of inductions.

Spontaneous Experiential and Cognitive Sequelae of Inductions

Discussions of the impact and significance of inductions have typically neglected the spontaneous sequelae experienced by participants following an induction. These phenomena, however, provide valuable information regarding changes in cognitive and perceptual functioning produced by an induction and their neurophysiological underpinnings and are likely to color the phenomenology of hypnotic responding more broadly as they reliably co-vary with individual differences in hypnotic suggestibility (Pekala & Kumar, 2007).

One line of research has sought to explore the spontaneous experiences reported in response to a standard induction using a self-report instrument, the *Phenomenology of Consciousness Inventory* (Pekala & Kumar, 2007). This research has consistently found that highly suggestible individuals reliably experience spontaneous alterations in body image, time perception, meaning, and awareness, increased affect and imagery, and decreased self-awareness, rationality, volition, and memory following an induction (see also Cardeña, 2014a). One study reported that direct and indirect inductions have similar effects on spontaneous phenomenology (Szabó, 1993), although a subsequent study found that direct inductions elicited greater spontaneous alterations in awareness (Robin et al., 2005).

One limitation of these studies is that they used standardized inductions drawn from scales such as the HGSHS:A (Shor & Orne, 1962). As described above, these inductions typically include references to sleep and repeated instructions and suggestions to promote relaxation and heaviness of the body and limbs, absorption in the words of the experimenter, and reduced awareness of the environment. Thus, any changes in different dimensions of consciousness following an induction may be driven by the inclusion of such components. In turn, the use of such inductions renders it difficult to disentangle which experiences are attributable to which components. Cardeña (2005) circumvented these limitations by using a minimal (neutral) induction with only a 1–30 count and a suggestion to go into hypnosis. Highly suggestible participants still exhibited pronounced changes in a variety of dimensions of consciousness similar to those reported by Pekala and Kumar (2007), although low suggestible individuals did not experience substantial changes (Cardeña et al., 2013). These results complement the observation that the word *hypnosis* enhances suggestibility (Gandhi & Oakley, 2005) and seem to suggest that many features of standardized inductions are not necessary to observe the rich spontaneous sequelae of an induction. Complicating matters, research has begun to show that spontaneous experiential response to an induction may comprise discrete patterns (Pekala & Kumar, 2007; Terhune & Cardeña, 2010). We previously found that highly suggestible participants exhibited one of two distinct response patterns: a *dissociative* response characterized by greater alterations in experience, greater negative affect, poorer attention, and reduced volitional control, and an *inward attention* response characterized by greater awareness of mental processes and greater imagery vividness (Terhune & Cardeña, 2010). These results suggest that inductions elicit a diverse array of spontaneous experiences that may form unique patterns of responding.

Such research can be further expanded upon by adopting a neurophenomenological orientation that integrates neurophysiological and experiential data (Cardeña, 2016; Lutz & Thompson, 2003). Following this approach, we investigated the electrophysiological correlates of spontaneous experiences following a neutral induction (Cardeña et al., 2013). Notably, spontaneous experiences of positive affect and transcendence, and hypnotic suggestibility (marginally), were inversely associated with global functional connectivity, suggesting that some spontaneous anomalous experiences following an induction are associated with reduced network communication. Complementary research has further shown that, following an induction, highly suggestible individuals exhibit reduced frontal-parietal connectivity (Terhune, Cardeña, & Lindgren, 2011a) and frontal connectivity (Jamieson & Burgess, 2014) in frequency bands related to a range of higher-order cognitive functions.

Using electroencephalography (EEG), De Pascalis (1993) found that during the early and middle stages of an induction (Morgan & Hilgard, 1979), highly suggestible participants exhibited greater power in the upper beta band than low suggestible participants. Offering better spatial resolution than EEG, resting state functional magnetic resonance imaging (fMRI) research (McGeown, Mazzoni, Venneri, & Kirsch, 2009) has shown that highly suggestible individuals exhibit greater deactivation of anterior medial prefrontal cortex following an induction than low suggestible participants (see also Deeley et al., 2012). Medial prefrontal cortex is activated during a range of psychological functions, so these data should be interpreted cautiously. Nevertheless, insofar as this region is similarly activated during metacognition of agency (Miele, Wager, Mitchell, & Metcalfe, 2011), it is plausible that changes in the activity patterns of this region reflect decreases in metacognition or self-related processing (see also Landry & Raz, 2015) that contribute to individual differences in hypnotic suggestibility. Additional research is required to clarify the neurophysiological basis of these experiences, but these converging results have begun to highlight how neurophysiological changes following an induction underlie spontaneous alterations in consciousness.

An independent line of research has sought to understand the impact of an induction on spontaneous cognition and perception. This research has been motivated by the desire to discriminate between competing theories of hypnosis (Woody & Sadler, 2008), but it also has implications for the role of inductions in hypnotic responding. Although not programmatic, multiple studies have suggested that a hypnotic induction impairs selective attention among highly suggestible, but not low suggestible, individuals (Jamieson & Sheehan, 2004; see also Farvolden & Woody, 2004). These results are arguably consistent with the phenomenological and neurophysiological sequelae of inductions described above. Inductions also seem to reliably produce contractions in the perception of duration relative to control conditions (Naish, 2014). These timing distortions are of theoretical importance given the overlapping neural circuitry between time perception and sense of agency (Yin, Terhune, Smythies, & Meck, 2016), changes in which constitute the primary phenomenological feature of hypnotic responding (K. S. Bowers, 1981; Kihlstrom, 2008; Weitzenhoffer, 1980).

As with other dimensions of hypnotic responding, individuals also vary in the extent to which their cognitive functioning is affected by an induction. In two independent studies with different samples, an induction selectively impaired sustained attention and cognitive control among high suggestible individuals who were highly dissociative, but not among those who exhibited few dissociative tendencies (Marcusson-Clavertz, Terhune, & Cardeña, 2012; Terhune, Cardeña, & Lindgren, 2011b). The former study used a relaxation-based induction that did not mention hypnosis, whereas the latter used a hand heaviness induction without mentioning relaxation (the two subtypes did not differ in relaxation across conditions), suggesting that these results are relatively robust and that some of the spontaneous responses to an induction may be restricted to, or elevated among, high dissociative highly suggestible individuals. Such effects may be related to other characteristics of this subgroup, including elevated involuntariness (Terhune, Cardeña, & Lindgren, 2011c) and reduced attentional effort (King & Council, 1998) during hypnotic responding, as well as in their spontaneous experiences in daily life (Cardeña & Marcusson-Clavertz, 2016). These findings suggest that an induction elicits spontaneous changes in cognition and perception in highly suggestible individuals, and that some of these effects are more pronounced in high dissociative highly suggestible individuals. How these results relate to other effects of an induction remains unclear and requires further research.

Optimizing Inductions

Although much of the discussion regarding the impact of inductions has focused on whether inductions are effective in enhancing suggestibility and which components of inductions are essential, a more substantive question is which components function to *optimize* inductions. In other words, researchers and clinicians should actively seek to better understand which components facilitate the largest increase in suggestibility and whether these components are uniformly efficacious across individuals. In this final subsection, we return to the components of inductions and consider ways to optimize inductions. We first describe a number of practical ways to improve inductions and then advocate for theory-driven optimization of inductions.

The most widely used measures of hypnotic suggestibility were developed more than half a century ago (Shor & Orne, 1962; Weitzenhoffer & Hilgard, 1962), and there are concerns regarding their efficacy (P. Bowers et al., 1988; Ruch et al., 1974; Terhune, 2015; Woody & Barnier, 2008). As research turns to the development of novel measures of hypnotic suggestibility, researchers and clinicians must also improve the inductions present in these scales. The efficacy of inductions can be easily enhanced with relatively minor adjustments. Standard inductions are excessively long, particularly in the HGSHS:A (Shor & Orne, 1962), and evidence from rapid inductions (Eitner, Wichmann, Schlegel, & Holst, 2006) suggests that this is unnecessary. For example, we have often noticed how all or most participants have already responded to the eye closure suggestion within the induction of the HGSHS:A long before the suggestion is completed, exemplifying the unnecessarily drawn-out nature of the induction. Inductions also sometimes make reference to antiquated ideas about hypnosis that are not empirically sound, such as the similarities between hypnosis and sleep, clear vestiges from previous eras (Hilgard, 1982) that should be excluded from standard inductions. We routinely omit such references in our own research, and we suspect that others do as well, but it is important for such omissions to become standard practice in order to ensure methodological uniformity across studies. Similarly, although they represent a core feature of the majority of inductions and are present in most of the major scales, the data indicate that there is mixed evidence as to how much, if at all, relaxation suggestions increase suggestibility (Bányai & Hilgard, 1976; Barber, 1969; Brown et al., 2001). Thus, we recommend that inductions in future scales and in experimental studies be more rapid and omit references to sleep and perhaps to relaxation. Standard inductions might also be strengthened by including absorption-specific instructions (Brown et al., 2001).

A further concern, the significance of which is not yet clear, is the uniformity of inductions across studies. Cognitive and neuroimaging studies often draw or adapt inductions from standard scales, which is beneficial because it ensures that readers are aware of the induction structure; however, this practice is not universal, and inductions are not always clearly specified. Perhaps more worrisome is that a number of neuroimaging studies on hypnosis have used inductions that include instructions and suggestions for visual imagery (for a review, see Oakley & Halligan, 2013). The inclusion of such specific suggestions, which do not have any clear value in the enhancement of suggestibility to our knowledge, only functions to cloud the interpretation of any phenomenological and neurophysiological data (Cardeña et al., 2013). For this reason, we think that the development of a battery of different inductions, with descriptions of their intended use and strengths and limitations, will prove useful across a range of contexts and procedures. This will advance the field by providing a common set of replicable procedures that provide much-needed standards for this understudied, but potentially important, feature of hypnosis. This battery should be developed with consideration to individual differences in hypnotic suggestibility (Terhune & Cardeña, 2015) and responsiveness to inductions (Braffman & Kirsch, 1999; Tart & Hilgard, 1966) as well as the characteristics of the subsequent suggestions. For example, analgesia suggestions may be better preceded by a relaxation than an active-alert induction (see also Woody et al., 2005). Moreover, such a battery may prove useful for clinicians working with dissociative patients as such individuals may feel more comfortable with an induction that emphasizes that they retain control over their experiences.

Inductions can be further optimized by approaching their development in a more theory-driven manner that integrates information from a range of sources to further enhance suggestibility. We find it unfortunate that relatively few of the previous comparisons of different inductions were grounded in contemporary theory. Theory-driven optimization has the potential to yield not only empirically-based induction modifications but also novel ways of testing such theories. A dominant strand present in a diverse array of theories of hypnosis is that hypnotic responding is characterized by a disruption of executive monitoring or meta-awareness (Dienes & Perner, 2007; Hilgard, 1977; Kunzendorf, 1985–1986). For example, Kirsch and Lynn (1998) proposed that individuals might intentionally respond to suggestions, but the volitional nature of their responses does not breach awareness. Dienes and Perner (2007) similarly proposed that the intention associated with the enactment of a response may not be accessible to consciousness because of a failure of metacognition, producing the perception that one was not the author of the response (i.e., the classic suggestion effect; K. S. Bowers, 1981; Weitzenhoffer, 1980). A corollary of these and similar accounts is that the experimental disruption of metacognition will augment suggestibility (Semmens-Wheeler, Dienes, & Duka, 2013). To our knowledge, only one study has explored this idea within the context of an induction. As described above, Brown and colleagues (2001) incorporated instructions and suggestions for reduced critical thinking, increased absorption, or further relaxation following a relaxation-based induction and found that the critical thinking (and, to a lesser extent, absorption) instructions enhanced behavioral and experiential suggestibility more than additional relaxation instructions. This suggests that promoting a reduction of mindfulness and disengagement from the critical evaluation of one's responses may augment hypnotic responding.

Other variables that should be targeted in inductions include response expectancies and rapport (Lynn et al., 2008). Although we believe that the magnitude of the role of response expectancies in hypnotic responding has sometimes been overstated, there is consistent evidence for an association between response expectancies and hypnotic suggestibility (Benham et al., 2006; Lynn et al., 2008), and increasing expectancies through different manipulations may prove to be a valuable way of enhancing suggestibility. For example, Klinger (1970) found that observing peers modeling high responsiveness increased the observers' own responsiveness. Although studies examining the extent to which manipulating variables that should augment response expectancies influences hypnotic suggestibility have produced mixed results (Benham et al., 1998; Lifshitz et al., 2012; Wickless & Kirsch, 1989), future research may benefit from considering ways to enhance response expectancies during the induction phase. By contrast, to our knowledge, no research has sought to systematically investigate ways by which rapport could be enhanced during the induction, but given its importance in both clinical and experimental contexts, this represents an important question that warrants attention.

Research on the optimization of inductions will also need to grapple with a number of methodological challenges. Between-groups designs involving the random allocation of participants to an induction condition or a control condition require larger sample sizes than within-groups designs in which participants undergo both conditions sequentially and thus are at increased risk of Type II errors, as demonstrated in failures to observe induction-specific differences in between-groups designs (Hilgard & Tart, 1966). Accordingly, any studies adopting between-groups designs will need to be prudent in the interpretation of null results and should consider using Bayesian statistical analyses (Dienes, 2014) and/or meta-analysis in order to more clearly weigh the respective evidence for or against the impact of an induction or specific components of an induction. In contrast, although within-groups designs have increased statistical power, they are susceptible to carryover effects. Although such effects do not always pose a concern in psychological research, they do represent a clear challenge in hypnosis studies. For instance, previous research has shown that the impact of an induction on suggestibility is *greater* when the induction condition precedes the baseline condition than when the baseline condition precedes the induction condition; this effect has been interpreted as participants "holding back" in the former baseline (Braffman & Kirsch, 1999). Further research has cited this as justification for administering the baseline condition prior to the induction condition with no counter-balancing (Milling, Coursen, Shores, & Waszkiewicz, 2010), but this may lead to an underestimation of the impact of an induction. Moreover, induction-specific differences observed in within-groups designs might also be related to fatigue, boredom, familiarity, or practice associated with repeated administration of the suggestion protocol. Future research on the impact of inductions should prioritize identifying the psychological variables that mediate any order effects in order to more robustly estimate the impact of an induction on suggestibility.

Summary and Conclusions

Although clinicians and researchers have made strong pronouncements regarding the importance, or lack thereof, of hypnotic inductions, a careful reading of the impact of inductions on suggestibility, spontaneous conscious states, cognition, and neurophysiology suggests a more nuanced perspective. Certain components of standard inductions appear to be efficacious in enhancing suggestibility, whereas others do not. The impact of an induction on suggestibility varies depending on a number of factors, including the type of suggestion and the mode of assessment, although the source of this variability is unknown. Moreover, inductions do not seem to uniformly impact suggestibility and cognition, and preliminary evidence suggests that typological and componential models may provide a valuable framework for understanding individual differences in the impact of an induction on suggestibility, spontaneous experience, and cognition. Despite the uncertainties surrounding the characteristics and mechanisms of inductions, theory-informed approaches offer new avenues for the optimization of inductions, a critical step in the development of novel measures of hypnotic suggestibility.

Funding

Devin B. Terhune acknowledges support from Bial foundation bursary 344/14.

References

Balthazard, C. G., & Woody, E. Z. (1992). The spectral analysis of hypnotic performance with respect to "absorption." *International Journal of Clinical and Experimental Hypnosis*, *40*, 21–43. doi:10.1080/00207149208409644

Bandler, R., & Grinder, J. (1975). *Patterns of the hypnotic techniques of Milton H. Erickson, M.D.* (Vol. 1). Cupertino, CA: Meta Publications.

Bányai, E. I., & Hilgard, E. R. (1976). A comparison of active-alert hypnotic induction with traditional relaxation induction. *Journal of Abnormal Psychology*, *85*(2), 218–224. doi:10.1037/0021-843X.85.2.218

Barber, T. X. (1969). *Hypnosis: A scientific approach*. New York, NY: Van Nostrand Reinhold.

Barber, T. X. (1984). Changing "unchangeable" bodily processes by (hypnotic) suggestions. In A. A. Sheikh (Ed.), *Imagination and healing* (pp. 69–127). Farmingdale, NY: Baywood.

Barber, T. X. (1999). A comprehensive three-dimensional theory of hypnosis. In I. Kirsch, A. Capafons, E. Cardeña-Buelna, & S. Amigo (Eds.), *Clinical hypnosis and self-regulation: Cognitive-behavioral perspectives* (pp. 21–48). Washington, DC: American Psychological Association.

Barnes, S. M., Lynn, S. J., & Pekala, R. J. (2009). Not all group hypnotic suggestibility scales are created equal: Individual differences in behavioral and subjective responses. *Consciousness and Cognition*, *18*, 255–265. doi:10.1016/j.concog.2008.07.006

Bates, B. L., & Brigham, T. A. (1990). Modifying hypnotizability with the Carleton skills training program: A partial replication and analysis of components. *International Journal of Clinical and Experimental Hypnosis*, *38*(3), 183–195. doi:10.1080/00207149008414517

Benham, G., Bowers, S., Nash, M., & Muenchen, R. (1998). Self-fulfilling prophecy and hypnotic response are not the same thing. *Journal of Personality and Social Psychology*, *75*(6), 1604–1613. doi:10.1037/0022-3514.75.6.1604

Benham, G., Woody, E. Z., Wilson, K. S., & Nash, M. R. (2006). Expect the unexpected: Ability, attitude, and responsiveness to hypnosis. *Journal of Personality and Social Psychology*, *91*(2), 342–350. doi:10.1037/0022-3514.91.2.342

Bowers, K. S. (1981). Do the Stanford Scales tap the "classic suggestion effect"? *International Journal of Clinical and Experimental Hypnosis*, *29*(1), 42–53. doi:10.1080/00207148108409142

Bowers, P., Laurence, J. R., & Hart, D. (1988). The experience of hypnotic suggestions. *International Journal of Clinical and Experimental Hypnosis*, *36*(4), 336–349. doi:10.1080/00207148808410523

Braffman, W., & Kirsch, I. (1999). Imaginative suggestibility and hypnotizability: An empirical analysis. *Journal of Personality and Social Psychology*, *77*(3), 578–587. doi:10.1037/0022-3514.77.3.578

Brown, R. J., Antonova, E., Langley, A., & Oakley, D. A. (2001). The effects of absorption and reduced critical though on suggestibility in an hypnotic context. *Contemporary Hypnosis*, *18*, 62–72. doi:10.1002/ch.220

Brown, R. J., Schrag, A., Krishnamoorthy, E., & Trimble, M. R. (2008). Are patients with somatization disorder highly suggestible? *Acta Psychiatrica Scandinavica*, *117*(3), 232–235. doi:10.1111/acp.2008.117.issue-3

Bryant, R. A., Guthrie, R. M., & Moulds, M. L. (2001). Hypnotizability in acute stress disorder. *American Journal of Psychiatry*, *158*(4), 600–604. doi:10.1176/appi.ajp.158.4.600

Cardeña, E. (2005). The phenomenology of deep hypnosis: Quiescent and physically active. *International Journal of Clinical and Experimental Hypnosis*, *53*(1), 37–59. doi:10.1080/00207140490914234

Cardeña, E. (2014a). Hypnos and psyche: How hypnosis has contributed to the study of consciousness. *Psychology of Consciousness: Theory, Research, and Practice*, *1*, 123–138.

Cardeña, E. (2014b). Spinning in circles. *Journal of Mind-Body Regulation*, *2*(2), 121–123.

Cardeña, E. (2016). Towards comprehensive neurophenomenological research in hypnosis and meditation. In A. Raz & M. Lifshitz (Eds.), *Hypnosis and meditation: Towards an integrative science of conscious planes* (pp. 281–301). Oxford, UK: Oxford University Press.

Cardeña, E., Alarcon, A., Capafons, A., & Bayot, A. (1998). Effects on suggestibility of a new method of active-alert hypnosis: Alert hand. *International Journal of Clinical and Experimental Hypnosis*, *46*(3), 280–294. doi:10.1080/00207149808410008

Cardeña, E., Jonsson, P., Terhune, D. B., & Marcusson-Clavertz, D. (2013). The neurophenomenology of neutral hypnosis. *Cortex*, *49*(2), 375–385. doi:10.1016/j.cortex.2012.04.001

Cardeña, E., & Krippner, S. (2010). The cultural context of hypnosis. In S. J. Lynn, J. W. Rhue, & I. Kirsch (Eds.), *Handbook of clinical hypnosis* (2nd ed., pp. 743–771). Washington, DC: American Psychological Association.

Cardeña, E., & Marcusson-Clavertz, D. (2016). The relation of hypnotizability and dissociation to everyday mentation: An experience-sampling study. *Psychology of Consciousness: Theory, Research, and Practice*, *3*(1), 61–79.

Cardeña, E., & Terhune, D. B. (2014). Hypnotizability, personality traits and the propensity to experience alterations of consciousness. *Psychology of Consciousness: Theory, Research, and Practice*, *1*, 292–307.

Cardeña, E., Terhune, D. B., Loof, A., & Buratti, S. (2009). Hypnotic experience is related to emotional contagion. *International Journal of Clinical and Experimental Hypnosis*, *57*(1), 33–46. doi:10.1080/00207140802463500

Carlson, E. B., & Putnam, F. W. (1989). Integrating research on dissociation and hypnotizability: Are there two pathways to hypnotizability? *Dissociation*, *2*, 32–38.

Comey, G., & Kirsch, I. (1999). Intentional and spontaneous imagery in hypnosis: The phenomenology of hypnotic responding. *International Journal of Clinical and Experimental Hypnosis*, *47*(1), 65–85. doi:10.1080/00207149908410023

Connors, M. H., Barnier, A. J., Coltheart, M., Cox, R. E., & Langdon, R. (2012). Mirrored-self misidentification in the hypnosis laboratory: Recreating the delusion from its component factors. *Cognitive Neuropsychiatry*, *17*(2), 151–176. doi:10.1080/13546805.2011.582287

Council, J. R., Kirsch, I., & Hafner, L. P. (1986). Expectancy versus absorption in the prediction of hypnotic responding. *Journal of Personality and Social Psychology*, *50*(1), 182–189. doi:10.1037/0022-3514.50.1.182

De Pascalis, V. (1993). EEG spectral analysis during hypnotic induction, hypnotic dream and age regression. *International Journal of Psychophysiology*, *15*, 153–166. doi:10.1016/0167-8760(93)90073-X

Deeley, Q., Oakley, D. A., Toone, B., Giampietro, V., Brammer, M. J., Williams, S. C., & Halligan, P. W. (2012). Modulating the default mode network using hypnosis. *International Journal of Clinical and Experimental Hypnosis*, *60*(2), 206–228. doi:10.1080/00207144.2012.648070

Dienes, Z. (2014). Using Bayes to get the most out of non-significant results. *Frontiers in Psychology*, *5*, 781. doi:10.3389/fpsyg.2014.00781

Dienes, Z., & Perner, J. (2007). Executive control without conscious awareness: The cold control theory of hypnosis. In G. A. Jamieson (Ed.), *Hypnosis and conscious states: The cognitive neuroscience perspective* (pp. 293–314). Oxford, UK: Oxford University Press.

Eitner, S., Wichmann, M., Schlegel, A., & Holst, S. (2006). Rapid induction of hypnosis by finger elongation: A brief communication. *International Journal of Clinical and Experimental Hypnosis*, *54* (3), 245–262. doi:10.1080/00207140600689405

Elkins, G. R., Barabasz, A. F., Council, J. R., & Spiegel, D. (2015). Advancing research and practice: The revised APA Division 30 definition of hypnosis. *American Journal of Clinical Hypnosis*, *57*(4), 378–385. doi:10.1080/00029157.2015.1011465

Farvolden, P., & Woody, E. Z. (2004). Hypnosis, memory, and frontal executive functioning. *International Journal of Clinical and Experimental Hypnosis*, *52*, 3–26. doi:10.1076/iceh.52.1.3.23926

Gandhi, B., & Oakley, D. A. (2005). Does 'hypnosis' by any other name smell as sweet? The efficacy of 'hypnotic' inductions depends on the label 'hypnosis'. *Consciousness and Cognition*, *14*(2), 304–315. doi:10.1016/j.concog.2004.12.004

Hammond, C. (Ed.). (1988). *Hypnotic induction & suggestion: An introductory manual*. Des Plaines, IL: American Society of Clinical Hypnosis.

Hilgard, E. R. (1965). *Hypnotic susceptibility*. New York, NY: Harcourt, Brace & World, Inc.

Hilgard, E. R. (1977). The problem of divided consciousness: A neodissociation interpretation. *Annals of the New York Academy of Sciences*, *296*, 48–59. doi:10.1111/nyas.1977.296.issue-1

Hilgard, E. R. (1981). Hypnotic susceptibility scales under attack: An examination of Weitzenhoffer's criticisms. *International Journal of Clinical and Experimental Hypnosis*, *29*(1), 24–41. doi:10.1080/00207148108409141

Hilgard, E. R. (1982). Hypnotic susceptibility and implications for measurement. *International Journal of Clinical and Experimental Hypnosis*, *30*(4), 394–403. doi:10.1080/00207148208407275

Hilgard, E. R., & Tart, C. T. (1966). Responsiveness to suggestions following waking and imagination instructions and following induction of hypnosis. *Journal of Abnormal Psychology*, *71*(3), 196–208. doi:10.1037/h0023323

Jamieson, G. A., & Burgess, A. P. (2014). Hypnotic induction is followed by state-like changes in the organization of EEG functional connectivity in the theta and beta frequency bands in high-hypnotically susceptible individuals. *Frontiers in Human Neuroscience*, *8*, 528. doi:10.3389/fnhum.2014.00528

Jamieson, G. A., & Sheehan, P. W. (2004). An empirical test of Woody and Bowers's dissociated-control theory of hypnosis. *International Journal of Clinical and Experimental Hypnosis*, *52*(3), 232–249. doi:10.1080/00207140490523491

Kihlstrom, J. F. (2008). The domain of hypnosis, revisited. In M. R. Nash & A. J. Barnier (Eds.), *The Oxford handbook of hypnosis* (pp. 21–52). Oxford, UK: Oxford University Press.

King, B. J., & Council, J. R. (1998). Intentionality during hypnosis: An ironic process analysis. *International Journal of Clinical and Experimental Hypnosis*, *46*(3), 295–313. doi:10.1080/00207149808410009

Kirsch, I., Cardeña, E., Derbyshire, S., Dienes, Z., Heap, M., Kallio, S., & Whalley, M. (2011). Definitions of hypnosis and hypnotizability and their relation to suggestion and suggestibility: A consensus statement. *Contemporary Hypnosis and Integrative Therapy*, *28*(2), 107–115.

Kirsch, I., Council, J. R., & Wickless, C. (1990). Subjective scoring for the Harvard group scale of hypnotic susceptibility, form A. *International Journal of Clinical and Experimental Hypnosis*, *38*(2), 112–124. doi:10.1080/00207149008414506

Kirsch, I., & Lynn, S. J. (1998). Social-cognitive alternatives to dissociation theories of hypnotic involuntariness. *Review of General Psychology*, *2*(1), 66–80. doi:10.1037/1089-2680.2.1.66

Kirsch, I., Milling, L. S., & Burgess, C. (1998). Experiential scoring for the Waterloo-Stanford Group C scale. *International Journal of Clinical and Experimental Hypnosis*, *46*(3), 269–279. doi:10.1080/00207149808410007

Kirsch, I., Silva, C. E., Comey, G., & Reed, S. (1995). A spectral analysis of cognitive and personality variables in hypnosis: Empirical disconfirmation of the two-factor model of hypnotic responding. *Journal of Personality and Social Psychology*, *69*, 161–175. doi:10.1037/0022-3514.69.1.167

Klinger, B. I. (1970). Effect of peer model responsiveness and length of induction procedures on hypnotic responsiveness. *Journal of Abnormal Psychology*, *75*, 15–18. doi:10.1037/h0028683

Kunzendorf, R. G. (1985–1986). Hypnotic hallucinations as 'unmonitored' images. *Imagination, Cognition, and Personality*, *5*, 255–270. doi:10.2190/KNE8-QT3L-RDB0-6KWK

Landry, M., & Raz, A. (2015). Hypnosis and imaging of the living human brain. *American Journal of Clinical Hypnosis*, *57*(3), 285–313. doi:10.1080/00029157.2014.978496

Lifshitz, M., Howells, C., & Raz, A. (2012). Can expectation enhance response to suggestion? De-automatization illuminates a conundrum. *Consciousness and Cognition*, *21*(2), 1001–1008. doi:10.1016/j.concog.2012.02.002

Litwin, R., & Cardeña, E. (2001). Demographic and seizure variables, but not hypnotizability or dissociation differentiated psychogenic from organic seizures. *Journal of Trauma & Dissociation*, *1*, 99–122. doi:10.1300/J229v01n04_06

Lutz, A., & Thompson, E. (2003). Neurophenomenology: Integrating subjective experience and brain dynamics in the neuroscience of consciousness. In A. Jack & A. Roepstorff (Eds.), *Trusting the subject* (pp. 31–52). Exeter, UK: Imprint.

Lynn, S. J., Kirsch, I., & Hallquist, M. (2008). Social cognitive theories of hypnosis. In M. R. Nash & A. Barnier (Eds.), *The Oxford handbook of hypnosis: Theory, research and practice* (pp. 111–140). Oxford, UK: Oxford University Press.

Lynn, S. J., Neufeld, V., & Mare, C. (1993). Direct versus indirect suggestions: A conceptual and methodological review. *International Journal of Clinical and Experimental Hypnosis*, *41*(2), 124–152. doi:10.1080/00207149308414543

Malott, J. M. (1984). Active-alert hypnosis: Replication and extension of previous research. *Journal of Abnormal Psychology*, *93*(2), 246–249. doi:10.1037/0021-843X.93.2.246

Marcusson-Clavertz, D., Terhune, D. B., & Cardeña, E. (2012). Individual differences and state effects on mind-wandering: Hypnotizability, dissociation, and sensory homogenization. *Consciousness and Cognition*, *21*(3), 1097–1108. doi:10.1016/j.concog.2012.04.002

Martinez-Tendero, J., Capafons, A., Weber, V., & Cardeña, E. (2001). Rapid self-hypnosis: A new self-hypnosis method and its comparison with the Hypnotic Induction Profile (HIP). *American Journal of Clinical Hypnosis*, *44*(1), 3–11. doi:10.1080/00029157.2001.10403451

McConkey, K. M., & Barnier, A. J. (2004). High hypnotizability: Unity and diversity in behavior and experience. In M. Heap, R. J. Brown, & D. A. Oakley (Eds.), *The highly hypnotizable person: Theoretical, experimental and clinical issues* (pp. 61–84). New York, NY: Routledge.

McConkey, K. M., Szeps, A., & Barnier, A. J. (2001). Indexing the experience of sex change in hypnosis and imagination. *International Journal of Clinical and Experimental Hypnosis*, *49*(2), 123–138. doi:10.1080/00207140108410063

McGeown, W. J., Mazzoni, G., Venneri, A., & Kirsch, I. (2009). Hypnotic induction decreases anterior default mode activity. *Consciousness and Cognition*, *18*(4), 848–855. doi:10.1016/j.concog.2009.09.001

Miele, D. B., Wager, T. D., Mitchell, J. P., & Metcalfe, J. (2011). Dissociating neural correlates of action monitoring and metacognition of agency. *Journal of Cognitive Neuroscience*, *23*(11), 3620–3636. doi:10.1162/jocn_a_00052

Milling, L. S., Coursen, E. L., Shores, J. S., & Waszkiewicz, J. A. (2010). The predictive utility of hypnotizability: The change in suggestibility produced by hypnosis. *Journal of Consulting and Clinical Psychology, 78*(1), 126–130. doi:10.1037/a0017388

Mitchell, Jr., G. P., & Lundy, R. M. (1986). The effects of relaxation and imagery inductions on responses to suggestions. *International Journal of Clinical and Experimental Hypnosis, 34*(2), 98–109. doi:10.1080/00207148608406975

Morgan, A. H., & Hilgard, J. R. (1979). The Stanford Hypnotic Clinical Scale for adults. *American Journal of Clinical Hypnosis, 21*, 134–147. doi:10.1080/00029157.1978.10403968

Naish, P. (2014). The perception of time in hypnosis. In V. Arstila & D. Lloyd (Eds.), *Subjective time: The philosophy, psychology, and neuroscience of temporality* (pp. 621–636). Cambridge, MA: MIT Press.

Nash, M. R. (2005). The importance of being earnest when crafting definitions: Science and scientism are not the same thing. *International Journal of Clinical and Experimental Hypnosis, 53*(3), 265–280. doi:10.1080/00207140590961934

Oakley, D. A., & Halligan, P. W. (2013). Hypnotic suggestion: Opportunities for cognitive neuroscience. *Nature Reviews Neuroscience, 14*(8), 565–576. doi:10.1038/nrn3538

Page, R. A., & Handley, G. W. (1991). A comparison of the effects of standardized Chiasson and eye-closure inductions on susceptibility scores. *American Journal of Clinical Hypnosis, 34*(1), 46–50. doi:10.1080/00029157.1991.10402959

Page, R. A., Handley, G. W., & Carey, J. C. (2002). Can devices facilitate a hypnotic induction? *American Journal of Clinical Hypnosis, 45*(2), 137–141. doi:10.1080/00029157.2002.10403511

Pekala, R. J., & Kumar, V. K. (2007). An empirical-phenomenological approach to quantifying consciousness and states of consciousness: With particular reference to understanding the nature of hypnosis. In G. A. Jamieson (Ed.), *Hypnosis and conscious states: The cognitive neuroscience perspective* (pp. 167–194). Oxford, UK: Oxford University Press.

Raz, A., Kirsch, I., Pollard, J., & Nitkin-Kaner, Y. (2006). Suggestion reduces the stroop effect. *Psychological Science, 17*(2), 91–95. doi:10.1111/j.1467-9280.2006.01669.x

Robin, B. R., Kumar, V. K., & Pekala, R. J. (2005). Direct and indirect scales of hypnotic susceptibility: Resistance to therapy and psychometric comparability. *International Journal of Clinical and Experimental Hypnosis, 53*(2), 135–147. doi:10.1080/00207140590927617

Roelofs, K., Hoogduin, K. A., Keijsers, G. P., Naring, G. W., Moene, F. C., & Sandijck, P. (2002). Hypnotic susceptibility in patients with conversion disorder. *Journal of Abnormal Psychology, 111*(2), 390–395. doi:10.1037/0021-843X.111.2.390

Ruch, J. C., Morgan, A. H., & Hilgard, E. R. (1974). Measuring hypnotic responsiveness: A comparison of the Barber suggestibility scale and the Stanford Hypnotic Susceptibility Scale, Form A. *International Journal of Clinical and Experimental Hypnosis, 22*(4), 365–376. doi:10.1080/00207147408413016

Semmens-Wheeler, R., Dienes, Z., & Duka, T. (2013). Alcohol increases hypnotic susceptibility. *Consciousness and Cognition, 22*(3), 1082–1091. doi:10.1016/j.concog.2013.07.001

Sheehan, P. W., & McConkey, K. M. (1982). *Hypnosis and experience: The exploration of phenomena and process*. Hillsdale, NJ: Lawrence Erlbaum.

Shor, R. E., & Orne, E. C. (1962). *Harvard group scale of hypnotic susceptibility, form A*. Palo Alto, CA: Consulting Psychologists Press.

Spanos, N. P. (1986). Hypnotic behavior: A social psychological interpretation of amnesia, analgesia and trance logic. *Behavioral and Brain Sciences, 9*(3), 449–467. doi:10.1017/S0140525X00046537

Spanos, N. P., Arango, M., & Degroot, H. P. (1993). Context as a moderator in relationships between attribute variables and hypnotizability. *Personality and Social Psychology Bulletin, 19*(1), 71–77. doi:10.1177/0146167293191008

Spanos, N. P., Lush, N. I., Smith, J. E., & De Groh, M. M. (1986). Effects of two hypnotic induction procedures on overt and subjective response to two measures of hypnotic susceptibility. *Psychological Reports*, *59*(3), 1227–1230. doi:10.2466/pr0.1986.59.3.1227

Spanos, N. P., Radtke, H. L., Hodgins, D. C., Bertrand, L. D., Stam, H. J., & Dubreuil, D. L. (1983). The Carleton University Responsiveness to Suggestion Scale: Stability, reliability, and relationships with expectancy and 'hypnotic experiences.' *Psychological Reports*, *53*(2), 555–563. doi:10.2466/pr0.1983.53.2.555

Spiegel, D., Hunt, T., & Dondershine, H. E. (1988). Dissociation and hypnotizability in posttraumatic stress disorder. *American Journal of Psychiatry*, *145*(3), 301–305. doi:10.1176/ajp.145.3.301

Straus, R. A. (1980). A naturalistic experiment investigating the effects of hypnotic induction upon creative imagination scale performance in a clinical setting. *International Journal of Clinical and Experimental Hypnosis*, *28*(3), 218–224. doi:10.1080/00207148008409847

Szabó, C. (1993). The phenomenology of the experiences and the depth of hypnosis: Comparison of direct and indirect induction techniques. *International Journal of Clinical and Experimental Hypnosis*, *41*(3), 225–233. doi:10.1080/00207149308414552

Tart, C. T., & Hilgard, E. R. (1966). Responsiveness to suggestions under "hypnosis" and "waking-imagination" conditions: A methodological observation. *International Journal of Clinical and Experimental Hypnosis*, *14*(3), 247–256. doi:10.1080/00207146608412967

Terhune, D. B. (2015). Discrete response patterns in the upper range of hypnotic suggestibility: A latent profile analysis. *Consciousness and Cognition*, *33*, 334–341. doi:10.1016/j.concog.2015.01.018

Terhune, D. B., & Cardeña, E. (2010). Differential patterns of spontaneous experiential response to a hypnotic induction: A latent profile analysis. *Consciousness and Cognition*, *19*(4), 1140–1150. doi:10.1016/j.concog.2010.03.006

Terhune, D. B., & Cardeña, E. (2015). Dissociative subtypes in posttraumatic stress disorders and hypnosis: Neurocognitive parallels and clinical implications. *Current Directions in Psychological Science*, *24*, 452–457. doi:10.1177/0963721415604611

Terhune, D. B., Cardeña, E., & Lindgren, M. (2011a). Differential frontal-parietal phase synchrony during hypnosis as a function of hypnotic suggestibility. *Psychophysiology*, *48*(10), 1444–1447. doi:10.1111/j.1469-8986.2011.01211.x

Terhune, D. B., Cardeña, E., & Lindgren, M. (2011b). Dissociated control as a signature of typological variability in high hypnotic suggestibility. *Consciousness and Cognition*, *20*(3), 727–736. doi:10.1016/j.concog.2010.11.005

Terhune, D. B., Cardeña, E., & Lindgren, M. (2011c). Dissociative tendencies and individual differences in high hypnotic suggestibility. *Cognitive Neuropsychiatry*, *16*(2), 113–135. doi:10.1080/13546805.2010.503048

Wagstaff, G. F. (2014). On the centrallity of the concept of an altered state to definitions of hypnosis. *Journal of Mind-Body Regulation*, *2*(2), 90–108.

Weitzenhofer, A., & Sakata, K. (1970). Role of visual fixation in the production of hypnotic behavior. *American Journal of Clinical Hypnosis*, *13*, 104–107. doi:10.1080/00029157.1970.10402089

Weitzenhoffer, A. M. (1980). Hypnotic susceptibility revisited. *American Journal of Clinical Hypnosis*, *22*(3), 130–146. doi:10.1080/00029157.1980.10403217

Weitzenhoffer, A. M. (2000). *The practice of hypnotism* (2nd ed.). New York, NY: Wiley.

Weitzenhoffer, A. M., & Hilgard, E. R. (1962). *Stanford Hypnotic Susceptibility Scale: Form C.* Palo Alto, CA: Consulting Psychologists Press.

Wickless, C., & Kirsch, I. (1989). Effects of verbal and experiential expectancy manipulations on hypnotic-susceptibility. *Journal of Personality and Social Psychology*, *57*(5), 762–768. doi:10.1037/0022-3514.57.5.762

Woody, E. Z., & Barnier, A. J. (2008). Hypnosis scales for the twenty-first century: What do we know and how should we use them? In M. Nash & A. J. Barnier (Eds.), *The Oxford handbook of hypnosis: Theory, research and practice* (pp. 255–281). Oxford, UK: Oxford University Press.

Woody, E. Z., Barnier, A. J., & McConkey, K. M. (2005). Multiple hypnotizabilities: Differentiating the building blocks of hypnotic response. *Psychological Assessment*, *17*(2), 200–211. doi:10.1037/1040-3590.17.2.200

Woody, E. Z., Drugovic, M., & Oakman, J. M. (1997). A reexamination of the role of nonhypnotic suggestibility in hypnotic responding. *Journal of Personality and Social Psychology*, *72*(2), 399–407. doi:10.1037/0022-3514.72.2.399

Woody, E. Z., & Sadler, P. (2008). Dissociation theories of hypnosis. In M. Nash & A. J. Barnier (Eds.), *The Oxford handbook of hypnosis: Theory, research and practice* (pp. 81–110). Oxford, UK: Oxford University Press.

Yin, B., Terhune, D. B., Smythies, J., & Meck, W. H. (2016). Claustrum, consciousness, and time perception. *Current Opinion in Behavioural Sciences*, *8*, 258–267. doi:10.1016/j.cobeha.2016.02.032

Conscious/Unconscious Dissociation Induction: Increasing Hypnotic Performance With "Resistant" Clients

Stephen Lankton

Milton H. Erickson promoted several approaches to psychotherapy using hypnosis. In the last decades of his life, his work moved away from the use of redundant suggestion and a predominance of direct suggestion in favor of indirect suggestion. In addition, he frequently employed a type of storytelling (that has come to be called therapeutic metaphor) to indirectly convey learning. Another change that occurred during the last decade was his definition of the cause of a symptom. However, there were two important areas of his work that he did not change during his career. These two components of his work he did not change were his definition of a cure and the importance of a naturalistic induction. This article concerns his naturalistic approach to hypnotic induction and especially his use of conscious/unconscious dissociation in the induction process and how indirect suggestion and therapeutic binds can be used to facilitate that type of induction and a cure.

Erickson continually modified aspects of his approach throughout his career. There has been disagreement about his approach between those who studied with him in the 1940s and 1950s and those who visited him in the 1970s. The reason for this becomes obvious when examining the progression of some of his ideas. I have explored this in detail elsewhere and will briefly summarize it here by way of introduction (Lankton, 2005).

For example, consider the changes in treatment duration reflected in his published cases. The cases he published in the 1950s reveal therapy lasting several months and even years: The man with a "fat lip" was seen for at least 11 months (Erickson & Rossi, 1979), and the "February Man" case continued for almost 2 years (Erickson, 1980). However, by the 1970s, his published cases reveal shorter durations. In 1973, the eight-year-old "stomper" case took 2 hours (Haley, 1973). In cases involving his "shock" technique, he spent as little as 1–2-hour-long sessions (Erickson & Rossi, 1980). In general, his therapy became briefer in the last decade(s) of his career.

It was not just his approach to treatment duration that changed over the course of his career; his use of suggestion also changed. In 1957, it was typical for Erickson to say to a subject, "Now I want you to *go deeper and deeper asleep*" (Haley, 1967; italics added). He also stated in an authoritarian manner, "*I can put you* in any level of trance" (Erickson, Rossi, & Rossi, 1976, p. 452; Haley, 1967; italics added). In the 1950s and 1960s, he was redundant: He repeated the word "sleep," and his manner was authoritarian. But in the last decade of his life's work, we find his reliance on indirect suggestion to be a "significant factor." Similarly, in 1981, Erickson wrote in sharp contradiction to the wording in the previous transcript, "I don't like this matter of telling a patient *I want you to get tired and sleepy*" (Erickson & Rossi, 1981, p. 4; italics added). And, contrary to his authoritarian approach, he added that he "*offers*" ideas and suggestions (Erickson & Rossi, 1981, pp. 1–2; italics added). Clearly, his early students and observers would correctly argue that he used redundant direct suggestions, while his later students would correctly argue that he typically used indirect suggestion in his inductions and therapy. It is obvious that such misunderstandings arise from the evolution of his approach.

There are at least two important areas in which Erickson did not change his view. The first is what constitutes a "cure." As early as 1948, Erickson argued that cure was *not* the result of suggestion; rather, it was due to the reassociation of experiences (Erickson, 1980; Erickson & Rossi, 1979, 1980, 1981).

The other concept that did not change in Erickson's approach is what he called "naturalistic induction." "Speaking the client's own experiential language" (Erickson, personal communication, April 1977) was a major component of naturalistic induction. Erickson (1958) defined and described the naturalistic techniques of hypnosis, in contrast to a ritualistic technique of induction, as

> the acceptance of the situation encountered and the utilization of it, without endeavoring to restructure it psychologically. In so doing, the presenting behavior of the patient becomes a definite aid and an actual part in inducing a trance, rather than a possible hindrance. For lack of a more definite terminology, the method may be termed a naturalistic approach, in which an aspect of the principle of synergism is utilized. (p. 3)

He enhanced the naturalistic approach with a therapeutic dissociation between the conscious and unconscious (he sometimes used the term subconscious) dissociation. His reason for using a naturalistic approach and dissociative approach was to increase hypnotic performance by reducing "resistance." My view is that clients who may have low motivation, have little or no expectations of success due to their learning history, and who do not attribute special prestige to the therapist are usually labeled as "resistant." However, Erickson stated that these are his techniques for "many types of difficult patients who seek psychotherapy and yet are openly hostile, antagonistic, resistant, defensive, and resent every appearance of being unwilling to accept the therapy they have come to seek" (Erickson, 1964, p. 8). The naturalistic approach is identified by speaking the client's language: "It is advantageous to modify it to include the patient's own style of speech, whether abrupt, impolite, or even outrageously profane" (Erickson, 1964, p. 12).

As soon as possible, he then introduces a style of language that will help develop a conscious/unconscious dissociation. "'Conscious mind' and 'unconscious mind' can be used, depending upon the educational level, and thus a second intimation is given of dissociation" (Erickson, 1964, p. 13). We find many examples of this in his transcripts. This approach is represented in his selection of language throughout his published works. For instance: "Just be comfortable while I am talking to your unconscious mind, since I don't care what your conscious mind does" (Erickson, 1964, p. 13). And he often used voice tone variations to reinforce the dissociation: "I use one tone of voice to speak to the conscious mind and another to speak to the unconscious. . .you are establishing a duality" (Erickson & Rossi, 1976, pp. 159–160). His method was intended to facilitate an experiential distinction between the recognizable operations of conscious and unconscious functioning.

Conscious/Unconscious Dissociation

"The functioning of autonomous mental (and bodily) mechanisms as well as the operations of synthetic and autonomous ego mechanisms constitute the bulk of that which is referred to as the unconscious. Consciousness, by comparison, operates in a linear way, and often with doubt, ambition, pride, confusion, and so on" (Lankton & Lankton, 1983/2008, p. 141).

Erickson saw the unconscious mind, in contrast to the conscious mind, as divided into right and left hemispheres of brain functioning. Rossi wrote: "it is clear that a neuropsychological model utilizing the differences between right and left-hemispheric functioning is also implicit in Erickson's work." This difference in hemispheric functioning is characterized by Erickson's co-authored chart (Erickson et al., 1976, p. 277).

LEFT HEMISPHERE (Awake)	*RIGHT HEMISPHERE (Trance)*
Linguistic	Pantomime, Kinesthetic, musical
Logical-Grammatical	Visuo-spatial
Rational	Intuitive
Abstract	Perceptual-synthetic
Directed	Spontaneous
Focal	Diffuse
Effort	Comfort

Building a Conscious/Unconscious Dissociation Induction

This dichotomy of mental functioning and, presumably, brain hemisphere lateralization (which is currently questioned) gives rise to a communication pattern that can be easily illustrated. Whether or not hemispheric lateralization is correct, the effect of the dichotomy is quite tangible with regard to conscious and unconscious brain processing.

And as a result, the following method of induction helps create the effect Erickson discussed. The following chart is not meant as a script to be followed verbatim. Rather, as a training tool, it illustrates how the conscious and unconscious dichotomies can be exacerbated to achieve a therapeutic (but not an actual personality) dissociation during an induction process. It should be apparent that the left side of the chart represents aspects of conscious mind functioning, while the right side of the chart mentions functional aspects of the unconscious mind.

"Your conscious mind…"	Link	"Your unconscious mind…"
Is listening to and hearing my words	and	Is doing something else
May be interested in learning one thing	and	Is interested in what's relevant
May have that doubt	and	Is developing its own line of thought
Is possibly curious	and	Isn't even interested
Operates linearly	and	Thinks globally
Won't do much that's very interesting	as	Is really acting spontaneously
Is interested in one depth of trance	while	Has its own diffuse ideas of what you need
Can focus on one spot	while	Is learning a great deal
Doesn't know how things will culminate	since	Makes things happen in your best interest
Is sorting, categorizing, and pigeonholing	just as	Understands the context
May be easily distracted	so	Can discover intuitively
May be wondering about certain things	because	Holds a vast storehouse of learnings and potentials
Is oriented to situations of the moment	at the same time	Acts on your own behalf at this moment (modified from Lankton & Lankton, 1983/2008, p. 155)

The above chart illustrates how entire sentences may be created from the dichotomy offered by Erickson et al. (1976). It has served as a learning exercise for trainees becoming aware of the types of sentences that can be created and modified to conform to the feedback of a real client in therapy.

The following narrative is taken from a recent induction with a 22-year-old man who was extremely reluctant to discuss an important issue (regarding violence against him) with his parents. He stated while he was reluctant to even come to a therapy session, he certainly cannot be hypnotized. The therapy can be seen to begin in this example because conscious/unconscious dissociation suggestions (CUDS), which help build the induction, integrate some of the therapeutically needed experiences in order to be relevant and speak the client's own language. This integration of induction and therapy is a hallmark of naturalistic induction.

This induction transcript includes several forms of indirect suggestion and therapeutic binds not yet discussed. For readers unfamiliar with indirection, indirect suggestions are defined as those suggestions that have a degree of ambiguity and allow for increased latitude in responding on the part of the subject as compared to a direct suggestion, which is a clear request for a particular response from the hypnotist to the subject. In the following transcript, these include only truism, implication, presupposition, focusing attention, bind of comparable alternatives, and conscious/unconscious double bind (Erickson & Rossi, 1980).

Transcript

Just continue to sit comfortably, and know that even though you can't go into trance, you're consciously listening to what I say; your unconscious is understanding in its own way. Consciously, you're probably thinking about what we just said, while unconsciously, you may have a great deal of connections and meanings that have not yet been mentioned.	Implication suggestion to "continue." Acknowledging that he "can't go into trance" but he has both a conscious and unconscious functioning. First CUDS linked from focusing attention suggestion on listening to "understanding" differently CUDS linked from the pre-trance discussion to "connections and meanings"
Sooner or later you'll recognize that, staring at me, your eyes are getting tired of being open, and maybe your unconscious will close your eyes so you can better concentrate on your thoughts. You may wonder if you will close your eyes while I speak, or if you're going to close your eyes in the pauses between my words. And you know that your conscious mind is in the habit of categorizing and finding labels for ideas and experiences, but your unconscious mind operates in a manner which is more global and intuitive. Your conscious mind would be easily distracted by noises in the hallway, while your unconscious mind continues to organize information according to what is of most interest to you. And which mind noticed your comfort?	Truism. CUDS omitting the word conscious and using "recognize." Bind of comparable alternatives for eye closure while speaking or silent. CUDS linked from categorizing to being global and intuitive. CUDS linked from distraction of noise in the hall (focusing attention) to organizing information of most interest. Focusing attention suggestion for comfort.
And you know that your left hand just raised up to brush your cheek because you consciously noticed that you had an itch, but you don't know why your unconscious made your cheek have that itch just at this moment. And, consciously you may be curious, searching for an answer, while unconsciously you have a vast storehouse of learning and potentials that contain answers to questions you have never asked. While you keep the comfort.	CUDS linked from the client brushing his cheek to the idea that the itch was caused by the unconscious for an unknown reason. CUDS linked from curiosity to the implication of a vast store of resources and potentials. Presupposition of keeping the comfort.
Your conscious mind may be wondering what you'll use this trance-like experience for, but sooner or later your unconscious will bring to your awareness feelings and memories and ideas so that you can make a new arrangement of your experiences. For example, your conscious mind might wonder how you're going to a sit-down with your parents and explain the things that are important while your unconscious locates feelings of safety and comfort. Or, it's even possible that while your conscious mind holds onto the feelings of safety and comfort, your unconscious is choosing how you are going to sit down with your parents and explain things that are important.	CUDS linked from wondering about the trance-like session to bringing desired experiences into awareness. (This has introduced the word "trance" and the client appears to accept it). Conscious/Unconscious Double Bind (see below) to intertwine his speaking to his parents about (the important issue not mentioned in this excerpt) and feelings of comfort and safety. (The experience of safety has been introduced without resistance and piggy-backed off of the previously accepted experience of comfort.)

State of Consciousness (SoC) Model and Conscious/Unconscious Dissociation

Erickson wrote, "that hypnotic trance is an altered *state* of consciousness" (Erickson & Rossi, 1974, p. 237; italics in original). Building upon his observations, I have presented a more complete SoC model of induction and therapy (Lankton, 2015). The integration of the conscious/unconscious dissociation model of induction with the SoC model I proposed earlier is elegant. The SoC model proposes that a trance state is constructed by assembling component experiences, or parts of ego states, from various SoC, such as the "feeling of floating" from, say, a scuba diving experience or "an experience of a detached observation," such as that provided from an automobile-repair frame of mind, etc. Of course, all the components may exist in the person's "normal" SoC. But when the experiences which are sought for a certain type of trance or therapy intervention are not present, the therapist would attempt to elicit them from other learned SoCs (pp. 369–376).

As the suggestions pertain to creating a conscious/unconscious dissociation induction, the comments spoken to the conscious mind are always directed to experiences in the "normal" SoC. This is the SoC the client almost always brings to the office and that contains useful and, if present, seemingly resistant experiences; therefore, the inclusion of conscious mind comments in the above transcript pertain to listening, pride in the parent-child relationship, doubt, etc.

The CUDS which speak of unconscious experiences attempt to elicit comfort, safety, images of speaking to parents, etc. These may or may not be a subset of the "normal" SoC. In the above transcript, attempts to elicit these appeared readily accessible. They were either existing subsets of the "normal" SoC or the client needed little additional excitation or communicational energy from the therapist to tap into other SoCs to find these experiences. If in other inductions, attempts to elicit the desired experiences do not appear successful with minimal attempts to elicit them, the therapist must stimulate and evoke another SoC that may contain the experience as a subset. For instance, if a requirement for the induction-set or therapy was "persistence" or "repeated trying and persevering until a task was accomplished," the therapist may attempt to evoke a SoC from learning a childhood skill like jumping rope. The use of therapeutic metaphor is a possible tool for such a therapeutic maneuver, as would be a more direct intervention of age regression. In these ways, the experiences in another existing SoC could be obtained and associated into the foreground from a series of suggestions on the unconscious "side" of the CUDS.

Indirect Suggestions

The author's formulas for constructing indirect suggestions and binds used in the above induction are discussed below. Each formula is based on the idea that the communication has a goal *in context* (e.g., relax, close eyes, become more absorbed, recall an experience, etc.). That context needs to be relevant to the client. Rather than directly demanding that the subject produce that goal, indirect suggestions approach the goal more conversationally. This approach allows the client to either produce the behavior or not produce it—but it ultimately means there can be little resistance because no performance demand is made. Each of the formulas below, therefore, state a goal, but only in the context of the type of indirections for which the suggestions are named.

Presupposition: Use a presupposition word and state the goal. That is, the hypnotist must use a form of presupposition such as "when," "since," "before," "one of the," "as," "after," etc., and then state the goal (e.g., "close your eyes," "relax," "recall," etc. For example, "Since you will be closing your eyes, let's continue."

Focusing attention: Use you or I "wonder" or "doubt" about a named goal. For example, "I wonder when you will close your eyes," or, "You may doubt that you will close your eyes."

Truism: Use "every person" or "in every culture," etc., and state the goal. For example, "Everybody closes their eyes at some point," or, "In every culture people find it appropriate to close their eyes," etc.

Bind of comparable alternatives: Use options "A" or "B," where both contain a form of the goal. For example, "You can close your eyes now or after you are in trance," or, "You can go into trance with your eyes open or with your eyes closed."

Conscious/unconscious bind: Use the form: "Your conscious mind is/may (some form of awareness) while (as, when, if, etc.) your unconscious is/may (retrieval of the goal)." This is the major form of suggestion for creating the conscious/unconscious dissociation trance. For example, "Your conscious mind may wonder when your unconscious mind will want you to close your eyes," or, "Your conscious mind may be surprised at how your unconscious mind makes you feel safe."

Double dissociative bind: Use the form above, and then reverse the conscious and unconscious and the two stated goals: "Your conscious mind may think 'A' as your unconscious mind does 'B,' or perhaps your conscious mind will do 'B;' while your unconscious does 'A'." For example, "Your conscious mind may think about talking to your parents as your unconscious mind makes you safe and comfortable, or perhaps your conscious mind will be aware of being safe and comfortable while your unconscious thinks about talking to your parents." This bind is most useful for associating together two desired goals.

Research Support

There has been no empirical research regarding the efficacy of naturalistic induction or conscious/unconscious dissociation induction. However, over the last few decades, there have been studies that attempted to compare participants' responses to direct and indirect suggestion. These are summarized as follows:

Alman and Carney (1980), using audio-taped inductions of direct and indirect suggestions, reported that *indirect suggestions were more successful in producing post-hypnotic behavior than were direct suggestions.*

McConkey (1984) concluded that "*indirection may not be the clinically important notion as much as the creation of a motivational context* [italics added] where the overall suggestion is acceptable such as making the ideas congruent with the other aims and hopes of a patient" (p. 312).

Van Gorp, Meyer, and Dunhar (1985) found that, for analgesia, *direct suggestion was more effective* as measured by verbal self-report and autonomic lability scores.

Stone and Lundy (1985) investigated body movements following suggestions and reported *indirect suggestions to be more effective than direct suggestions in eliciting the target behaviors.*

Matthews, Bennett, Bean, and Gallagher (1985) compared participants' responses on the Stanford Hypnotic Clinical Scale (Morgan & Hilgard, 1978) to responses on the same scale re-written to include only indirect suggestions. They found *no significant behavioral differences* between the two scales. However, they did report that *individuals who received the indirect suggestions perceived themselves to be more hypnotized* than those who received direct suggestions.

Matthews and Mosher (1988) compared direct and indirect hypnotic induction. *The results did not support the efficacy of indirect induction and suggestion over direct induction and suggestion.*

Weeks and Lynn (1990) compared direct and indirect suggestions for a range of hypnotic behaviors and *found no significant behavioral differences* but did find that *subjects who received direct suggestions perceived their hypnotic responses to be more involuntary* than those who received indirect suggestions.

Robin, Kumar, and Pekala (2005) reported results contrary to Groth-Marnat and Mitchell's (1998) findings and to "the popular held view among Ericksonians that highly resistant [clients] respond better to nondirective or paradoxical interventions (p. 325)." Robin et al. (2005) concluded, "There seem to be repeated difficulties in replicating some of the confident predictions made from the Ericksonian model, whether comparing behavioral or subjective responses on the direct and indirect methods" (p. 142). While these findings appear interesting, there are two caveats in interpreting them: (a) their findings, like other studies, are based on self-selected introductory psychology students; and, (b) their study context was not clinical; rather, they tested students for hypnotizability using the Alman-Wexler Indirect Hypnotic Susceptibility Scale and the Harvard Group Scale of Hypnotic Susceptibility, Form A.

Further, the transparency of an indirect suggestion such as to scratch one's ankle is likely to create resistance or even irritability. In contrast, the direct suggestion to do the same, whether denied or not, does not carry a condescending aspect of attempting trickery on the student. Indirect suggestion in a therapeutic setting is not, and should not be, used to create irrelevant or non-essential performances on the part of a client. Thus, research at its current best has not teased out the crucial features and impact of indirect suggestions, especially their clinical effectiveness.

The research to date would appear to be mixed at best in support of indirect suggestion as compared to direct suggestion in producing trance depth and a range of hypnotic and post-hypnotic behaviors. However, in most of this research, the reader should remember that the tests were often done with audio taping or written texts to standardize the interventions, and therefore *it was not possible to tailor the suggestions* (whether direct or indirect) and stories to the individual, and thus do not emphasize the importance Erickson attached to adapting and utilizing the unique responses of the individual. Similarly, and perhaps more importantly, these *tests were not designed in a context which attempted to address relevant goals of each individual.* In this regard, therefore, this research *may not represent an accurate picture* of how a clinical client would experience the interventions (Lankton & Matthews, 2010, pp. 225–228).

Summary

Erickson's clinical observations and goals for the use of naturalistic induction, conscious/unconscious dissociation, and indirection were twofold. One was to bypass resistance in difficult clients, and the other was to gain access to unconscious resources. His rationale was that any limitation or resistance coming from the conscious mind should be accepted and unchallenged. At the same time, the dichotomy of the dissociation presupposes the existence of unexamined and unused experiences from memories, events, skills, etc. that can be elicited, brought into the foreground during the trance, and associated with (Wolpe, 1990) or conditioned to (e.g., see Bandura, 1969), no-trial learning, problem solving efforts, and future situations.

His techniques were not solely for clients who might be considered resistant. Rather, these techniques were seen as bringing maximum benefit to all clients. This article has summarized the approach and rationale, provided examples for naturalistic induction, and reflected on the existing research for indirect suggestion. Further research is necessary to tease out the important and valuable aspects of Erickson's work with naturalistic induction and conscious/unconscious induction and the impact it may have on increasing the therapeutic performance of clients. Yet the requirement that each trance be modified to the client's personal goals and language complicates the application of customary research paradigms.

References

Alman, B., & Carney, R. (1980). Consequences of direct and indirect suggestion on success of posthypnotic behavior. *American Journal of Clinical Hypnosis*, *23*, 112–118. doi:10.1080/00029157.1980.10403249

Bandura, A. (1969). *Principles of behavior modification*. New York, NY: Holt Rinehart and Winston, Inc.

Erickson, M. (1958). Naturalistic techniques of hypnosis. *American Journal of Clinical Hypnosis*, *1*(1), 3–8. doi:10.1080/00029157.1958.10401766

Erickson, M. (1964). An hypnotic technique for resistant patients: The patient, the technique, and its rationale and the filed experiments. *American Journal of Clinical Hypnosis*, *7*(1), 8–32. doi:10.1080/00029157.1964.10402387

Erickson, M. (1980). February man: Facilitating new identity in hypnotherapy. In E. L. Rossi (Ed.), *The collected papers of Milton H.: Erickson on hypnosis: Vol. 4. Innovative hypnotherapy* (pp. 525–542). New York, NY: Irvington.

Erickson, M., & Rossi, E. (1976). Two-level communication and the microdynamics of trance and suggestion. *American Journal of Clinical Hypnosis*, *18*(3), 153–171. doi:10.1080/00029157.1976.10403794

Erickson, M., & Rossi, E. (1979). *Hypnotherapy: An exploratory casebook*. New York, NY: Irvington.

Erickson, M., & Rossi, E. (1980). Indirect forms of suggestion. In E. L. Rossi (Ed.), *The collected papers of Milton H.: Erickson on hypnosis: Vol. 1 The nature of hypnosis and suggestion* (pp. 452–477). New York, NY: Irvington.

Erickson, M., & Rossi, E. (1981). *Experiencing hypnosis: Therapeutic approaches to altered state*. New York, NY: Irvington.

Erickson, M., & Rossi, L. (1974). Varieties of hypnotic amnesia. *American Journal of Clinical Hypnosis*, *16*(4), 225–239. doi:10.1080/00029157.1974.10403687

Erickson, M., Rossi, L., & Rossi, S. (1976). Hypnotic realities: The induction of clinical hypnosis and forms of indirect suggestion. In L. Rossi, R. Erickson-Klien, & K. Rossi (Eds.), *The collected works of Milton H. Erickson, volume 10: Hypnotic realities: The induction of clinical hypnosis and forms of indirect suggestion* (pp. 1–351). Phoenix, AZ: The Milton H. Erickson Foundation Press.

Groth-Marnat, G., & Mitchell, K. (1998). Responsiveness to direct versus indirect hypnotic procedures: The role of resistance as a predictor variable. *International Journal of Clinical and Experimental Hypnosis*, *46*, 324–333. doi:10.1080/00207149808410012

Haley, J. (1967). *Advanced techniques of hypnosis and therapy: Selected papers of Milton H. Erickson, M. D*. New York, NY: Grune & Stratton.

Haley, J. (1973). *Uncommon therapy: The psychiatric techniques of Milton H. Erickson, M.D*. New York, NY: Norton.

Lankton, S. (2005). Foreword. In D. Short, B. A. Erickson, & R. Erickson-Klein (Eds.), *Hope & resiliency: Understanding the psychotherapeutic strategies of Milton H. Erickson, M.D.* (pp. iii–ix). Norwalk, CT: Crown House Publishing.

Lankton, S. (2015). A SoC model of hypnosis and induction. *American Journal of Clinical Hypnosis*, *57*, 367–377. doi:10.1080/00029157.2015.1011461

Lankton, S., & Lankton, C. (2008). *The answer within: A clinical framework of Ericksonian hypnotherapy*. Bethel, CT: Crown House Publishing. (Original work published 1983)

Lankton, S., & Matthews, W. (2010). An Ericksonian model of clinical hypnosis. In S. J. Lynn, J. W. Rhue, & I. Kirsch (Eds.), *Handbook of clinical hypnosis* (2nd ed., pp. 209–238). Washington, DC: American Psychological Association.

Matthews, W., Bennett, H., Bean, W., & Gallagher, M. (1985). Indirect versus direct hypnotic suggestions—an initial investigation: A brief communication. *International Journal of Clinical and Experimental Hypnosis*, *33*(2), 19–223. doi:10.1080/00207148508406650

Matthews, W., & Mosher, D. (1988). Direct and indirect hypnotic suggestion in a laboratory setting. *British Journal of Experimental and Clinical Hypnosis*, *5*(2), 63–71.

McConkey, K. (1984). The impact of indirect suggestion. *International Journal of Clinical and Experimental Hypnosis*, *32*, 307–314. doi:10.1080/00207148408416021

Morgan, A., & Hilgard, J. (1978). The Stanford hypnotic susceptibility scale for adults. *American Journal of Clinical Hypnosis*, *21*, 148–169. doi:10.1080/00029157.1978.10403969

Robin, B., Kumar, V. K., & Pekala, R. J. (2005). Direct and indirect methods of hypnosis: Therapeutic resistance and psychometric comparability. *International Journal of Clinical & Experimental Hypnosis*, *53*, 135–147. doi:10.1080/00207140590927617

Stone, J. A., & Lundy, R. M. (1985). Behavioral compliance with direct and indirect body movement suggestions. *Journal of Abnormal Psychology*, *3*, 256–263. doi:10.1037/0021-843X.94.3.256

Van Gorp, W. O., Meyer, R. O., & Dunhar, K. D. (1985). The efficacy of direct versus indirect hypnotic induction techniques on reduction of experimental pain. *International Journal of Clinical and Experimental Hypnosis*, *4*(3), 19–328.

Weeks, J. R., & Lynn, S. J. (1990). Hypnosis, suggestion type and subjective experience: The order effects hypothesis revisited. *International Journal of Clinical and Experimental Hypnosis*, *38*, 95–101. doi:10.1080/00207149008414504

Wolpe, J. (1990). *The practice of behavior therapy* (4th ed.). New York, NY: Pergamon.

Perspectives on Pathways to Induction: Confronting Unexpected Challenges

Richard P. Kluft

In clinical practice, the process of induction may prove more complex and nuanced than its presentation in workshop training would suggest. The relatively straightforward cognitive and instrumental educational domains address defining the concept of induction and instructing workshop participants about how inductions can be performed. However, in work with patients, factors relevant to the attitudinal domain of education become increasingly salient and speak to the importance of how the person inducing hypnosis relates to the person in whom hypnosis is to be induced and how that person goes about crafting a constructive rather than formulaic approach to the induction of hypnosis for a unique individual. Considerations relevant to relational issues and the optimization of inductions in a clinical context will be addressed. These include assessing aspects of hypnotic talent and individual preference, identifying distressing dynamics, attention to the clinician's manner of speech, patience, achieving congruent expectations about how help is given and received, attention to shame dynamics, relational dimensions, contributions from self-psychology, collaboration with other caregivers, and issues related to autohypnosis and spontaneous trance in the clinical setting.

Healthcare providers from many disciplines employ hypnosis in their efforts to alleviate pain and suffering. Their scopes of practices entail many responsibilities, skill sets, and competencies shared in common and others unique to their particular professions and the spectra of interventions for which each individual practitioner is trained. They address the needs of somewhat overlapping but considerably divergent patient populations. Within each of these groups of patients, significant differences exist across individual recipients of care.

Notwithstanding the diversities indicated above, in workshop settings, hypnotic induction, the process of deliberately guiding and assisting a participant into trance in the context of preparing the way for making hypnosis-facilitated interventions, is usually taught to all disciplines in a similar manner. Those standardized approaches may then be employed by health professionals whose clinical practices are far from uniform.

In this communication, I will argue that induction is a multifaceted process, a far more complex and nuanced event than workshop instruction would generally imply. Focusing on the induction process in terms of techniques to facilitate a patient's entry into a form of trance useful for therapeutic purposes, while useful in conveying a set of basic skills, profoundly oversimplifies induction as a clinical phenomenon, a change of state/expectations, and an interpersonal/relational process as well as a circumscribed event. The usefulness of more nuanced and complex perspectives may not become apparent in the general course of clinical work and may seem completely irrelevant to those accustomed to a relatively predictable and circumscribed area of practice. However, when difficulties and/or unwanted events are encountered, the problems associated with misunderstanding induction as a simple, straightforward endeavor may become apparent.

These concerns are crucial not only for optimizing the effectiveness of particular clinical interventions, but also because most of those who take hypnosis training but abandon the use of hypnosis rather rapidly do so because their efforts to induce hypnosis, a process that may appear smooth and effortless in workshop environments and demonstrations, often prove profoundly problematic in clinical practice. When neophytes attempting to do inductions experience a series of failures, not infrequently they discontinue their efforts to utilize hypnosis.

Here I will argue that notwithstanding concerns about issues that might be classified under the cognitive (e.g., learning about induction) and instrumental (e.g., learning how to do techniques of induction) domains of education, attention is long overdue to considerations more relevant to the affective or attitudinal domain (e.g., attitudes and feelings that may impinge upon the induction process, and how they can be addressed).

My interest in exploring a broader view of induction that embraces the attitudinal domain stems from several sources, including my consultations to colleagues, my ongoing studies of the experiences of participants in hypnosis workshop settings (Kluft, 2012a, 2012b, 2012c), my daily endeavors to make the benefits of hypnosis available to facilitate the treatment of patients (including those who have suffered trauma and those with long histories of failed psychotherapies), and a never-completed project to explore why so many colleagues who take hypnosis training do not make use of hypnosis in their clinical work.

Difficulties in "making hypnosis work" surface frequently in consultations. The categories of considerations discussed were drawn from my tabulation of problems that proved to be causing difficulty in the situations presented to me as a consultant.

In my study of 30 individuals who had suffered unwanted negative effects during hypnosis training, I discovered that most of these unfortunate occurrences were neither recognized by faculty nor reported by participants. Numerous pressures combined to deter both groups from acknowledging and addressing difficulties, some of which were quite serious. The impact of these events could have been dealt with more effectively had they been identified and addressed promptly (Kluft, 2012c).

In my work with highly traumatized individuals, I have found that many feared hypnosis and/or resisted hypnosis, often without being aware of their own concerns or acknowledging their misgivings to me. Further, some alleged mistreatment by persons who stated they had used hypnosis, or who had taken actions that these patients had inferred or assumed to be hypnosis. I found that exquisitely slow and stepwise introductions to hypnotic experiences and phenomena usually succeeded when more rapid conventional methods and pacing had failed or had led to insurmountable resistances even after trance had been induced (Kluft, 2016).

Those who have suffered unwanted negative sequelae to prior hypnosis and those who have been traumatized and/or fear traumatization serve as paradigms for those patients with whom induction efforts are likely to fail. Often they either do not know or will not share why they covertly oppose induction. They are defending themselves against discomfort experienced in reaction to the induction suggestions themselves or arising in response to incipient dysphoria as they begin to follow those suggestions.

During my years as an officer of the American Society of Clinical Hypnosis, I became concerned about how frequently I was told that many of those who took beginning workshops rapidly discontinued their use of hypnosis. Casual interviews with over two dozen "hypnosis drop-outs" revealed that they found that their efforts to induce hypnosis in actual practice with the methods they had been taught in workshop settings were generally frustrating and disappointing.

These four categories of experience motivated me to ask a different sort of question: When does a hypnotic induction actually begin? If the induction technique is part of a larger process that is neither being recognized nor taught, could significant aspects of induction problems reside in elements of that larger process and generally escape being taken into consideration?

Putting aside for the moment individual differences in hypnotic responsivity and comorbidity, if the same procedures could yield such different results in different settings, factors other than the procedures themselves might have been exerting major influences upon the induction process.

This brought to mind two dramatic experiences from the early 1970s. I asked one of my professors, Martin T. Orne, M.D., Ph.D., to share his favorite approach to induction. Dr. Orne replied that his preferred method was very simple. Given his reputation, he said, people were very eager to see him, and willing to wait a long time for an appointment. He said that he would always give new patients an appointment time some six months in the future. By the time they arrived, they were so eager and motivated that all he had to do was intone the word "Sleep!" in a commanding manner, and his patients would enter a profound trance.

It seemed to me that the most potent interventions in Dr. Orne's approach occurred well in advance of his formal induction procedure. He relied heavily on social-psychological variables, expectation, and the demand characteristics inherent in his unique position in American psychiatry and the world of hypnosis at the time. It is dubious whether such an approach would be deemed acceptable, or even ethical, in current practice.

Shortly thereafter I observed that the potent variables noted above can be rendered powerless unless they are consensually validated by clinician and patient alike. A patient was presented to a famous Ericksonian, a man widely admired and respected as a teacher and clinician. The patient, however, had neither prior knowledge of nor antecedent respect for the Ericksonian mystique and this master practitioner. Neither infatuated with nor socialized to Ericksonian methods, he could make no sense of the practitioner's approaches. Unlike Orne's patients, he had not been schooled to appreciate the specialness of what was being offered to him. His response to confusional techniques and double binds was to remain unmoved by any of the interventions that were attempted, and to decline all alternative responses suggested. Again, we might wonder whether such a magical stance without meaningful informed consent would be regarded positively by today's standards.

Our patients are under no obligation to be predictable or to respect our preferences and/or narcissism. They often provide us with humbling reminders that sometimes one has to hit the ball where it is pitched.

Two years ago I evaluated a businesswoman in her 30s seeking help for a distressing symptom. We agreed to proceed to hypnosis at our next meeting. However, my next patient canceled, providing an unexpected opportunity to move forward. She rapidly entered what appeared to be a deep trance. The first hypnoprojective exploration after trance ratification revealed the dynamics of her problem. After a tearful abreaction and further exploration both within trance and subsequent to realerting, the symptom disappeared and has not recurred on 2-year follow-up.

Successful interventions of this sort are often recounted in workshops. A participant might believe such interventions and results are typical. However, uncomplicated patients are uncommon visitors to my consulting room. In fact, this was the only occasion in which I had been able to use a simple, straightforward workshop-style induction to initiate a problem-free treatment and achieve such a rapid outcome in my practice for several years. This means that when I teach in a basic workshop, I am educating others in techniques I rarely employ in the course of my professional activities.

My comments here are based primarily upon my experiences in consulting to colleagues who encountered difficulties using hypnosis in their own diverse practices and only secondarily from my work with the traumatized and my research on difficulties occurring in hypnosis workshops.

My cumulative observations strongly suggest that fear of unwanted experiences drives patients' misgivings about hypnosis and their lack of cooperation and/or success in participating with the induction process across all settings. An apprehensive anticipation of possible trauma is shared by those who are fearful on the basis of conscious or unconscious fantasies of some unwanted consequences, those confronted with the need to cope with unpleasant realities and stressors, and those who have already been subjected to severe traumata (the types of severe trauma associated with acute stress disorder, post-traumatic stress disorder, and most of the dissociative disorders) and are fearful of recurrent or additional hurt.

Anticipating arguments made below, largely on the basis of the work of Diamond (1984, 1987), whether an individual is an apprehensive workshop participant, the victim of severe trauma, or a patient with some concern about his or her condition and the treatment to be rendered, the primary consideration in optimizing the likelihood of a successful induction is related to the degree to which the individual who is about to undergo hypnosis can be helped to achieve a sense of safety.

Induction is invariably imbricated within a situational, expectational, and relational therapeutic matrix. Within that therapeutic matrix, induction requires the formation of a specialized helping alliance (Luborsky & Crits-Cristoph, 1990) designed to facilitate treatment by harnessing the focusing power and other useful characteristics of trance. What will be required to move toward the formation of this alliance and the attainment of its goals may vary tremendously depending on the unique characteristics of the therapeutic dyad, what must be achieved to lay the foundation for the overall success of the treatment in an optimal manner, and the particular nature, stressors, goals, and demands of each unique therapeutic encounter.

Beyond technique per se, induction inevitably involves and/or elicits expectancies and elements of the transference, the therapeutic alliance, and the real relationship within the therapeutic dyad. Some argue that it initiates a fourth manner of relating, unique to hypnosis, which Diamond (1987) describes as a symbiosis, a matter to be discussed below. Working toward induction offers a powerful and often unrecognized opportunity to establish, explore, and recognize obstacles to the establishment of a therapeutic alliance capable of optimizing the treatment process. This "preview of coming attractions" in terms of problems likely to be encountered in the ongoing treatment, and what is learned about how they may be overcome, is profoundly helpful in preparing both members of the therapeutic dyad and the relational matrix they co-create between them to prepare to confront the work ahead.

In an earlier publication (Kluft, 1992), I described the problem of paradigm exhaustion, the stalling and/or stalemating of treatment when the clinician persists in applying a paradigm, be it expressed in an orientation or a pattern of intervention, that has lost its credibility to the patient. Induction failures threaten to destroy the usefulness of hypnosis. Patients may feel they have failed (usually once again) and lose confidence in themselves as competent individuals. Iatrogenic shame may be superimposed upon an already uncomfortable individual. Alternatively or additionally, such failures may undermine patients' ability to repose confidence in the healer, who may be perceived as a failure by one or both parties and/or may create fear, hostility, contempt, and other negative feelings toward that healer and/or all healers. Further still, the uncomfortable ambience of the aftermath of induction failures may undermine the clinician's confidence in hypnosis and/or him or herself. Incompetence breeds shame, and the antidote to shame is competence (Nathanson,

1992, 2009). Competence is unlikely to be reestablished by repeating a failed strategy.

Preliminary Considerations—Setting the Stage for Induction

Loading the Dice, Stacking the Deck

In clinical work, uniformity of approach determined by the preference or convenience of the clinician represents a countertransference error that risks bypassing the individuality and dignity of the patient (Hirsch, 2008; Kluft, 2016). The patient is best served by optimizing the likelihood that what is said and suggested in the process of induction will be well received.

Two simple measures and one caution have served me well in this regard: the "Apple Test" (Strauss, 1991); my assumption that my patients would rather be somewhere else doing something else; and my effort to eliminate from consideration approaches to induction that may have an unacceptable cost/benefit ratio for a particular patient.

In Strauss's (1991) method, the patient is asked to imagine an apple, seeing it, holding it, and beginning to eat it. Questions are asked that educate the clinician about which sensory modalities are most responsive to suggestion. Notwithstanding Kroger and Fezler's (1976) powerful argument for anchoring imagery in all five sensory modalities, we often encounter patients whose ability to respond to suggestions varies widely across different sensory modalities.

At this moment in the history of hypnosis, visual imagery suggestions seem predominant in many workshop settings. Yet in almost every workshop I observed during my research (Kluft, 2012a, 2012b, 2012c), a number of participants were frustrated by their inability to immerse themselves in visual imagery suggestions. While these participants simply may have had minimal hypnotic talent, I reflected that when I was learning hypnosis, workshop directors routinely approached such participants with inductions appealing to different sensory modalities and usually were able to help them experience a range of hypnotic phenomena. The apple exercise protects both my patients and me from considerable frustration.

One need not use an apple to benefit from Strauss's model. In the last year, I have used ice cream, cheesecake, a pricey wine, and a porterhouse steak. Sometimes recalling a patient's preference pays unexpected dividends. One patient said, "Give me something I'd really like to eat!" She chose mint chocolate chip ice cream. Years later, she had to undergo a series of endoscopic procedures. Complex medical problems indicated that any type of chemical anesthesia might prove problematic. She was able to "eat" mint chocolate chip ice cream until every part of her upper gastrointestinal track beyond her taste buds had been numbed by her chilly delicacy of choice. She underwent two such procedures without additional chemical anesthesia.

It is customary to ask a patient to choose a place that is pleasant and positive to serve as a useful image. Then, the patient is brought into this scene and the scene is elaborated by the clinician while the patient's mind remains relatively passive. Mindful of Stolar and Fromm's (1974) distinction between ego passivity and ego activity, and of my impression that my patients would rather be elsewhere rather than in my office, I prefer to ask my patients where they would rather be and then follow my patient's lead in what I add to the mix. I find this often makes my patients more invested in the deepening and success of the imagery suggestions. If I know little about the patient's preferred activity, I do not hesitate to make inquiries before proceeding.

Some caveats: I do not work with imagery associated with anything too elaborate for clinical use, dangerous, or inappropriate. I will not work with activities of which the patient is incapable. Wishful fantasies collapse all too easily and, if they do not, their illusory success risks encouraging problematic grandiosity.

In one instance, a patient wanted to climb Mount Everest. The task was beyond his capacities. Constructing a satisfactory experience would have required too much in terms of time and specialized knowledge. We bargained down to Mount Washington, which he thought he could climb and which I had climbed myself. It was easy to create a convincing and successful "climb" for him. Mount Washington "mastered" and trance achieved in a manner involving inherent ego strengthening dimensions, the obstacles to his attaining his therapeutic objectives were easily surmounted. (However, the major ego strengthening, which involved the corrective impact of my suggesting to him and his accepting a reasonable objective, was to initiate a way of thinking designed to protect him against his often-problematic grandiosity and his disintegration anxiety [Kohut, 1977] when his grandiosity was punctured by reality.)

Finally, some inductions are simply inappropriate for some patients. Those involving suggestions of heaviness may unsettle patients with weight and eating issues. Those involving fists, or hands coming closer to the face, may upset survivors of physical abuse. For example, one of my favorite inductions, the Chiasson (1973) method involves the patient's hand coming closer to the patient's face. The eyes are to close when the hand touches the face. This is so analogous to the model of a victim of violence closing her eyes in terror as an attacker's hand nears her face that its use with such patients is contraindicated.

Notice Subtle Hints of Distressing Dynamics

Research by Lester Luborsky and his colleagues (Luborsky & Auerbach, 1969; Luborsky & Mintz, 1974) has demonstrated that disruptions in therapeutic communication are usually heralded by references to some discomfort in connection with the therapeutic dyad (presumed to be transferential). Therapeutic success is correlated with the degree to which the therapist addresses the recurrent central concerns of the patient, which are characterized as the Core Conflictual Relationship Theme (Luborsky

& Crits-Cristoph, 1990). While early slight indicators of change in the patient's expression may be due to the onset of trance phenomena, if some fluctuation of uncertain nature is observed, it is useful to wonder, and sometimes even to inquire, whether one's words have triggered any concerns or discomforts and to make inquiries. It is easier to clarify and start again than continue along the lines of an oversight or error and be forced to deal with the aftermath of a misadventure.

Be Sensitive to How You Begin to Change When You Start to Do an Induction

When taught in workshops and demonstrations, inductions are presented without providing more than rudimentary data concerning the contexts of interactions antecedent and subsequent to the induction per se. In workshops, perfunctory preliminaries completed, attention is turned to induction. At this juncture in clinical settings, the tenor of the clinical interaction often undergoes a sudden and a significant transition. What had been a conversational back and forth is exchanged for a pattern characterized by the relative activity of one party, the clinician, and the relatively passivity of the second, the patient. Usually this occurs uneventfully.

Some patients, however, are disconcerted by the transition from the clinician's more habitual style of self-expression to the clinician's "hypnotic voice." By comparison to one's usual pattern of interaction, one's hypnotic voice, often lowered, slowed, and replete with suggestions, may be experienced as asserting control and/or as frankly seductive. Since many inductions go awry during this transition, it may be helpful as we proceed to inquire whether there are elements of discomfort in what our patients are experiencing.

Refrain From Imposing Your Subjective Experience of Time and Pressure Upon the Patient

While many patients share an experience of the passage of time congruent with that of the clinician, others do not. Clinicians learn hypnosis in workshop settings, in a context in which constraints and limitations of time are understood and accepted. Social, psychological, and group pressures collude to deceive the student that the constricted time lines of practice groups and demonstrations generate reasonable temporal facsimiles of clinical encounters. Deviations from such expectations may demoralize patient and clinician alike.

Not only is there great individual variation in trance capacity and in the ease with which it can be mobilized, but working in an office with a suffering individual is very different from attempting to induce hypnosis with others present as witnesses, with performance pressures and time restrictions perceived and experienced by the participants inducing and experiencing hypnosis alike, and with an instructor prepared to assume the role of deus ex machina should things be taking too long or should something go awry. In contrast, clinical encounters are private events that may evoke any number of reactions unconstrained by pressures generated by others and may introduce other demand characteristics, all of which fall to the clinician to recognize and address.

Clinical patience, like clinical tact, is an undervalued virtue. When working with a new patient and/or a patient who cannot articulate his or her prior experience of hypnotic phenomena, the nature of the hypnotic components of the interaction of patient and clinician about to take place are initially unknown to either party. While comparing the responses of an individual to those of others might appear at first glance to be a reasonable application of one's experience and clinical judgment, it may prove to be an insult to the individuality and dignity of the patient (see Hicks, 2012; Levine, 2016) and can become a subtle but toxic countertransference error (see Hirsch, 2008; Kluft, 2016).

D. Corydon Hammond (1990) reminded us that the master clinicians of earlier generations were often phenomenally patient, unfazed by the passage of long periods of time during which little appears to transpire. On two occasions, I watched Hammond work with seemingly unhypnotizable workshop participants, waiting quietly, making only the occasional kind remark. Hammond's gentle, unrushed efforts ultimately elicited phenomena characteristic of hypnotic virtuosos from both.

In my own practice, when I encounter individuals who respond quite slowly to suggestions either by observation or per information from a referral source, I often will schedule a session of indeterminate duration. Once the patient and I have reached a satisfactory way of working toward trance, I usually make suggestions to facilitate subsequent hypnotic efforts, such as cues to reinstitute a desirable trance more quickly.

Craft Inductions Congruent With the Model of Helping Inherent in Your Treatment Approach and With Your Patient's Expectations

The act of helping is studied in the disciplines of sociology, anthropology, and social psychology as well as by the helping professions, formal and otherwise. Brickman et al. (1982) distinguished four models of helping classified by patterns of attribution of responsibility for a problem (who is to blame for a past event) and attributions of responsibility for a solution (who is to control future events).

In what they called the medical model, individuals are neither held responsible for their problems nor for the resolution of their problems. They need to receive treatment. In the moral model, individuals are held responsible for both their problems and the solutions of their problems. People need motivation. In the enlightenment model, individuals are seen as responsible for their problems, but need help from responsible others to find and implement solutions to those problems. They are understood to need discipline. Finally, in the compensatory model, individuals are not held responsible for their problems, but are held accountable for the solution of those problems. People need the knowledge that provides them with tools and capability to do what needs to be done.

These authors regard rational-emotive therapy (Ellis, 1962) and existential psychotherapy (Frankl, 1969) as embodying the assumptions of the moral model and psychoanalysis as an exemplar of the medical model. They propose therapeutic communities and Alcoholics Anonymous as illustrations of the enlightenment model and cognitive behavioral therapy as an illustration of the compensatory model.

While the models of Brickman et al. (1982) might seem to have little relationship to the logistics of a hypnotic induction and often will be of marginal relevance, they raise two potentially helpful concerns. First, given the importance of the induction to the therapeutic process, especially in making a contribution to the therapeutic alliance in psychotherapies facilitated with hypnosis, it is useful to employ an induction method congruent with the nature of the psychotherapy to follow. For example, employing an induction method replete with extensive poetic imagery would be jarringly discordant with the tone and stance of rational-emotive treatment, and might confuse the patient about the roles of both therapist and patient in hypnosis as compared to the overall treatment.

Second, it is important to match the model of helping embodied in the induction with the expectations of the patient. Brickman et al. (1982) summarized data suggesting that sociological and social-psychological considerations may determine which models of intervention a given patient is likely to accept. For example, blue-collar workers tend to expect and do best with approaches embracing a medical model.

My predecessor in treating a machinist recovering from a work-related injury had attempted an imagery induction. When I asked what had gone wrong, his answer was blunt: "She told me to imagine some place I can't afford to go, and she didn't tell me what to do. So, I opened my eyes." A classic Spiegel and Spiegel (2004) eye-roll induction delivered with a kindly but firm and authoritative directive stance, consistent with a medical model approach, followed by restructuring, was quite effective.

In hypnosis workshop trainings, participants are practicing their skills with peers who share many of their values and understandings and are learning from experts to whom patients often come already expecting hypnosis. It is important to appreciate that transposing expectations derived from these settings into the consulting room of the average practitioner may encourage a destructive countertransference blindness (Hirsch, 2008; see also Kluft, 2016). A few questions about how the patient believes the helping process works or should work often provide instructive information.

Affect-Related Concerns in Induction

Hypnosis is well known to hold the potential to mobilize and/or intensify affect and/or to trigger the release of strong affect. Here I address a different and more specialized concern.

Diligent efforts to present hypnosis in a manner that dispels patients' fears of passivity and mitigates worries that entering trance constitutes a weakness that labels successful patients as weak, submissive, and unable to fend for themselves are often far less successful than they appear to be on the surface. Motivation to receive the hoped-for benefits often overrides unresolved concerns, or at least their expression or manifestation.

However, when motivation is weak or conflicted, or when patients present already burdened by their sense that failure in a more conventional (or at least an unfacilitated) modality has already defined them as damaged goods and/or unlikely to be helped, the practitioner should consider the possibility that the shadows of demoralization and shame already loom large over the current therapeutic enterprise. Such awareness should be prominent in patients with a history of mistreatment, especially childhood mistreatment, because shame usually accompanies traumatization and its aftermath.

A discussion of shame and its impact upon treatment is beyond the scope of this article. Interested readers are referred to Nathanson (1992, 2009). The crucial consideration in planning an induction is respect for Nathanson's pithy observation that the antidote to shame is competence. Inductions for patients known to suffer considerable shame or whose circumstances make it reasonable to expect severe shame will be encountered should be built upon a number of very easily achieved suggestions selected to be congenial to the patient and chosen to steer far from the risk of failure and potentially upsetting subject material. Stock imagery is always potentially dangerous. It may inadvertently trigger traumatic associations or memories. Considerable conversation with the patient may be necessary to select relatively problem-free elements from which suggestions can be built and from which a workable induction can be framed.

A decade ago, a workshop director instructor began a group induction using images derived from her love of the seashore, which she assured the group would be safe and pleasant for all participants. Unfortunately, one participant had been raped on a beach very much like the one in the imagery being suggested. She began to experience terrible flashbacks and became acutely suicidal (Kluft, 2012a, 2012b, 2012c). The participant left the workshop in turmoil. When she could not calm herself, she asked me to intervene. Before she was safely stabilized, what we both had anticipated would be a brief intervention had mushroomed into several hours of horrendous abreactions, during which she repeatedly tried to hurl herself out of a window to her death.

Conversely, in dealing with one horribly abused and profoundly depressed woman who had been exploited by a previous therapist, her belief that all humans were perfidious and dangerous invalidated many approaches from the start. Fortunately, she loved and trusted dogs. I elicited a list of 20 species of which she was particularly fond, and encouraged her to envision a puppy of one species after another in her mind's eye, suggesting only the species of the puppy of the moment. After going through all 20 species, I wondered if she could let them bark ferociously if I said anything that was problematic, and suggested that she report their barking to me, should any occur. She was delighted with her success in creating "my own puppy TV channel," and things went well, although there was some growling along the way.

Relational Perspectives on Induction

Diamond (1984, 1987) addressed the well-known observation that some clinicians are far more successful than others in their use of hypnosis. He makes a powerful argument that notwithstanding patients' innate differences in hypnotic talent, relational factors play a considerable role in how and to what extent the hypnotic endeavor will succeed. The clinician's success in establishing safety within the therapeutic dyad, in creating a holding environment in which the patient will feel protected, establishes a strong foundation for the therapeutic enterprise.

He advised careful attention to the relational matrix that develops between clinician and patient. While transference and the therapeutic alliance as they are defined in classic psychoanalysis take time to develop, transference elements, expectancies, and connections based on past experiences are present from the first. Likewise, while a therapeutic alliance based on an identification with the therapist's work ego must emerge slowly and grow stronger over time, basic elements of cooperation and impediments to cooperation are always in evidence. The real relationship between clinician and patient begins with (or even before) first in-person impressions and is further elaborated with every verbal exchange. While most clinicians allow themselves to appreciate the wide range of reactions they experience to their patients as people, many succumb to the common narcissistic self-deception of assuming that they will be well received by every patient they endeavor to assist.

Diamond (1987) and others believe that a fourth dimension of relatedness occurs in hypnosis-facilitated treatments, a hypnotic symbiosis or fusion in which the hypnotist briefly becomes part of the patient and participates in the working of the patient's mind during hypnosis. This aspect of collaboration in connection with hypnosis is important, but attempts to formulate it in the above terms are problematic. They rely on older psychoanalytic concepts that no longer enjoy universal acceptance even within psychoanalysis. They are articulated in language that implies that a considerable (and somewhat shared) psychodynamic regression takes place in hypnosis, involving the breaking down of ego boundaries between clinician and patient. Some of the phenomena described in discussing these concepts strongly imply that both parties enter trance and that both are high in hypnotic talent.

Most difficulties noted above in describing these matters are bypassed if the hypnotic relationship is reformulated using the theoretical framework of Heinz Kohut (1971, 1977), the founder of self-psychology, who developed the concept of the self-object (the experience of another person as a part of or as a purveyor of functions to the mind of the individual). Because Kohut's conceptual matrix expresses these ideas most clearly, his contributions will be discussed separately below.

Rather than elaborate relational considerations on a theoretical level, I will illustrate their potential for intrusion into an induction process by reflecting on four words I hear used repeatedly in hypnosis workshops and by consultees, and emphatically advise students against saying: "I want you to...."

"I want you to" is far more than a helpfully intended directive. "I want you to" invites the patient to become the narcissistic object of the hypnotist, to become an extension of the hypnotist's will. Indeed, people who tell us what they want us to do may be beseeching us, but it is more likely that they are laying claim to an authority over us and claiming the power to issue commands. Unless they are combined with other instructions, such as "I want you to be able to accomplish exactly what you want to accomplish," which place the speaker in a position potentially dedicated to serve the interests of the patient, these are the words of a person who expects to give orders and be obeyed, the antithesis of a permissive stance.

Imagine the impact of such a verbalization upon a victim of mistreatment, a person who presents with difficulties in assertiveness, an individual enmeshed in a contentious or painful relationship, someone struggling to individuate him- or herself, etc. Imagine how such words, if uttered by an assertive male clinician, would be received by a woman who holds strong feminist values.

In one fell swoop, the speaker taints him- or herself with transference elements related to negatively perceived authority figures, indicates to the patient that the therapeutic alliance will have a dominance/submission atmosphere, conveys that the real relationship will be with someone who wants to have his or her way, and communicates that any temporary borrowing of aspects of the clinician's mind by the patient in trance may be of an unwelcome variety, to be defended against rather than to be openly embraced.

Taking such considerations into account prior to deciding upon an approach to induction and choosing which verbalizations to employ is a worthwhile effort.

Self-Psychological Perspectives on Induction

Kohut (1971, 1977) understood man to be perpetually interdependent rather than atomistic and complete unto himself, even when reasonably secure and mature. Defining the self as, among other things, a center of initiative and experience, this aspect of the human psyche, whether early development has been kind and nurturing or troubled and unsupportive, is often distressed by the vicissitudes of life. Those experiencing an unsettled and/or fragmenting sense of self seek out connectedness with others to restore and restabilize themselves.

In childhood, these forms of connectedness optimally involve empathic connections that understand us and reflect both us and that empathic form of understanding back to ourselves (mirroring self-objects). In addition, the child needs to be able to identify with a powerful individual who is competent, capable, strong, and with whom one can feel safe (idealizing self-objects). As the child grows older, connection with peers with whom one has a sense of sameness, the sense that one is one of many and not alone in the world, enters the picture (the alter-ego or twinship self-object).

When many key psychoanalytic reflections on hypnosis were being written in the 1980s, authors often used aspects of Kohut's language and thought without citing him, alluding to their wish to avoid undue confusion by introducing new and controversial terminology. Their decisions led to three unfortunate consequences. Kohut was not given due credit for his contributions, even when others used terms and concepts he created. The normalizing of various forms of narcissistic relatedness, all of which are necessary in normal development and function throughout the lifespan, especially in responding to life's vicissitudes, did not become part of the psychodynamic understanding of aspects of hypnosis. This left the all-important study of the form of relatedness considered unique to the hypnotic situation in a conceptual and linguistic quagmire often biased toward describing the interaction of a highly hypnotizable patient and a highly hypnotizable clinician in confusing impressionistic/metaphoric terms, such as "symbiosis" or "symbiotic fusion" (e.g., Diamond, 1987).

Kohut offers a more pragmatic stance. If we understand the hypnotic situation as one in which self-object relationships are relevant, we can appreciate the clinician not as fusing or entering a symbiotic relationship, implying a lysis of ego boundaries, primitive stages of development, and a shared altered state. Instead, the clinician is temporarily lending one or more series of functions: (1) a strong, dependable, and idealized figure to provide safety and with whose strength the patient can identify (idealizing self-object); and/or (2) a sense of acceptance, understanding, and positive regard (mirroring self-object); and/or (3) a sense of sameness that reestablishes the interpersonal bridge between the individual and others, potentially pulling him or her out of the loneliness and isolation of shame (see Nathanson, 1992, 2009) (twinship or alter-ego self-object). Applying these Kohutian constructs to hypnosis reveals striking similarities with Ferenczi's (1955, 1988) oft-forgotten distinctions between "father hypnosis," characterized by strength, authority, and clear suggestions to be followed (hypnotist as idealizing self-object), and "mother hypnosis," characterized more by nurture and support (hypnotist as mirroring self-object).

The importance of discerning and empathizing with the self-object needs of the patient and responding to them in one's choice of induction strategies can hardly be overemphasized. While many clinicians accomplish this intuitively, careful listening and thoughtful responding are skills that can be mastered by all.

In my clinical work, if I do not discover a particular form of self-object hunger, I generally try to include elements of all three forms of relatedness in my induction patter. When it is clear that a patient is insecure and looking to me for structure and strength, I speak with a firm calmness and assurance with which I hope my patient can identify (analogous to Ferenczi's "father hypnosis"). When a patient conveys a fear of being misunderstood or hurt, I will identify the patient's concerns in a sensitive rather than critical or blandly reassuring manner and make several inquiries as we proceed to make sure that the patient knows that I am trying to track and respond sensitively to the patient's concerns (analogous to Ferenczi's "mother hypnosis"). I inquire into any indication of increasing distress or consternation. Again, the reassurance given takes the form of making the patient aware that I am eager to keep the patient's concerns in mind. Direct reassurance often fails to impact a patient with a trauma history or a long history of feeling misunderstood or depreciated. They usually have received ample reassurance and expressions of sentiments to the effect, "I understand," usually followed by ample evidence that the reassurance did not address their most important concerns accurately and/or honestly, and that they were not understood very well at all. If I cannot make an empathic connection with my patient, voice it, and receive a response that indicates that my empathic remark was on target, I am not inclined to proceed with an induction until I am more confident in my understanding of my patient's frame of mind.

In consultations, I often find that an induction failed because the clinician proceeded with the planned induction without touching base with a patient who actually was experiencing misgivings and discomforts. Usually, the induction seemed to be going well until the patient abruptly opened his or her eyes in distress, or with a comment to the effect of, "It's not working."

Thoughts on Providing Hypnosis in Collaborative Therapeutic Endeavors

At times a clinician is asked to contribute hypnotic expertise and experience to the efforts of a treatment team. During such endeavors, the consulting room is crowded by many more presences than the two visible to an observer and those that can be inferred from transference phenomena. Further, the transference and therapeutic alliance themselves are split and distributed across members of the treatment team.

Under these circumstances, it may be useful to avoid bravura inductions that demonstrate the highly developed skills of the clinician providing hypnosis-facilitated interventions, or inductions that please that clinician to employ, but which may be difficult both for the patient to comprehend and describe. At the end of the day, the others collaborating in a patient's care are more likely to provide collateral support for the provider of hypnosis if the nature of the hypnotic work is easily explained and understood both by patients and by colleagues with little or no familiarity with hypnosis. I have been consulted in several instances after impressive initially effective interventions were so unfamiliar to the patients and the other participating clinicians alike that they were not embraced and validated. Instead, their effectiveness rapidly deteriorated, and the artistry of the clinicians was wasted.

What About BYOT (Bring Your Own Trance) Inductions?

Both heterohypnosis (hypnosis subsequent to induction in a subject or patient by a second party) and autohypnosis or self-hypnosis (hypnosis subsequent to an induction by a subject or patient by that subject or patient) are deliberate and thoughtful interventions. However, a third form of hypnosis exists, spontaneous trance, in which neither formal induction, deliberation, nor thoughtful planning can be assumed.

Clinical anecdotes abound in which use has been made of a patient's spontaneous and autohypnotic trance phenomena. Some clinicians prefer to proceed in a conversational manner, with minimal use of discrete techniques. Some believe either that there is no clear or absolute demarcation between trance and an absence of trance, or define trance in an idiosyncratic manner. Indeed, patients may be more comfortable with indirect approaches that avoid formal elements and bypass whatever mixed feelings may be associated with hypnosis and "being hypnotized."

Gruzelier (2000) argued convincingly that polarizing trance and non-trance implies a false dichotomy, drawing attention to many partial and incomplete transitional or "in between" situations. Further, Gruzelier (2000), J. Hilgard (1974), Howard (n.d.), MacHovec (1986), and Kluft (2012a), among others, have noted the frequency with which unwanted events linked to hypnosis are associated with ongoing and incompletely terminated trance phenomena.

Over a decade's research on these matters leads me to recommend that a patient's first introduction to hypnosis should involve a discrete beginning and end, i.e., formal induction and formal dehypnosis. Until the patient's response to hypnosis has been studied carefully, it seems foolhardy to assume that simply allowing the patient to enter and exit trance in a poorly understood and incompletely characterized manner serves the best interests of the patient. I am concerned that beginning the use of hypnosis in this manner disrespects the dignity of the patient, may be experienced as manipulative and dishonest, and may fail to respect the Hippocratic injunction, "firstly, do no harm" (see Kluft, 2016).

In addition, I have become increasingly convinced that assessing a patient's alertness before and after a trance experience is a useful way to avoid the inadvertent persistence of trance phenomena and concomitant unwanted sequelae, a step difficult to take except in connection with discrete induction and dehypnosis procedures. I find the recently developed Howard Alertness Scale (HAS; Howard, 2008, n.d.) is quite useful both to establish a prehypnotic baseline and to identify unwanted trance remnants, which must be addressed to prevent the patient's leaving the consultation room inadequately realerted. It is effective in both heterohypnotic and autohypnotic contexts.

Mindful of the risks associated with leaving patients in persistent trances of uncharacterized qualities, I am of the opinion that until the response of a given individual to circumscribed trance experiences with discrete beginnings and deliberately defined end points has been explored, it is unwise and potentially dangerous to simply avail one's self of what appear to be spontaneous or self-induced hypnotic phenomena, especially in patients who appear to be highly or readily hypnotizable. Too often, they prove to be indicators of an unrecognized dissociative disorder.

Patients' unfortunate posthypnotic discomforts constitute a powerful disincentive to the optimal use of hypnosis, disenchanting both healthcare professionals and patients alike with this modality. The HAS is a valuable and easily implemented safeguard for the clinical use of hypnosis.

This protocol and my personal approach to its use were reprinted, with the permission of Dr. Howard, in a recent text (Kluft, 2013).

Conclusion

Induction is a complex and nuanced process, not simply a matter of applying various techniques to effect an individual's entry into trance. The success of this process, involving as it does a series of responses to a series of suggestions, paves the way for successful responses to more specifically targeted therapeutic interventions involving suggestions and other communications as well. Unless hypnosis is being introduced into an already established therapeutic relationship, it may serve as the paradigm for problem solving and relating within the therapeutic dyad, i.e., the therapeutic alliance.

From this perspective, whatever facilitates the establishing of a constructive model in the approach to and the process of induction is beneficial to the overall therapeutic enterprise, and whatever impedes achieving such an outcome is potentially detrimental to that endeavor. Also, from this perspective, the specific technique of induction employed is of less consequence than the efforts made to anticipate and remove impediments to its success.

References

Brickman, P., Rabinowitz, V., Karuza, J., Coates, D., Cohn, E., & Kidder, L. (1982). Models of helping and coping. *American Psychologist*, *37*, 368–384. doi:10.1037/0003-066X.37.4.368

Chiasson, S. (1973). Chiasson's method. In *Syllabus on hypnosis and a handbook of therapeutic suggestions*. Chicago, IL: The American Society of Clinical Hypnosis—Education and Research Foundation.

Diamond, M. (1984). It takes two to tango: Some thoughts on the neglected importance of the hypnotist in an interactive hypnotherapeutic relationship. *American Journal of Clinical Hypnosis*, *27*, 3–13. doi:10.1080/00029157.1984.10402582

Diamond, M. (1987). The interactional basis of hypnotic experience: On the relational dimensions of hypnosis. *International Journal of Clinical and Experimental Hypnosis*, *35*, 95–115. doi:10.1080/00207148708416046

Ellis, A. (1962). *Reason and emotion in psychotherapy.* New York, NY: Lyle Stuart.

Ferenczi, S. (1955). Confusion of tongues between adults and the child—the language of tenderness and of passion. In *Final contributions to the problems and methods of psycho-analysis* (pp. 156–167). London, UK: Hogarth Press.

Ferenczi, S. (1988). *The clinical diary of Sándor Ferenczi* (J. Dupont, Ed.). Cambridge, MA: Harvard University Press. (Original work printed 1932 [in Hungarian])

Frankl, V. E. (1969). *The will to meaning: Foundations and applications of logotherapy.* New York, NY: New American Library.

Gruzelier, J. (2000). Unwanted effects of hypnosis: A review of the evidence and its implications. *Contemporary Hypnosis*, *17*, 163–193. doi:10.1002/(ISSN)1557-0711

Hammond, D. C. (1990). *Handbook of hypnotic suggestions and metaphors*. New York, NY: Norton.
Hicks, D. (2012). *Dignity*. New Haven, CT: Yale University Press.
Hilgard, J. R. (1974). Sequelae to hypnosis. *International Journal of Clinical and Experimental Hypnosis*, *22*, 281–298. doi:10.1080/00207147408413008
Hirsch, I. (2008). *Coasting in the countertransference: Conflicts of self-interest between analyst and patient*. New York, NY: Routledge.
Howard, H. (n.d.). *The role of an alertness scale in clinical hypnosis*. Manuscript under review.
Howard, H. (2008). The Howard Alertness Scale. *Focus*, *50*(2–3), 3–4.
Kluft, R. P. (1992). Paradigm exhaustion and paradigm shift and thinking through the therapeutic impasse. *Psychiatric Annals*, *22*, 502–508. doi:10.3928/0048-5713-19921001-06
Kluft, R. P. (2012a). Enhancing workshop safety: Learning from colleagues' adverse experiences (Part I—structure/content). *American Journal of Clinical Hypnosis*, *55*, 85–103. doi:10.1080/00029157.2012.659359
Kluft, R. P. (2012b). Enhancing workshop safety: Learning from colleagues' adverse experiences (Part II—structure/policy). *American Journal of Clinical Hypnosis*, *55*, 104–122. doi:10.1080/00029157.2011.650800
Kluft, R. P. (2012c). Issues in the detection of those suffering adverse effects in hypnosis training workshops. *American Journal of Clinical Hypnosis*, *54*, 213–232. doi:10.1080/00029157.2011.631228
Kluft, R. P. (2013). *Shelter from the storm*. Charleston, SC: Create Space Independent Publishing Platform.
Kluft, R. P. (2016). You have to be carefully taught: Dignity considerations in clinical practice, scholarship, and trauma treatment. In S. Levine (Ed.), *Dignity matters: Psychoanalytic and psychosocial perspectives* (pp. 141–158). London, UK: Karnac Books.
Kohut, H. (1971). *The analysis of the self.* Chicago, IL: The University of Chicago Press.
Kohut, H. (1977). *The restoration of the self.* Chicago, IL: The University of Chicago Press.
Kroger, W., & Fezler, W. (1976). *Hypnosis and behavior modification: Imagery conditioning*. New York, NY: J. B. Lippincott.
Levine, S. (Ed.). (2016). *Dignity matters*. London, UK: Karnac Books.
Luborsky, L., & Auerbach, A. (1969). The symptom-context method—quantitative studies of symptom formation in psychotherapy. *Journal of the American Psychoanalytic Association*, *17*, 68–99.
Luborsky, L., & Crits-Cristoph, P. (1990). *Understanding transference: The core conflictual relationship theme method*. New York, NY: Basic Books.
Luborsky, L., & Mintz, J. (1974). What sets off momentary forgetting during a psychoanalysis? Investigation of symptom-onset conditions. *Psychoanalysis and Contemporary Science*, *3*, 233–268.
MacHovec, F. (1986). *Hypnosis complications: Prevention and risk management*. Springfield, IL: Thomas.
Nathanson, D. (1992). *Shame and pride*. New York, NY: Norton.
Nathanson, D. (2009). Affect and hypnosis: On paying friendly attention to disturbing thoughts. *International Journal of Clinical and Experimental Hypnosis*, *57*, 319–342. doi:10.1080/00207140903098361
Spiegel, H., & Spiegel, D. (2004). *Trance and treatment* (2nd ed.). Washington, DC: American Psychiatric Press.
Stolar, D., & Fromm, E. (1974). Activity and passivity of the ego in relation to the superego. *International Review of Psychoanalysis*, *1*, 297–311.
Strauss, B. (1991). The use of a multimodal image, the apple technique, to facilitate hypnosis: A brief clinical communication. *International Journal of Clinical and Experimental Hypnosis*, *39*, 1–5. doi:10.1080/00207149108409614

Induction Technique: Beyond Simple Response to Suggestion

Arreed Barabasz and Marianne Barabasz

The hypnotic induction is intended to induce hypnosis. This implies that what is sought is intended to go beyond what might be wrought by mere suggestion, expectancy, and social influence. The experimentally controlled research showing that the induction makes a difference and how small changes in wording of suggestions can produce orthogonal responses is briefly reviewed. This article explains the principles of induction and three critical phases of hypnotic induction in detail. An arm levitation scripted protocol demonstrating how to respond to the patient using the three phases to maximize responses to hypnotic suggestions is presented.

As defined by the American Psychological Association (APA) Division 30, a hypnotic induction is "A procedure designed to induce hypnosis" (Elkins, Barabasz, Council, & Spiegel, 2015, p. 4). The APA definition committee intended to clearly distinguish between hypnosis (the product) and procedures that are used to induce the hypnotic state. Thus, it did not specify what the procedures might involve or the contexts in which they may occur. This feature of the definition allows for procedures that involve interaction between a therapist and client, self-hypnosis, or advanced technology procedures such as virtual reality hypnosis (Patterson, 2010, pp. 50–55). Laudable as this definition may be, it allows for just about any sort of induction without specifying what is likely needed to go beyond mere response to suggestion.

Expectancies

To obtain more than simple responses to suggestions, let us first consider the effect of expectancies on hypnotic responding. Benham, Woody, Wilson, and Nash (2006, p. 342) addressed what has become, in our view, a highly overblown notion. In this elegantly designed study, Benham et al. (2006) reported substantial evidence that the strength of the linkages between expectation and hypnotic performance simply did not support the extreme position that expectations are the "sole determinants" or the "essence" of hypnosis (Kirsch, 1991, pp. 460–461). The Kirsch model fails to adequately consider empirically the cognitive ability underlying hypnotizability. Furthermore, Benham, Bowers, Nash, and Muenchen (1998) directly tested the effects of expectation using a manipulation to significantly increase participants' expectation. Unfortunately for the "expectation is everything" believers, increasing expectation failed to lead to higher hypnotizability scores. Across each of two independent samples, hypnotic responsiveness of participants receiving the enhanced-expectations treatment was no different than the hypnotic responsiveness of control participants who did not receive the treatment. Most recently Black and Green (2016) successfully manipulated expectations to enhance participants' subjective estimates of the number of anagrams they would solve using a sample of 257 undergraduate students. However, the expectancy manipulation did not statistically enhance actual anagram performance. More recently, Tomé-Pirez, Ludena, and Lopez Pirez (2015) shed further light on research design flaws in expectation model studies.

Given that expectation is not the key to hypnotic responsiveness, what is the key if the induction itself is nothing more than "an extended initial suggestion" (Green, Barabasz, Barrett, & Montgomery, 2005, p. 262)? The words used in the initial induction may not be crucial, but the manner in which the induction progresses can be (Barabasz & Barabasz, 2016; Christensen, Barabasz, & Barabasz, 2013). Furthermore, experimentally controlled research has shown that the wording of suggestions, once hypnosis has been successfully induced, can be critical (Barabasz et al., 1999; Calvin, 2000; Christensen, Barabasz, & Barabasz, 2009; Grogan, Barabasz, Barabasz, & Christensen, in press; Jensen, Barabasz, Barabasz, & Warner, 2001).

The Wording of Hypnotic Suggestions Makes a Difference

Barabasz et al. (1999) determined in controlled experiments that electroencephalographic cortical event-related potentials (ERPs) are affected by information processing strategies, thus making them particularly appropriate for the examination of hypnotic alterations in perception. The effects of positive obstructive and negative obliterating instructions on visual and auditory P300 ERPs were tested. Twenty participants, stringently selected for hypnotizability from an initial sample of over 100, performed identical tasks during waking and alert hypnotic conditions. Alert hypnosis was used to preclude the effects that might be due to relaxation per se. High hypnotizables showed greater ERP amplitudes while experiencing negative hallucinations and lower ERP amplitudes while experiencing positive obstructive hallucinations, in contrast to low hypnotizables and their own waking imagination-only conditions. Consistent findings among investigations (Barabasz, 2000; Barabasz & Lonsdale, 1983; Barabasz et al., 1999; Calvin, 2000; Jensen et al.,

2001; Spiegel & Barabasz, 1988; Spiegel, Cutcomb, Ren, & Pribram, 1985) revealed that when responses are time-locked to events, robust physiological markers of hypnosis emerge that reflect alterations in consciousness that correspond to participants' subjective experiences of perceptual alteration and that even apparently minor alterations in hypnotic suggestion wording can produce orthogonal differences in the electroencephalographic (EEG) ERPs' produced. These effects were not produced by suggestion alone but only once hypnosis was effectively induced in hypnotizable participants. The induction (Barabasz, 2000) makes a difference, and the wording of suggestions, once a person is experiencing hypnosis, can be crucial.

Maximize Responsiveness

We (Barabasz & Barabasz, 2016) recently noted that throughout our 40+ years in the field, we have observed not only academic researchers but sometimes acclaimed expert clinicians speed through inductions and then offer up suggestions without even a veiled attempt to assure that the participants were experiencing veridical hypnosis. Given such an inadequate induction technique, why would anyone expect to observe little more than what might be wrought by mere suggestion, compliance, and/or social influence without hypnosis?

Far too often, an audio-recorded induction is played or a protocol read verbatim without any ongoing real-time systematic assessment of the participant's responses to the induction instructions during the induction process. Inductions tailored to the individual participant produce better clinical responses (Barabasz & Barabasz, 2006), but what should we attend to during the heterohypnotic induction procedure for the typical mid-range average hypnotizable patient or research participant?

Principles of Induction

1. To narrow the perceptual field, the participant is asked to concentrate on some aspect of his or her physical or psychological functioning. Concentrating on a single aspect removes attention from other aspects of his or her being. Thus, one may be told to gaze at an eye-fixation object ("Please stare at that thumbtack up on the wall."), to sense the feelings in their hand ("Just look at that hand and notice what you can notice."), or to visualize a certain scene ("Imagine yourself on a tropical island.").
2. To minimize conscious and volitional effort, the participant may be told that he or she need not attend to the words of the hypnotist. "My words will enter your mind without you trying to listen, do not to try to do anything, just let happen whatever happens."
3. To dissociate the hand from control of the participant and turn normal self or "subject" movements into not self or "object" actions. The participant may be

told (upon observation of movement), "*The* hand is moving toward *your* face." (Not, "*Your* hand is moving toward *your* face.")

4. Milton Erickson (Erickson, Rossi, & Rossi, 1976) seemed to prefer a confusion technique to bypass voluntary or ego participation. For example, the participant might be told, "You are not really concerned about the fact that you can achieve many things without having to think about them."
5. To induce regression, emphasize comfort, relaxation, passivity, or even infantile dependency, the participant can be told, "You are in a soft, warm place where all your needs are taken care of, and you can enjoy this experience with every fiber of your being" (a womb fantasy).
6. To tie together hypnotic responses with ordinary suggested behaviors, the participant can be told, "As you sit there, you seem so calm and relaxed in the chair, you *will* begin to notice a sensation of lightness coming into your hand."
7. To use repetition as an aid to creating a dissociative response, the participant can be told, "You *will* become sleepier and sleepier and sleepier." (It makes no difference to the participant that the hypnotic state itself has nothing to do with the actual sleep state [Haley, 2015]). By contrast, an alert induction might involve wording such as, "You will become more alert, more and more alert, more awake and completely alert."
8. To focus attention on tiny normal movements and expand them into behaviors involving larger parts of the body, the participant can be told (upon observation), "The eyes are blinking and the eyes *will* get heavier and want to come down, down, and close."
9. To establish a set for entry into trance, the participant can be told, "I will count up to 20. Your arm, which I am holding, *will* get heavier and heavier. At the count of twenty, when I drop it, you *will* drop rapidly with it into a deep state of calmness." This is like "on your mark, get set, go!" A readiness for hypnotic response is suggested. The participant anticipates its occurrence.
10. Finally, to facilitate a natural entry into a trance state, the participant can simply be asked to imagine a kind of fantasy or dream. "let any kind of dream come, any sort of fantasy." If part of the therapeutic goal is self-esteem building you might say, "Just think about a time when you were especially happy with yourself, perhaps when you achieved a difficult goal or just any time that felt so very good."

The Three Phases of Hypnotic Induction

1. The *preparatory phase*, as explained by Barabasz and Watkins (2005, pp. 121–-124) consists of descriptions of hypnotic responding, which are embedded in the

hypnotic induction. The preparatory phase is entirely future tense oriented. Wording may include suggestions such as:

> Your eyelids *will* become heavier and heavier and you *will* want to close your eyes, *eventually* your eyes will be so tired you will close them—it *will* become impossible to keep them open, the pressure of your hand resting on your leg *will* become less and less—*that* hand will become lighter and lighter (the word "that" is used to facilitate dissociation of the hand from the person; from an analytic view [Watkins & Barabasz, 2008], this implies that the hand becomes 'object energized' instead of remaining "ego energized"). *Eventually it will* begin to rise, to lift on its own. You may notice that you *will* get an increase in salivation as you go into hypnosis, some people have that response, you might too, it's just one of those perfectly normal responses some people have at this stage, maybe you will have it too, maybe not, but all of the time *you will become* more and more calm (or more alert, if an alert induction is preferred for the response anticipated; these are specific responses indicating what *will* be felt, rather than a call for relaxation).

The key element of the preparatory phase is that you are protected from loss of rapport (Barabasz & Barabasz, 2016) when suggesting responses in the future tense when there is no behavioral evidence of them displayed by the participant yet.

Patience is also essential. I (A. B.) once took nearly an hour for an arm levitation induction to evoke minimal rising of a hand from a patient's leg. However, once accomplished, the response to the induction became so profound that future hypnotic rapport was assured. Deep rapid inductions became the norm for this patient, which, in due course, helped to produce significant therapeutic gains and lasting positive life changes.

2. The *transition phase* consists of descriptions of hypnotic responding as you observe them (Barabasz & Watkins, 2005, p. 122). The induction terminology shifts to using the present tense. The participant's concentration becomes effortless as they begin to dissociate and become unaware of all but the hypnotic activity. Moving on to this phase prematurely is a recipe for failure to achieve genuine hypnotic responsivity. This is the most common induction mistake. Then, even if you obtain an apparently positive response, it may only represent some sort of simple social compliance. In such cases, you might achieve nothing more than simple relaxation at best (in contrast to hypnotic relaxation, Elkins, 2014, pp. 32–34; Johnson, Johnson, Barton, & Elkins, 2016) or simple effort-laden non-hypnotic responses to easy suggestions. Such effortful responses are those that could be evoked without hypnosis per se. Those who still hold to the socio-cognitive belief that hypnosis is nothing more than an artifact of social influence, role-playing or simple suggestibility are known to instruct their research participants to "try as hard as you can" or "just try harder" (Spanos & Coe, 1992).

   To obtain veridical hypnotic responses, initiate the transition phase only when you have in reality observed the patient's responses suggested in the preparatory phase. As you become familiar with the phases of hypnosis, you will be able to observe your patient more closely as you will be less pre-occupied with carrying out the specifics of the induction procedure. As a result, you will be able to use these subtle clinical observations of hypnotic responding in the transition phase, regardless of whether you suggested them in the earlier phase because our patients and research participants frequently repeat their own idiosyncratic responses in the process of entering hypnosis. Wording typical of the transition phase might be as follows: (e.g., upon noticing eye flutter) " Your eyes are beginning to flutter, they may close soon," then as the eyes close for an instant say, "There the eyes closed, yes so much more comfortable closed than open."

3. The hypnotic *rapport phase* (Barabasz & Watkins, 2005, pp. 122–123) constitutes the true hypnotic experience where the patient's responses to hypnotic suggestions are perceived to be automatic (involuntary) and effortless. There is a shift toward primary processes (Barabasz & Christensen, 2006; Fromm, 1992) while maintaining some aspects of secondary processes where vigilance and defenses relax (Barabasz, 1982). Rapport phase wording involves whatever is required by the clinical demands of the situation or the research protocol. Hypnotic deepening, as well as depth checks, should correspond to the difficulty of the hypnotic response required.

Confidence in the hypnotic modality is important. Consider, for a moment, that your patient is regressed at least to some degree. Why would you expect to be trusted to use hypnosis in therapy any further if you were viewed as unsure of yourself or fail to convey that you understand that the hypnotic state is real (Elkins et al., 2015)? It is no surprise that inductions carried out by graduate students who may have had little or no training in clinical hypnosis from an academician psychologist who prizes suggestibility over hypnotic responsiveness per se and puts "hypnosis" in quotation marks in their writings obtains nothing more than mere response to suggestion or conscious compliance. No therapist, no matter how clever, can resonate with a patient while attempting to hide disbelief in the reality of the modality they are attempting to use (Newton, 2000). To obtain difficult responses (Pekala et al., 2006) to hypnotic suggestions (pain relief, surgery without anesthesia, amnesia, trauma resolution, etc.), you must absolutely expect it to work. As the late Bruner 'Fig' Newton explained (Newton, 2000), "You must know it will work."

Once the rapport phase is established, develop a series of graded hypnotic suggestions. Do not interrupt the process by calling for simple voluntary behaviors. In the rapport phase, the subject shows true hypnotic phenomena, including (a) increased responsiveness to suggestion, (b) attentional redistribution (if told to listen only to your voice, all else will be effortlessly ignored), (c) no desire to make plans—the here and now is all that they will focus on, (d) a reduction in reality testing where reality distortions are readily accepted (may uncritically accept hallucinated experiences, such as petting an imaginary rabbit), (e) the response of posthypnotic amnesia when so instructed as well as a restoration of what has transpired by posthypnotic signal, and

(f) the ability to readily enact unusual roles when instructed to do so, such as reenacting behaviors characteristic of an earlier age or reconstruction, "re-living" of a significant prior event.

An Arm Levitation Technique: A Phased Approach

Let us use an updated and modified version of the Barabasz and Watkins (2005, pp. 136–143) arm levitation induction as an example of how one might proceed. Starting with aroused focal attention, there is a corresponding, diminution in peripheral awareness (Alladin & Amundsen, 2016; Elkins et al., 2015). Attention, directed perception, and tiny movements are spread to larger ones. At each stage of the induction, there are overt movements, which indicate the extent of hypnotic involvement so that the hypnotist is continually receiving cues from and responding to the participant based on those cues. This makes it possible to continue each step with repetition as needed until it is successfully executed before proceeding with the next phase.

To facilitate analysis of each step and the principals involved, the following verbalizations have been numbered (the numbers are not part of the verbalization):

(1) Please place your hand on the table. (2) Please concentrate all your attention on *that* hand. You can look at it and see if you can be aware of all the sensations and feelings in *the* hand. (3) For example, you are aware that it is sitting on the table. There is weight there. You may be aware of the texture of the table; you may keenly sense the position every finger has toward every other finger. (4) Now please notice the temperature of *that* hand, and as you look at *that* hand with this concentration, you will begin to notice that one of the fingers in *that* hand will feel different from the others. (5) Now, *it* might be the thumb or the little finger or perhaps the index finger, but one of them *will* feel distinctly different from the others. (6) And that feeling may be that it's a little more warm or that it's a little cold. *It* could be that it kind of stings a little or that it's numb. *It* could feel lighter or heavier, I am not sure which, (7) but if you can concentrate, you will be able to know which finger it is that has the different sensation from the others, (8) and as you pay even closer attention, *that* finger *will* lift itself a little bit from the table. Now concentrate on that, and you will notice that one of *the* fingers will tend to lift itself up from the table a little. (9) [*Upon observing it lift even slightly*] It's that (little?) finger. (10) Please concentrate still further and you may find *that* finger becoming kind of numb; (*upon observation)* it's sticking straight out; perhaps it's almost as if it were made out of wood, (11) and that wooden feeling, or whatever it feels like, will start spreading to the other fingers close to it, and they too *will* begin to lift themselves and straighten. And you will find that next the finger will come up. And now you will find that same lifting feeling coming into the finger, and it sort of stiffens and straightens itself. And these feelings translate into a kind of tension that *will become* a light feeling, a wooden-like feeling, and then it moves into the (little) finger, and that, too, gets light and feels like it's floating, and then it gradually spreads into the hand. (12) And the hand may begin to feel like it is made out of wood or cork, and like cork, it sort of wants to float as if it were in water and wants to come up. (13) Or perhaps you can imagine there is a balloon attached to the wrist, and this hand keeps wanting to float up. (14) [*upon observation of lifting*] I'm not sure, and perhaps you are not sure, where the hand is lifting, but it's lifting toward your face, and it *will* get higher and higher and higher, (15) and you may feel a drowsy sensation as it comes closer to the face. (16) [*Upon observation*] It's about twelve inches (or whatever approximate distance is observed) away, then it's about eleven

inches (or whatever), (17) and the higher the hand comes, the drowsier you *will* feel, (18) and you *will* begin to think that when the hand touches the face, you *will* go into a deep relaxed state. (19) [*Upon observation*] Now, it's only five inches away. And now, it's four inches away. Closer and closer. It's *going to* touch pretty soon. Three inches away. (20) And when it touches, you will go into a very deep state. (21) Almost touching, almost touching, almost touching. An inch away. Coming closer and closer. (22) Touching, touching. (23) And you just feel a sense of relaxation, (24) and now as you let *that* hand go down, you go down, too, into a deep, deep, deep relaxed state. [*Upon observation of indicants of calmness*] And you feel yourself go down to a deep, comfortable, relaxed state. (A version of this induction is fully analyzed for each of the numbered sentences by Barabasz and Watkins, 2005, pp. 137–143.)

A variation of the technique preferred by the first author does not involve a table as the initial resting point of the participant's dominant hand. Instead, it begins with the hand on the participant's leg. This alternative approach allows the hypnotist to focus the participant's attention rather differently. After drawing attention to small finger movements, as in the protocol above, you can proceed with "(1) Notice the warmth generated between the hand and the leg." The warmth and pressure of the hand on the leg can then more easily be reframed as (2) "A kind of special tension *will* form between the hand and the leg. I don't know when and you don't know when it *will* happen, but it *will* be a kind of tension, ... perhaps it's already there; I do not know, and you might not know, but the tension *will* mount, the tension *will* grow and grow. (3) Now as that tension grows between your hand and your leg, it *will* push the hand up from the leg, the hand and the arm become lighter and lighter. (4) [*after some very minor confirmation that the hand is lifting—usually the fingers at first keep contact with the leg as the hand rises from the center of the back of the hand*] "Yes, there it goes lifting, lifting up, rising up. (5) Now, I do not know exactly where that hand is going, but it is rising up, moving in some way toward your face." If the hand lifts about one foot high or more, follow-up and persist with: "It continues to rise up, rise up toward your face, all the time watching it move on its own, fascinating it is to see your hand move up toward your face —and when it touches your face, you will go down into a deep state of hypnosis, as deeply down as you ever wished, to help make hypnosis work best for you." If after 20 or more minutes the hand has barely risen from the leg, continue with, "Amazing isn't it how the hand has moved up like that, all by itself, up off your leg—and now it's finally OK to let yourself go into a deep state of hypnosis, as deeply down as you ever wished, but try to keep from going too deeply into hypnosis like that until the hand falls back on to your leg...." Remember, the participant has no clue as to how high the hand might have gone up. A slight effortless rising of their hand as a prerequisite may be all that is necessary to help the participant to reach a substantial depth of hypnosis. Also, remember to be patient and completely confident throughout the induction; there is no time limit and no advantage to rushing the induction. For the patient I (A. B.) spent an entire hour with to achieve even minimal results, a slight effortless rising of their hand was all that was necessary to allow that patient to obtain a depth of hypnosis sufficient for noticeable pain relief. Subsequently, use of pain medication reportedly ceased entirely within a few weeks. The patient was proud they had learned a new skill and had overcome the use of pain relievers.

In summary, it appears that when hypnotic inductions are carried out with attention to the participant's responses and the established sequential progression of the three phases of induction, the changes produced by hypnosis can be surprising to the participant. Based on our observations of both patients and research participants, alterations in perception are often the most convincing of the potency of hypnosis per se because they go beyond simple motoric responses, such as arm immobilization and arm levitation, which can easily be produced by mundane responses to simple suggestion or compliance.

References

Alladin, A., & Amundson, J. (2016). Cognitive hypnotherapy as a transdiagnostic protocol for emotional disorders. *International Journal of Clinical and Experimental Hypnosis*, *64*, 147–166. doi:10.1080/00207144.2016.1131585

Barabasz, A. (1982). Restricted environmental stimulation and the enhancement of hypnotizability: EEG alpha, skin conductance and temperature responses. *International Journal of Clinical and Experimental Hypnosis*, *30*(2), 147–166. doi:10.1080/00207148208407380

Barabasz, A. (2000). EEG markers of alert hypnosis: The induction makes a difference. *Sleep and Hypnosis*, *2*(4), 164–169.

Barabasz, A., & Barabasz, M. (2006). Effects of tailored and manualized hypnotic inductions for complicated irritable bowel syndrome patients. *International Journal of Clinical and Experimental Hypnosis*, *54*(1), 100–112. doi:10.1080/00207140500322982

Barabasz, A., & Barabasz, M. (2016). Hypnotic phenomena and deepening techniques. In G. Elkins (Ed.), *Handbook of medical and psychological hypnosis: Foundations, applications, and professional issues*. New York, NY: Springer.

Barabasz, A., Barabasz, M., Jensen, S., Calvin, S., Trevisan, M., & Warner, D. (1999). Cortical event related potentials show the structure of hypnotic suggestions is crucial. *International Journal of Clinical and Experimental Hypnosis*, *47*(1), 5–22. doi:10.1080/00207149908410019

Barabasz, A., & Christensen, C. (2006). Age regression: Tailored versus scripted inductions. *American Journal of Clinical Hypnosis*, *48*(4), 251–261. doi:10.1080/00029157.2006.10401532

Barabasz, A., & Lonsdale, C. (1983). Effects of hypnosis on P300 olfactory evoked potential amplitudes. *Journal of Abnormal Psychology*, *92*, 520–523. doi:10.1037/0021-843X.92.4.520

Barabasz, A., & Watkins, J. G. (2005). *Hypnotherapeutic techniques* (2nd ed.). New York, NY: Brunner – Routledge.

Benham, G., Bowers, S., Nash, M., & Muenchen, R. (1998). Self-fulfilling prophecy and hypnotic response are not the same thing. *Journal of Personality and Social Psychology*, *75*, 1604–1613. doi:10.1037/0022-3514.75.6.1604

Benham, G., Woody, E. Z., Wilson, K. S., & Nash, M. R. (2006). Expect the unexpected: Ability, attitude, and responsiveness to hypnosis. *Journal of Personality and Social Psychology*, *91*(2), 342–350. doi:10.1037/0022-3514.91.2.342

Black, K. N., & Green, J. P. (2016, August). *Meditation focused attention, hypnotic susceptibility, and problem solving*. Paper presented at the 124th Annual Convention of the American Psychological Association. Denver, CO.

Calvin, S. (2000, October). *Effects of alternative hypnotic instructions on the N200 EEG event-related potential*. Paper presented at the Annual Scientific Program of the Society for Clinical and Experimental Hypnosis, Seattle, Washington.

Christensen, C., Barabasz, A., & Barabasz, M. (2009). Effects of an affect bridge for age regression. *International Journal of Clinical and Experimental Hypnosis*, *57*(4), 402–418. doi:10.1080/00207140903098817

Christensen, C., Barabasz, A., & Barabasz, M. (2013). Efficacy of abreactive ego state therapy for PTSD: Trauma resolution, depression and anxiety. *International Journal of Clinical and Experimental Hypnosis*, *61*(1), 20–37. doi:10.1080/00207144.2013.729386

Elkins, G. (2014). *Hypnotic relaxation therapy: Principles and applications*. New York, NY: Springer.

Elkins, G., Barabasz, A. F., Council, J. R., & Spiegel, D. (2015). Advancing research and practice: The revised APA division 30 definition of hypnosis. *International Journal of Clinical and Experimental Hypnosis*, *63*(1), 1–9. doi:10.1080/00207144.2014.961870

Erikson, M. H., Rossi, E. L., & Rossi, S. (1976). *Hypnotic realities: The induction of clinical hypnosis and forms of indirect suggestion*. New York, NY: Irvington.

Fromm, E. (1992). An ego psychological theory of hypnosis. In E. Fromm & M. Nash (Eds.), *Contemporary hypnosis research* (pp. 131–138). New York, NY: Guilford Press.

Green, J. P., Barabasz, A., Barrett, D., & Montgomery, G. H. (2005). Forging ahead: The 2003 Division 30 definition of hypnosis. *International Journal of Clinical and Experimental Hypnosis*, *53*, 259–264. doi:10.1080/00207140590961321

Grogan, G., Barabasz, A., Barabasz, M., & Christensen, C. (in press). Effects of hypnosis on regression to primary process thinking. *International Journal of Clinical Experimental Hypnosis*.

Haley, J. (2015). An interactional explanation of hypnosis. *International Journal of Clinical and Experimental Hypnosis*, *63*, 422–443. doi:10.1080/00207144.2015.1062696

Jensen, S., Barabasz, A., Barabasz, M., & Warner, D. (2001). EEG P300 event related markers of hypnosis. *American Journal of Clinical Hypnosis*, *44*(2), 127–139. doi:10.1080/00029157.2001.10403468

Johnson, A. K., Johnson, A. J., Barton, D., & Elkins, G. (2016). Hypnotic relaxation therapy and sexual function in postmenopausal women: Results of a randomized clinical trial. *The International Journal of Clinical and Experimental Hypnosis*, *64*, 213–224. doi:10.1080/00207144.2016.1131590

Kirsch, I. (1991). The social learning theory of hypnosis. In S. J. Lynn & J. W. Rhue (Eds.), *Theories of hypnosis: Current models and perspectives* (pp. 439–465). New York, NY: Guilford Press.

Newton, B. (2000, October). *Is your hypnosis what you think it is?* Paper presented at the Annual Workshops and Scientific program of the Society for Clinical and Experimental Hypnosis, Seattle, WA.

Patterson, D. R. (2010). *Clinical hypnosis for pain control*. Washington, DC: American Psychological Association.

Pekala, R., Kumar, K., Maurer, M., Elliott, N., Moon, E., & Salinger, M. (2006). "How deeply hypnotized did I get?" Predicting self-reported hypnotic depth from a phenomenological assessment instrument. *International Journal of Clinical and Experimental Hypnosis*, *54*, 316–339. doi:10.1080/00207140600691344

Spanos, N., & Coe, W. (1992). A socio-psychological approach to hypnosis. In E. Fromm & M. Nash (Eds.), *Contemporary hypnosis research* (pp. 102–130). New York, NY: Guilford.

Spiegel, D., & Barabasz, A. (1988). Effects of hypnotic hallucination on P300 evoked potential amplitudes: Reconciling conflicting findings. *American Journal of Clinical Hypnosis*, *31*(1), 11–17. doi:10.1080/00029157.1988.10402762

Spiegel, D., Cutcomb, S., Ren, C., & Pribram, K. (1985). Hypnotic hallucination alters evoked potentials. *Journal of Abnormal Psychology*, *94*, 249–255. doi:10.1037/0021-843X.94.3.249

Tomé Pirez, C., Ludena, M. A., & Lopes Pirez, C. (2015). Expectancies and hypnotic responsiveness: An experimental-design flaw revealed. *International Journal of Clinical and Experimental Hypnosis*, *63*(2), 129–143. doi:10.1080/00207144.2014.1002713

Watkins, J. G., & Barabasz, A. (2008). *Advanced hypnotherapy: Psychodynamic techniques*. New York, NY: Routledge.

A Comparison of Hypnotic Induction, Task Motivation, and a "Cold Start" Control Group on Hypnotizability

Stephen Krystek and V. K. Kumar

Groups of participants (N = 164) were randomly assigned to three conditions: Group 1 received a trance induction, Group 2 received task-motivational instructions, and Group 3—"cold start" control—was simply told, "We will begin the hypnosis procedure now." All participants received the Creative Imagination Scale suggestions and then completed the Creative Imagination Scale and Inventory Scale of Hypnotic Depth. The three conditions did not differ significantly either on the Creative Imagination Scale or in reported hypnotic depth. These results are consistent with prior studies which show that trance induction and task-motivational yield similar results, but they are inconsistent inasmuch as the trance induction and task-motivational groups did not differ from the control group. These results, however, are predictable from socio-cognitive perspectives that the context of hypnosis itself can elicit hypnotic behaviors.

The use of a formal hypnotic induction prior to administering suggestions is often predicated on the assumption that induction causes a trance state which facilitates hypnotic responsiveness (Heap et al., 2001). Stanton (1975) noted that hypnosis books commonly stress, "The deeper the trance, the more effective the suggestion" (p. 330). Formal inductions may include requesting cooperation, fixation on a visual stimulus, repetitive suggestions to enter a hypnotic or trance state, and repetitious deepening (e.g., counting up or down) suggestions to enhance the hypnotic state before suggesting the actual hypnotic tasks.

In many studies, Barber and his associates investigated if trance induction (TI) is a necessary and sufficient condition for improved hypnotic performance. Barber (1958, 1960) challenged such notions as trance states, unconscious awareness, preconscious, and subconscious states and argued, "*Hypnosis is not a 'state' of any kind*" (1958, p. 115, italics in original). Barber (1958) further argued that hypnosis would remain as an unexplained phenomenon if conceptualized in such aforementioned terms. Instead, Barber suggested that hypnosis is a matter of a participant assuming the role of a good hypnotic participant who is motivated, views hypnosis favorably, and expects to be hypnotized.

Based on many studies, Barber formulated his cognitive-behavioral theory of hypnosis (see Barber & Wilson, 1977), which stresses that hypnotic induction is not a necessary condition for hypnotic behavior to occur. Non-induction participants instructed on how to think along with suggestions, use imagination, and not have a passive or negative attitude tend to be just as proficient as participants who receive an induction in eliciting hypnotic behaviors. Barber (1956) tested participants on seven suggestions (e.g., finger clasp, finger rigidity, thirst) when "lightly asleep" (p. 405), after receiving a standard hypnotic induction, and when they were normally awake (control). The study was based on the assumption that lightly asleep individuals, being detached from their environment, would be in a trance state that should facilitate hypnotic responding. He noted that some of the "lightly asleep" participants responded as if they were in the second stage of hypnosis as noted by Davis and Husband's (1931) hypnotic depth scale. The scale assigns a depth score from 0–30 under five categories: insusceptible, hypnoidal (e.g., relaxation, closing of eyes), light trance (e.g., eye and limb catalepsy), medium trance (e.g., partial amnesia, complete amnesia), and somnambulistic trance (e.g., positive hallucinations, negative hallucinations). The "lightly asleep" and "hypnotic induction" conditions' scores did not differ significantly on any of the seven suggestions, but the "lightly asleep" condition scores were significantly higher than the control group on 5/7 suggestions. However, Barber argued that it was not the trance state that helped the "lightly asleep" participants to respond to suggestions; rather, because of the permission he had sought from them to approach them during light sleep for a test of suggestibility, they were positively set to implement the suggestions. To confirm his hunch, he surprised some of the participants by testing them during light sleep, and he found that they did not perform as well (Barber, 1958).

Glass and Barber (1961) found that a placebo administered as a hypnosis-producing oral drug was as effective as a formal induction (eye fixation, metronome, repetitive suggestions of relaxation, drowsiness, and sleep) in enhancing suggestibility. During session 1, participants received a formal TI, and 2 days to a week later they participated in session 2—a control session where participants were told, "You will not be hypnotized today," and suggestions were given as a test of imagination (p. 539). He noted that two-thirds of the participants showed a decline in scores when tested in the control condition. Per participants' reports, Barber interpreted that the decline in scores was because of the way the two conditions were defined, one as a hypnotic test and the other as a test of imagination, and not due to the effects of TI. He subsequently took 12 participants whose scores had declined in the control condition and administered to them a placebo hypnotic drug described as "a powerful hypnotic drug" that increases "suggestibility without producing relaxation or sleepiness" (p. 540). He found that the placebo drug and TI conditions' scores did not differ significantly.

Given Barber's (1956, 1958) and other prior studies' results, Weitzenhoffer and Sjoberg (1961) tested if a formal induction facilitated hypnotic behavior. Their results revealed that a conventional TI produced higher average gains relative to the initial waking condition (i.e., where participants were told that they will not be hypnotized) compared with the waking-waking group that showed no significant average gains on the second testing. However, they observed, "some individuals can produce hypnotic-like behavior in the absence of any formal induction of hypnosis" (p. 218). However, subjective reports suggest that the high performers had to work harder during the waking state to implement the suggestions, but when hypnotized, "it was the hypnotist 'who did all the work'" (p. 218). By repetition, the hypnotist is "doing the concentration" for the subject (p. 218). They speculated that during the waking state, the high performers use autosuggestions. They cited Martin Orne, who suggested, "it is not the procedure used *per se*, but whether or not it is perceived by the subject as a 'legitimization' to exhibit hypnotic behavior" (p. 219). They also mention the possibility that just saying, "I am now going to hypnotize you" can implicitly suggest some subjective changes needed to experience hypnosis (p. 218).

Barber and Glass (1962) produced more evidence that a formal TI is not necessary to elicit hypnotic behaviors. Barber and Glass observed that direct suggestions given alone (i.e., participants were told they would not be hypnotized, but were instructed to imagine to the best of their ability) were less effective on average than when suggestions were preceded by an induction (i.e., participants explicitly told they would be "deeply hypnotized"). However, they noted that 50% of the participants in the TI condition attained higher scores than in the direct suggestion condition; the other 50% scored either the same or lower scores in the direct suggestion condition, implying that the induction did not play a role with half the participants. Barber and Calverly (1963c) reported similar results using the same 8 suggestions as in the 1962 study later titled (possibly the first time in Barber & Calverly, 1963a) as the Barber Suggestibility Scale (BSS). Specifically, on both objective and subjective scores, they found that both TI and task-motivational (TM) groups performed significantly better than the control group, but the TI and TM groups did not differ significantly.

Barber and Calverley's (1963b) study employed four conditions: TM alone; TM with TI; TI alone; and control (neither TM nor TI: Test of Imagination). They found that the three experimental groups did not significantly differ from each other on the BSS, but they all scored significantly higher than the control group. They concluded that adding TM to TI does not make the instructions more effective; rather, each alone is effective in producing superior hypnotic performance compared to the control (imagination) group.

Barber and Calverley (1965a) tested 5 groups in their experiment 3: Group 1 participants were simply told that they were assigned to a hypnosis group, then instructed to close their eyes, and subsequently, "*without further preliminaries* were assessed on the Barber Suggestibility Scale" (p. 103, italics in original). Participants in Groups 2–4 were told that they were assigned to a hypnosis group, instructed to close their eyes, and then given "repeated suggestions of relaxation, drowsiness, and sleep for 1, 5, and 10 minutes, respectively" before being assessed on the BSS. Group 5 was defined as control; the participants were given motivational instructions and also told making responses to the suggestions is easy before being assessed on the BSS. They found that on both objective and subjective BSS scores, Groups 2–5 did not differ significantly from each other, but Group 5 (motivational instructions combined with ease of responding) was more effective than Group 1 (simply defining the situation as hypnosis). Barber and Calverley (1965a) noted that this result was different from their experiment 2, which showed that defining the situation as hypnosis led to better responsiveness than the control condition. There were no significant differences among groups 2–5, suggesting that the duration of TI had little impact on the hypnotic response compared to the TM group. However, the three groups (2–4) were equally more effective than Group 1.

Barber and De Moor (1972) identified nine conditions that help augment responses to test suggestions: (a) define the situation as hypnosis, (b) remove fears or misconceptions regarding hypnosis, (c) secure cooperation, (d) ask participants to keep eyes closed, (e) suggest relaxation, sleep, and hypnosis, (f) maximize the phrasing and vocal aspects, (g) use suggestions that correspond with naturally occurring events (e.g., eye heaviness or arm heaviness), (h) stimulate goal-directed imagery, and (i) reinterpret failed suggestions as successful. These conditions help stimulate positive attitudes, motivations, and expectancies to produce the hypnotic response, a trance-like appearance, feelings of being hypnotized, and changes in body.

Hilgard and Tart (1966) conducted a study in response to Barber and Calverley's (1962, 1963b) results which suggests that TM and TI are equally effective in eliciting hypnotic behaviors. Their experiments used both within-subjects and between-subjects designs. On the first day, they tested three groups: (a) a control waking instruction group (explicitly told that they would not be hypnotized), (b) a second control group (told that they will not be hypnotized, but were told the better they imagined, the better their performance would be, and (c) traditional TI group. All groups received a formal hypnotic induction on the second day. Using a within-subjects design to compare means, they found that hypnotic induction led to a statistically significant improved hypnotic performance, but the gains were small. They noted that such effects were not seen in a between-subjects design because the low hypnotizables did not make any gains.

Yet another study by Barber and Calverley (1969) examined differences among three groups: hypnotic induction, "place yourself in hypnosis" (PYHYP), and a control group (asked only to close their eyes for 5 minutes). They did not find the three groups to differ on reported loss of spontaneity, alterations of body or body parts, or changes in equilibrium. The hypnotic induction group and the PYHYP groups did not differ on pre-experimental expectations of hypnotic depth, loss of spontaneity, disappearance of body or body parts, feelings of unreality, changes in experienced temperature, experimenter's voice very close or far, or the testimony of having been hypnotized. There was a significant one-point difference between the two groups in favor of the induction group on ten suggestions of the Stanford Hypnotic Susceptibility Scale (SHSS), Form A (Weitzenhoffer & Hilgard, 1959). The control group did not receive the SHSS:A.

Thus, they emphatically questioned the need for complex induction procedures derived from complex theories when simple TM instructions would suffice and urged that the significance of TI in hypnotic responsiveness needed to be rigorously demonstrated.

Barber and Wilson (1977) tested the effectiveness of their "Think-With" instructions with their Creative Imagination Scale (CIS) using three groups: Think With Instruction, TI, and control ("focus your thoughts and to imagine to the best of ability," p. 37). They found that the mean Think-With scores were significantly higher than the TI and control groups, which did not differ from each other.

Kirsch's (1991) socio-cognitive theory stresses the role of expectancies in understanding hypnotic phenomena. While how much expectancies contribute to hypnotic responsiveness has been debated, most investigators do not deny their role in hypnosis. Council, Kirsch, Vickery, and Carlson (1983) tested performance on the SHSS: Form C (Weitzenhoffer & Hilgard, 1962) and CIS (administered in that order) under five conditions: (a) TI (eye closure, relaxation suggestions of the SHSS:C), (b) cognitive-behavioral skill induction with modeling, (c) cognitive-behavioral skill induction without modeling, (d) placebo induction, and (e) base-rate control (close eyes, sit quietly and comfortably, pay close attention, respond naturally). The various inductions produced similar levels of performance but higher than the control group on both the SHSS:C and CIS. However, on the Field Depth Inventory (a measure of trance depth), TI results were superior to skill inductions and the control. Council et al. (1983) argued that given that there were no differences on the behavioral measures, alterations in consciousness do not matter in the production of the hypnotic response.

Lynn, Laurence, and Kirsch (2015) reviewed what is typically called for in a hypnotic induction and suggested, "defining the situation as hypnosis activates sociocultural schemas and expectancies, including the idea that hypnosis produces an altered state of consciousness that enhances suggestibility" (p. 318). Thus, they inferred that it is no wonder that, given an induction, participants experience such alterations. They also observed that "most individuals do not in fact, experience hypnosis as a 'trance' and virtually all of the effects ... during hypnosis can be obtained with motivating instructions in the absence of defining the situation as hypnosis" (p. 318). They also cited earlier studies (e.g., Kirsch & Lynn, 1995) to suggest that instructions to imagine are mostly sufficient to elicit hypnotic behaviors and that the small advantage conferred by hypnotic inductions may be explained by response expectancies and enhanced motivation generated by instructions included in them. An interesting study by Lynn, Vanderhoff, Shindler, and Stafford (2002) had four groups: (1) standard induction (SI), (2) request for cooperation removed from SI instructions (CR), (3) altered state (AS; participants were told experiencing hypnosis depends upon their ability to experience altered states of consciousness or hypnotic trance, but request for cooperation was omitted), and (4) no induction group (NI; session defined as hypnosis during introductory information, but induction portion associated with the instrument was omitted). All subjects received the Carlton

University Responsiveness to Suggestion Scale (CURSS; Spanos, Radtke, Hodgins, Stam, & Bertrand, 1983). They found (1) omitting cooperation from induction affected objective but not subjective scores; (2) instructions on altered states reduced scores (i.e., CR < SI) on the behavioral but not the subjective measure compared with SI (i.e., AS < SI); (3) although NI scores averaged somewhat higher than in SI, they did not differ significantly; it is this latter result that is most relevant to the present study, as it is consistent with results of prior studies cited earlier.

In an applied study, Stanton (1975) tested if induction facilitated the effectiveness of ego-enhancing suggestions on reducing neuroticism, fear of social situations, fear of negative evaluation, and improving self-assertiveness. He used three experimental groups: (a) induction followed by ego-enhancement suggestions, (b) no induction, only ego-enhancement suggestions, and (c) no induction and no ego-enhancement suggestions (control group). His results were mixed: (a) the induction and no induction groups showed comparable improvement on neuroticism and self-assertion, (b) the induction group showed greater improvement on social avoidance and fear of negative evaluation, suggesting a "facilitative effect" of induction (p. 334), and (c) the control group showed no improvement on the four variables.

Gandhi and Oakley (2005) tested the effects of expectations (hypnosis versus relaxation) and induction (TI versus control). They found that TI produced slightly better performance, and, consistent with other studies (e.g., Charlesworth & Doughtie, 1982; Wickless & Kirsch, 1989), labeling the session as "hypnosis" led to significantly better performance than labeling it as "relaxation."

In summary, various studies suggest that hypnotic inductions, often modeled after the induction of the Stanford and Harvard scales, enhance hypnotic performance, but other types of inductions (including placebo) also yield similar effects. Compared with TM instructions, hypnotic induction does not confer any advantage. Studies do, however, show that TI provides superior performance than control groups (typically asked to imagine and do their best, accompanied by statements such as, "You will not be hypnotized today," and/or "Place yourself in hypnosis." Responsiveness to suggestions can be also enhanced if the hypnotist simply defines the clinical or testing situation as hypnosis, instructs them to close their eyes, and suggests relaxation, drowsiness, and sleepiness.

The Present Study

The present study was an attempt to revisit the question of superiority of TI versus TM instructions against a "cold start" control group simply instructed that "we will begin the hypnosis procedure now." All participants were informed that they would be experiencing hypnosis when they signed up for the study.

After the respective preliminary instructions (TI, TM, or Control), all participants were administered the 10 suggestions of the CIS, Barber & Wilson, 1978). Participants then completed the 10 CIS items and the Field's Inventory Scale of Hypnotic Depth (ISHD).

This study's purpose was to examine (a) if the experimental groups differed on responsiveness to the CIS, (b) if the experimental groups differed on reported subjective experiences on the ISHD (overall hypnotic depth and alterations on subscales of absorption and unawareness, automaticity and compulsion, and discontinuity), and (c) if hypnotic responsiveness was correlated with hypnotic depth and ISHD subscales. Since individuals experience hypnosis in different ways (Barber, 2000; Barrett, 1990; Forbes & Pekala, 1996; Terhune & Cardeña, 2010), it was deemed important to see if hypnotic responsiveness was not modified by the experimental manipulations, participants may still experience certain alterations in consciousness to support the use of induction. For example, if participants report greater feelings of absorption or automaticity as a result of induction, then that may justify the use of induction since these changes are typically regarded as hallmark characteristics of hypnotic states and may contribute to facilitating clinical work, provided, of course, such altered experiences are correlated with performance.

Given Barber and Wilson's (1977) results, we expected TM to produce higher CIS scores than either the TI or the control group. However, given some of the earlier studies, TM may be as effective as TI, but each would produce higher scores than the control group. Also, given Council et al.'s (1983) study that found no differences on overall hypnotic depth, we predicted that TM and TI groups would not differ significantly from each other, but each would differ from the control group. However, if expectancies based on prevalent historical and cultural myths pertaining to hypnosis and altered states predominate, then there should be no significant differences across the three conditions on any of the measures. From the perspective of dissociation theories that subscribe to the notion of alterations in consciousness, the TI group would be expected to show higher scores on overall hypnotic depth and the ISHD subscales compared to the TM and control groups.

Method

Experimental Design

The sample size calculated for this study was 50 participants in each experimental condition in order to obtain a power of 0.883 and a medium effect size of 0.70 at a 0.05 level of significance. Groups of participants were randomly assigned to the three conditions with the restriction that there would be an approximately equal number of participants in each condition.

Participants

Participants were recruited from Introduction to psychology classes who are required to participate in a research study or complete an independent assignment. Participation was voluntary, and the participants were free to terminate their participation at any time during the study with impunity. Participants ($N = 164$) were between the ages of 18–32 (male $n = 37$, female $n = 125$; White $n = 127$, Black $n = 18$, Asian $n = 9$, and Latino $n = 8$). Twenty-three participants reported having experienced hypnosis prior to the study; 139 participants did not report such prior experience.

The participants were recruited online via software installed in the Psychology Department for a study titled "The Role of Induction in Hypnotizability Assessment." The study was described in the following manner: (a) The purpose of the study is to compare three types of instructions in facilitating hypnotic responsiveness, (b) participants will be assigned to one of three experimental groups randomly, (c) participants will be given preliminary instructions before they receive the suggestions of a standard hypnotic responsiveness scale, (d) following hypnosis they will be asked complete questionnaires to assess their responses to the suggestions, (e) many people find the experience interesting and enjoyable, and (f) participants will learn what hypnosis is like and also help advance knowledge.

Instruments

CIS

The CIS was chosen specifically for this study because it has no specific induction or TI associated with it, and an experimenter has the flexibility of designing instructions or an induction to go with it. The scale includes 10 items (corresponding to 10 suggestions) that are scored on Likert scales (0–4). Each item describes the imaginative task and then asks if the experience was "not at all the same (0%)," "a little the same (25%)," "between a little and much the same (50%)," "much the same (75%)," or "almost exactly the same (90+%)" as the actual experience (Barber & Wilson, 1978). The CIS has been used in several studies; its Cronbach α in the present study was 0.76.

The ISHD

The scale (Field, 1965) is a 38-item true–false measure of "spontaneous subjective experiences during a hypnosis procedure" (Cardeña & Terhune, 2014, p. 295). The ISHD continues to be used in various studies to assess subjective experiences associated with hypnosis. In the present study, the Cronbach αs for the different scores were as follows: Total ISHD (overall hypnotic depth) = 0.84, absorption and unawareness = 0.69, automaticity and compulsion = 0.66, and discontinuity from normal experience = 0.68.

Procedure

Students were all tested in groups of 2–30 in the same 99-seat lecture hall with dimmed lighting. After participants arrived at the session, the first author thanked them and informed participants that the study was being conducted for his Master's thesis under the second author, who was present to assist in data collection. They were also told that (a) the purpose of the study was to examine what contributes to hypnotic performance, (b) after receiving some general instructions, they would receive 10 hypnotic suggestions, and then complete two questionnaires, and (c) they should not write any identifying information on the questionnaires. Following these general instructions, participants were asked to read and sign the Informed Consent Form, modeled after the university's Institutional Review Board requirements. The consent form explained the study's purpose, its voluntary nature (they could withdraw from the study at any time with impunity), the research credits being awarded for participation as required by the Psychology Department, benefits, risks, etc. The informed consent forms were collected immediately after obtaining consent to keep them separate from the data. Then they were also told to remove chewing gum and to turn off cell phones but were instructed to keep wearing glasses or contact lenses.

Instructions for the TI Group

Phrases taken from Harvard Group Scale of Hypnotic Susceptibility, Form A (HGSHS: A; Shor & Orne, 1962) were used to construct the induction:

> I am sure that you will find hypnosis a most interesting experience. Hypnosis is nothing fearful or mysterious. It is merely a state of strong interest in some particular thing. In a sense you are hypnotized whenever you see a good movie and forget that you are part of the audience but instead feel a part of the story. Nothing will be done that will in any way cause you any embarrassment. We are here for serious scientific purposes to examine what contributes to hypnotic responsiveness. Your ability to be hypnotized depends on your willingness to cooperate. It has nothing to do with your intelligence or your willpower. If you pay close attention to what I say and follow what I tell you, you can easily experience a state of hypnosis and you will be able to experience the interesting things that I will tell you to experience.
>
> Now relax and make yourself entirely comfortable. Keep your eyes on the little light.... Relax completely. Relax every muscle of your body, every muscle of your body.... Relax more and more, more and more.... You feel tired and sleepy, tired and sleepy, drowsy and sleepy, drowsy and sleepy. Your breathing is slow and regular, slow and regular. The strain in your eyes is getting greater and greater, greater and greater. You would like to close your eyes and relax completely ... completely relaxed ... feeling warm and comfortable ... tired and drowsy, tired and sleepy. Sleepy ... you are going to become much more drowsy and sleepy. Soon you will be deep asleep, but you will have no trouble hearing me. You will not wake up until I tell you to open your eyes. I will now begin to count. At each count you will feel yourself going deeper and deeper asleep. One—you are going to go deeply asleep. Two—down, down, into a deep, sound sleep. Three ... four ... deeper and deeper asleep. Five ... six ... seven. You are sinking, sinking into a deep, deep sleep. Nothing will disturb you.... You are feeling comfortable, relaxed, thinking of nothing, nothing but what I say.... You are feeling comfortable, relaxed, thinking of nothing, nothing but what I say ... more and more relaxed, more and more comfortable ... comfortable and relaxed ... in a deep sound sleep ... deeper and deeper ... in deepest trance ... you will be prepared to experience the many interesting things I will tell you to experience.

Instructions for the Task Motivation Group (TM)

The Barber and Wilson (1978) Think-With instructions were modified to remove outdated cultural references:

> In a short while, I'm going ask you to imagine and to visualize certain things for you to experience what hypnosis is like. How well you do on these tasks will depend entirely upon your willingness to try, your imagination, and your visualization. All of us use our ability to imagine and visualize on a daily basis when, for example, we plan to write a paper, or think about what groceries we want to buy, or how would I look if I wear a certain type of shirt. If I ask you to close your eyes, and think as if you are looking at a TV program, one way to respond is to say "there is no TV out there, this is ridiculous, this cannot be done"; this way is not helpful. A second way to respond is to wait passively for things to happen as if something magical is going to happen; this also is not helpful. A third way to respond is to say to yourself "let me try and close my eyes and try to see my favorite program in my mind's eye." When you let your imagination work for you, you can vividly see the characters, cars, buildings, and how the story moves in your favorite TV program. Keeping a positive attitude will help you to use your creative imagination to experience the hypnotic suggestions that I will give you. Having a negative attitude will make you feel this is all silly and ridiculous. So I am asking you to think with the suggestions that I give you, to focus your thinking on the tasks suggested, and to imagine to the best of your ability. Just let your thinking and your creative imagination go along with the instructions so that you can fully experience the many interesting and useful things that your mind can do.

Instructions for the "Cold Start" Control Group

The participants were simply told, "We will begin the hypnosis procedure now." Then they were asked to close their eyes and were administered the CIS. These instructions were similar to those used by Barber and Calverley (1965b) for one of their groups in their experiment 3 discussed earlier, but different from those used in most other prior studies which asked the participants in the control group to use imagination, to do their best, to pay attention, or "place yourself in hypnosis."

After the hypnosis, all participants anonymously completed a response booklet including the CIS followed by the ISHD and a few demographic questions.

Results

Hypnotic Performance by Experimental Group

A multivariate analysis used to test for significant differences on the CIS and the three ISHD subscales showed no significant differences among the three conditions (F[8, 298] = 0.52) on the four variables. A univariate analysis of variance used to test for differences on the overall hypnotic depth scale (ISHD-total score) revealed no significant differences among the three groups (F[2, 154] = 0.115). Table 1 summarizes the

TABLE 1
Means, *SD*s, and *F*-Values for CIS and ISHD Subscales

Scale/Subscale	*Experimental Group*	n	M	SD	F*(2, 151)*	p	eta^2
CIS	Induction	50	19.98	6.99	0.93	0.40	0.01
	TM	49	20.82	6.38	0.93	0.40	0.01
	No Induction	55	18.98	7.22	0.93	0.40	0.01
Absorption and Unawareness	Induction	50	5.22	2.53	0.28	0.76	0.00
	TM	49	5.22	2.32	0.28	0.76	0.00
	No Induction	55	4.91	2.57	0.28	0.76	0.00
Automaticity and Compulsion	Induction	50	2.54	1.81	0.12	0.89	0.00
	TM	49	2.69	1.88	0.12	0.89	0.00
	No Induction	55	2.71	2.02	0.12	0.89	0.00
Discontinuity	Induction	50	4.1	1.79	0.36	0.70	0.01
	TM	49	3.92	1.47	0.36	0.70	0.01
	No Induction	55	3.82	1.88	0.36	0.70	0.01
ISHD Total	Induction	50	11.86	5.16	0.12	0.89	0.00
	TM	49	11.84	4.73	0.12	0.89	0.00
	No Induction	55	11.44	5.38	0.12	0.89	0.00

*Multivariate analysis was used for the CIS, absorption and unawareness, automaticity and compulsion, and discontinuity. Univariate analysis was used for the ISHD Total.

means, standard deviations (SDs), *F*-values, significance, and η^2 values (effect size) for differences among the experimental groups on each of the scales/subscales.

Group Differences on Individual CIS Items

A between (three experimental conditions) × within (10 CIS items) multivariate analysis was used to determine if there was an interaction effect between item difficulty (order effects) and type of inductions. The multivariate analysis did not yield a significant main effect of Experimental conditions $F(2, 190) = 0.87$. While the main effect of CIS items was significant ($F[9, 151] = 19.62$, $p = 0.000$), the experimental condition × CIS items interaction was not significant ($F[18, 304] = 0.39$). The means, SDs, and *n*s for each CIS item by group are shown in Table 2. The between groups correlations of CIS item difficulty levels were induction/task motivation = 0.97; induction/control = 0.95; task motivation/control = 0.92.

Correlations of CIS With ISHD Scales/Subscales

Correlations between the CIS, overall hypnotic depth, and the ISHD subscales scores were computed for each condition to examine if they differed among the three experimental groups (Table 3). Given 12 tests, the Boneferroni $p = 0.004$ was used to evaluate the significance for each test for an overall alpha of 0.05. The correlations in the TI and Control groups were significant at $p < 0.004$ level but not in the TM group. Further, 12

TABLE 2
Group Differences on Individual CIS Items

CIS Item	*Experimental Group*	M	SD	n
CIS1	Induction	2.57	1.05	53
	TM	2.50	1.02	54
	No Induction	2.35	1.13	55
CIS2	Induction	1.62	1.23	53
	TM	1.67	1.10	54
	No Induction	1.40	1.23	55
CIS3	Induction	1.79	1.13	53
	TM	1.89	1.13	54
	No Induction	1.75	1.22	55
CIS4	Induction	1.55	1.25	53
	TM	1.81	1.23	54
	No Induction	1.49	1.18	55
CIS5	Induction	1.49	1.25	53
	TM	1.65	1.31	54
	No Induction	1.38	1.11	55
CIS6	Induction	2.11	1.28	53
	TM	2.44	1.40	54
	No Induction	2.11	1.23	55
CIS7	Induction	2.00	1.13	53
	TM	2.04	1.18	54
	No Induction	1.84	1.12	55
CIS8	Induction	2.23	1.42	53
	TM	2.35	1.38	54
	No Induction	2.44	1.17	55
CIS9	Induction	1.89	1.30	53
	TM	2.00	1.36	54
	No Induction	1.82	1.32	55
CIS10	Induction	2.40	1.32	53
	TM	2.44	1.22	54
	No Induction	2.53	1.26	55

Z tests between pairs of correlations between conditions did not reveal any significant differences (*Z* values ranged between 0.08 to 1.95 [$p = 0.052$]), assuming Bonferroni $p = 0.004$.

Discussion

The results revealed no significant differences among the three groups on the CIS total, the CIS items individually, overall hypnotic depth, or on the ISHD subscales. These results suggest that TI and TM instructions had no significant effects either on overall hypnotic responsiveness or on alterations in subjective experiences compared with the control group. Furthermore, the between conditions item difficulty levels were

TABLE 3
Correlations of CIS With ISHD for the Three Groups

Scale/Subscale		*Induction*	*TM*	*Control*
Absorption	*r*	0.59	0.38	0.43
	p	0.000	0.005	0.001
	n	53	53	56
Automaticity	*r*	0.48	0.20	0.55
	p	0.000	0.15	0.000
	n	53	52	56
Discontinuity	*r*	0.52	0.28	0.59
	p	0.000	0.048	0.000
	n	52	51	55
ISHD Total	*r*	0.61	0.34	0.62
	p	0.000	0.016	0.000
	n	50	49	55

correlated 0.92 and above for the 10 items, suggesting similarity of item responsiveness in the three conditions.

The CIS scores had moderately high correlations with the overall hypnotic depth scores in the TI ($r = 0.61$, $p = 0.000$) and control conditions ($r = 0.62$, $p = 0.001$); the same correlation in the TM condition was lower ($r = 0.34$, $p = 0.016$), but it was not significantly lower than the other two. These results suggest that the more hypnotically responsive participants reported achieving greater overall hypnotic depth in all three conditions. The pattern of correlations was similar with respect to absorption and unawareness, automaticity and compulsion, and discontinuity from waking experience. The lower correlations in the TM group are likely due to chance, assuming Bonferroni $p = 0.004$. This finding is in agreement with previous research, which shows that hypnotic scales such as the CIS, ISHD, HGSHS:A, and the BSS are inter-correlated (Cardeña & Terhune, 2014; Field, 1965; Sapp, 1997). However, the lower correlations in the TM group warrant further investigation to see if the lower correlations are due to the task-related (not altered states) expectancies generated by the TM instructions.

The lack of a significant difference between the TI and TM conditions on hypnotic responsiveness is consistent with earlier studies (e.g., Barber, 1965; Barber & Calverley, 1963b; Barber & Glass, 1962; Barber & Wilson, 1977; Council, Kirsch, & Hafner, 1986; Glass & Barber, 1961). However, inconsistent with other studies' (Barber & Calverley, 1965a, experiment 3; Barber & Wilson, 1977; Council et al., 1983) results, we found no significant differences between the control and the TM and TI groups. That there were also no significant differences among conditions on subjective experiences (overall hypnotic depth or ISHD subscales) was also inconsistent with results of Council et al. (1983) that showed lower overall hypnotic depth scores in the control condition than in the trance or skill type inductions.

Nevertheless, despite the above-mentioned inconsistencies, the lack of differences of either experimental group from the "cold start" control group on hypnotic responsiveness and depth is predictable from Kirsch's (1994) socio-cognitive theory, which suggested that merely labeling the session as "hypnosis" is sufficient to elicit hypnotic behaviors (Charlesworth & Doughtie, 1982; Wickless & Kirsch, 1989). The socio-cognitive theories assert that hypnotized individuals' responses are based on perceived task demands and prior cultural schemas of what happens in hypnosis instead of entering a special hypnotic or trance state by means of an induction.

Conclusions and Limitations

In this study, all participants, regardless of the experimental condition, signed up for an experiment on hypnosis, and they were duly reminded of it before starting the experiment via verbal instructions and the Informed Consent Form. Thus, the mere expectations of being hypnotized may have caused participants to respond in similar ways in the three conditions as perhaps occurred in Barber's sleep and placebo drug studies. An alternative explanation is that hypnotizability is an inherited trait and consequently, not easily modifiable; thus it would not matter if one uses induction or not, as long as participants believe they are experiencing hypnosis, they will respond accordingly. Another likely explanation is that the TM and TI did not significantly improve performance because they were very brief, and consequently did not allow enough time for instructions to be fully processed; perhaps longer, more repetitive instructions would work better. A study comparing differences due to variations in length of TI and TM instructions may be informative. It may, however, be noted that Barber and Calverley's (1965a) study found TI length (1, 5, or 10 min.) did not differ from each other using the BSS, although they were superior to the group which was simply told that it had been assigned to the hypnosis group. A future study may examine if the effects of TI duration vary with the complexity of hypnotic response required.

On the surface, these results suggest, TI or even TM instructions are no more effective than simple instructions that, "We will begin the hypnosis procedure now." However, this conclusion is not warranted, since extant studies do show that the TI and TM are effective when compared to control groups (e.g., Barber & Calverley, 1963c; Council et al., 1983; Hilgard & Tart, 1966). Perhaps, studies to examine if inductions are useful for certain types of hypnotizable individuals (e.g., Forbes & Pekala, 1996; Terhune & Cardeña, 2010) and for certain types of suggestions may show more productive results.

A limitation of this study was the size of the groups tested in different sessions. Students were allowed to sign up for any available timeslot, and although the groups were randomly assigned, their size ranged between 2–30 students. A future study might ensure that all groups tested are approximately the same size. Further research might test the effect of group size on hypnotic responsiveness. The study has limited generalizability inasmuch as only one sample of volunteer undergraduate students was tested, and the results may indeed vary with another similar sample. Further, this study used an assessment instrument in a non-clinical context; thus, its results have little generalizability to assessment in clinical contexts, where different expectancies operate.

References

Barber, T. X. (1956). Comparison of suggestibility during "light sleep" and hypnosis. *Science*, *31*, 405. doi:10.1126/science.124.3218.405

Barber, T. X. (1958). The concept of hypnosis. *The Journal of Psychology*, *45*, 115–131. doi:10.1080/00223980.1958.9916245

Barber, T. X. (1960). The necessary and sufficient conditions for hypnotic behavior. *American Journal of Clinical Hypnosis*, *3*, 31–42. doi:10.1080/00029157.1960.10404345

Barber, T. X. (1965). Measuring "hypnotic-like" suggestibility with and without "hypnotic induction"; Psychometric properties, norms, and variables influencing response to the Barber Suggestibility Scale (BSS). *Psychological Reports*, *16*, 809–844. doi:10.2466/pr0.1965.16.3.809

Barber, T. X. (2000). A deeper understanding of hypnosis: Its secrets, its nature, its essence. *American Journal of Clinical Hypnosis*, *42*, 208–273. doi:10.1080/00029157.2000.10734361

Barber, T. X., & Calverley, D. S. (1962). "Hypnotic motivation" as a function of task motivation. *Journal of Psychology*, *54*, 363–389. doi:10.1080/00223980.1962.9713126

Barber, T. X., & Calverley, D. S. (1963a). "Hypnotic-like" suggestibility in children and adults. *Journal of Abnormal and Social Psychology*, *66*, 589–597. doi:10.1037/h0041709

Barber, T. X., & Calverley, D. S. (1963b). The relative effectiveness of task-motivating instructions and trance-induction procedure in the production of "hypnotic-like" behaviors. *The Journal of Nervous and Mental Disease*, *137*, 107–116. doi:10.1097/00005053-196308000-00001

Barber, T. X., & Calverley, D. S. (1963c). Toward a theory of hypnotic behavior: Effects on suggestibility of task motivating instructions and attitudes toward hypnosis. *Journal of Abnormal and Social Psychology*, *67*, 557–565. doi:10.1037/h0047040

Barber, T. X., & Calverley, D. S. (1965a). Empirical evidence for a theory of hypnotic behavior: Effects on suggestibility of five variables typically included in hypnotic induction procedures. *Journal of Consulting Psychology*, *29*, 98–107. doi:10.1037/h0021932

Barber, T. X., & Calverley, D. S. (1965b). Empirical evidence for a theory of hypnotic behavior: The suggestibility-enhancing effects of motivational suggestions, relaxation-sleep suggestions, and suggestions that the s will be effectively "hypnotized." *Journal of Personality and Social Psychology*, *33*, 256–270. doi:10.1111/j.1467-6494.1965.tb01385.x

Barber, T. X., & Calverley, D. S. (1969). Multidimensional analysis of "hypnotic behavior." *Journal of Abnormal Psychology*, *74*, 209–220. doi:10.1037/h0027114

Barber, T. X., & De Moor, W. (1972). A theory of hypnotic induction procedures. *The American Journal of Clinical Hypnosis*, *15*, 112–135. doi:10.1080/00029157.1972.10402228

Barber, T. X., & Glass, L. B. (1962). Significant factors in hypnotic behavior. *Journal of Abnormal and Social Psychology*, *64*, 222–228. doi:10.1037/h0041347

Barber, T. X., & Wilson, S. C. (1977). Hypnotic suggestions and altered states of consciousness. Experimental evaluation of the new cognitive-behavioral theory and the traditional trance state theory of "hypnosis." *Annals of the New York Academy of Sciences, 296*, 34–74. doi:10.1111/j.1749-6632.1977.tb38159.x

Barber, T. X., & Wilson, S. C. (1978). The Barber Suggestibility Scale and the Creative Imagination Scale: Experimental and clinical applications. *American Journal of Clinical Hypnosis, 21*, 84–108. doi:10.1080/00029157.1978.10403966

Barrett, D. (1990). Deep trance subjects: A schema of two distinct subgroups. In R. G. Kunzendorf (Ed.), *Mental imagery* (pp. 101–112). New York, NY: Plenum Press.

Cardeña, E., & Terhune, D. B. (2014). Hypnotizability, personality traits, and the propensity to experience alterations of consciousness. *Psychology of Consciousness: Theory, Research, and Practice, 1*, 292–307.

Charlesworth, E. A., & Doughtie, E. B. (1982). Modification of baseline by differential task presentation as either hypnosis or "learned" relaxation. *Perceptual and Motor Skills, 55*, 1131–1137. doi:10.2466/pms.1982.55.3f.1131

Council, J. R., Kirsch, I., & Hafner, L. P. (1986). Expectancy versus absorption in the prediction of hypnotic responding. *Journal of Personality and Social Psychology, 50*, 182–189. doi:10.1037/0022-3514.50.1.182

Council, J. R., Kirsch, I., Vickery, A. R., & Carlson, D. (1983). "Trance" vs "skill" hypnotic inductions: The effects of credibility, expectancy, and experimenter modeling. *Journal of Consulting and Clinical Psychology, 51*, 432–440. doi:10.1037/0022-006X.51.3.432

Davis, L. W., & Husband, R. E. (1931). A study of hypnotic susceptibility in relation to personality traits. *Journal of Abnormal and Social Psychology, 26*, 175–182. doi:10.1037/h0074985

Field, P. B. (1965). An inventory scale of hypnotic depth. *The International Journal of Clinical and Experimental Hypnosis, 13*, 238–249. doi:10.1080/00207146508412946

Forbes, E. J., & Pekala, R. J. (1996). Types of hypnotically (un)susceptible individuals as a function of phenomenological experience. *Australian Journal of Clinical and Experimental Hypnosis, 24*, 92–108.

Gandhi, B., & Oakley, D. A. (2005). Does 'hypnosis' by any other name smell as sweet? The efficacy of 'hypnotic inductions depends on the label 'hypnosis'. *Consciousness and Cognition, 14*, 304–315. doi:10.1016/j.concog.2004.12.004

Glass, L. B., & Barber, T. X. (1961). A note on hypnotic behavior, the definition of the situation and the placebo effect. *Journal of Nervous and Mental Disease, 132*, 539–541. doi:10.1097/00005053-196106000-00009

Heap, M., Alden, P., Brown, R. J., Naish, P., Oakley, D. A., Wagstaff, G., & Walker, L. G. (2001). *The nature of hypnosis: A report prepared by a working party at the request of The Professional Affairs Board of The British Psychological Society.* Leicester, UK: The British Psychological Society.

Hilgard, E. R., & Tart, C. T. (1966). Responsiveness to suggestions following waking and imagination instructions and following induction of hypnosis. *Journal of Abnormal Psychology, 71*, 196–208. doi:10.1037/h0023323

Kirsch, I. (1991). The social learning theory of hypnosis. In S. Jay Lynn & J. W. Rhue (Eds.), *Theories of hypnosis: Current models and perspectives* (pp. 439–465). New York, NY: The Guilford Press.

Kirsch, I. (1994). Clinical hypnosis as a nondeceptive placebo: Empirically derived techniques. *American Journal of Clinical Hypnosis, 37*, 95–106. doi: 10.1080/00029157.1994.10403122

Kirsch, I., & Lynn, S. J. (1995). The altered state of hypnosis: Changes in the theoretical landscape. *American Psychologist, 50*, 846–858. doi:10.1037/003-066X.50.846

Lynn, S. J., Laurence, J. R., & Kirsch, I. (2015). Hypnosis, suggestion, and suggestibility: An integrative model. *American Journal of Clinical Hypnosis, 57*, 314–329. doi:10.1080/00029157.2014.976783

Lynn, S. J., Vanderhoff, H., Shindler, K., & Stafford, J. (2002). Defining hypnosis as a trance vs. cooperation: Hypnotic induction, suggestibility, and performance standards. *American Journal of Clinical Hypnosis, 44*, 231–240. doi:10.1080/00029157.2002.10403483

Sapp, M. (1997). Hypnotizability scales: What are they, and are they useful? *The Australian Journal of Clinical Hypnotherapy and Hypnosis*, *17*, 25–32.

Shor, R. E., & Orne, E. C. (1962). *Harvard group scale of hypnotic susceptibility.* Palo Alto, CA: Consulting Psychologists Press.

Spanos, N. P., Radtke, H. L., Hodgins, D. C., Stam, H. J., & Bertrand, L. D. (1983). The Carleton University Responsiveness to Suggestion Scale: Normative data and psychometric properties. *Psychological Reports*, *53*(2), 523–535. doi:10.2466/pr0.1983.53.2.523

Stanton, H. E. (1975). Is hypnotic induction really necessary? A study of ego-enhancing suggestions and their effects. *Psychotherapy and Psychosomatics*, *26*, 330–336. doi:10.1159/000286949

Terhune, D. B., & Cardeña, E. (2010). Differential patterns of spontaneous-experiential response to a hypnotic induction: A latent profile analysis. *Consciousness and Cognition*, *19*, 1140–1150. doi:19:1016/j.concog.2010.03.006

Weitzenhoffer, A. M., & Hilgard, E. R. (1959). *Stanford Hypnotic Susceptibility Scales, Forms A and B.* Palo Alto, CA: Consulting Psychologists Press.

Weitzenhoffer, A. M., & Hilgard, E. R. (1962). *Stanford Hypnotic Susceptibility Scales, Forms C.* Palo Alto, CA: Consulting Psychologists Press.

Weitzenhoffer, A. M., & Sjoberg, B. M. (1961). Suggestibility with and without "induction of hypnosis". *The Journal of Nervous and Mental Disease*, *132*, 204–220. doi:10.1097/00005053-196103000-00002

Wickless, C., & Kirsch, I. (1989). The effects of verbal and experimental expectancy manipulations on hypnotic susceptibility. *Journal of Personality and Social Psychology*, *57*, 762–768. doi:10.1037/0022-3514.57.5.762

The Hypnotic Induction in the Broad Scheme of Hypnosis: A Sociocognitive Perspective

Steven Jay Lynn, Reed Maxwell

and Joseph P. Green

Researchers and clinicians typically divide hypnosis into two distinct parts: the induction and the suggestions that follow. We suggest that this distinction is arbitrary and artificial. Different definitions of hypnosis ascribe different roles to the hypnotic induction, yet none clearly specifies the mechanisms that mediate or moderate subjective and behavioral responses to hypnotic suggestions. Researchers have identified few if any differences in responding across diverse hypnotic inductions, and surprisingly little research has focused on the specific ingredients that optimize responsiveness. From a sociocognitive perspective, we consider the role of inductions in the broader scheme of hypnosis and suggest that there is no clear line of demarcation between prehypnotic information, the induction, suggestions, and other constituents of the hypnotic context. We describe research efforts to maximize responses to hypnotic suggestions, which encompass the induction and other aspects of the broader hypnotic framework, and conclude with a call for more research on inductions and suggestions to better understand their role within hypnotic interventions in research and clinical contexts.

Hypnosis has fueled the popular and scientific imagination for centuries. The roots of hypnosis stretch back to prehistory and surely to ancient times, and the ritual induction of altered experiential states for spiritual and physical healing remains a key feature in Western and non-Western religious practices as well (Pintar & Lynn, 2008). The now virtually mythic figure, Mesmer, was an icon of the charismatic person who wields amazing and ineluctable power over the participant. This image was firmly implanted in the public mind following the publication of De Maurier's novel, *Trilby* (1894/2009), in which Svengali—whose name today connotes a ruthless manipulator—uses hypnosis to dominate the hapless *Trilby*.

The very idea of inducing hypnosis still reverberates with connotations of power and control, as depicted stereotypically in popular culture, dramatized vividly in books, movies, and television. In recent years, the Internet has touted hypnotic inductions that push the envelope of the bizarre and absurd, claiming that conversational hypnosis can be used to "get people to do anything you want" (http://undergroundhypnosissecretsre vealed.blogspot.com/), and males can use special induction techniques to feminize their bodies to transform each body part into a desired feminine shape (http://www.hypnosis blacksecrets.com).

Such nonsense aside, practitioners of hypnosis have concocted a potpourri of approaches to produce whatever at the historical time or the whim of the hypnosis operator has been considered to be "hypnotic." A small sample of these inductions include flashing lights; focusing on the breath; fixating the eyes on an object, such as a moving watch popularized in the media; applying pressure to participants' heads; clanging gongs; and suggesting relaxation and alertness (Gibbons & Lynn, 2010). It seems that the only constraint on the nature of hypnotic inductions is the imagination of the hypnotist, although the inductions used in standardized scales of hypnosis, and incorporated in the repertoire of many clinical practitioners, are generally quite tame, emphasizing relaxation, sleepiness and drowsiness, imagination, focused attention, and cooperation. Moreover, as we will describe, inductions differ along multiple dimensions, such as their length, whether the wording is authoritative or permissive, whether they are individualized, and whether they are standardized for research or clinical purposes or administered on an individual or group basis or on a self versus hypnotist initiated basis. These highly diverse possibilities for inductions underscore the problems inherent in making generalizations about hypnotic inductions and in finding commonalities among them. Nevertheless, we attempt to identify such commonalities in our account of the role of the induction in the broader hypnotic scheme in an effort to move toward a more comprehensive understanding of how the induction works from a sociocognitive perspective.

Our review is limited to a consideration of behavioral and subjective responses associated with inductions. We do not discuss the thorny question of psychophysiological/ neurological correlates or concomitants of inductions, because interested readers will find an in depth and critical discussion elsewhere of findings and methodological issues pertinent to this topic examined from a sociocognitive perspective (Lynn, Kirsch, Knox, & Lilienfeld, 2006).

Definitions of Hypnosis

Given the rich diversity in inductions, it is not surprising that they have been defined only in the most general terms by three definitions of hypnosis crafted by the hypnosis division of American Psychological over more than two decades. The 1994 definition simply states: "The hypnotic context is generally established by an induction procedure. Although there are many different hypnotic inductions, most include suggestions for relaxation, calmness, and well-being. Instructions to imagine or think about pleasant experiences are also commonly included in hypnotic inductions" (Kirsch, 1994, p. 143).

This definition implies that establishing the context as "hypnotic" is an important, if not a primary, function of the induction. We agree and cite Sheehan and Perry (1976) to exemplify this point: "It is not the procedural conditions per se that are important but whether or not the subject perceives them as part of a context that is 'appropriate' for displaying hypnotic behavior" (p. 72).

We will argue that a key aspect of inductions is that they contribute to and are embedded in a far broader experiential context that establishes and reinforces the idea that the transaction between the hypnotist and the participant is "hypnotic" in nature. That is, the induction contextualizes whatever occurs subsequent to it as "hypnotic" and as a departure from mundane social interaction and communication, marking the proceedings as special in kind and conducive to altered and enhanced experiences and responses.

The induction—simply by framing the situation as hypnosis—potentially expands participants' beliefs and expectancies about what is possible to think, feel, and do, thereby enhancing motivation to respond and involvement in imaginative suggestions. At its heart, an induction amplifies, focuses, and channels (1) thoughts (imaginings) and feelings/emotions consistent with a positive response; (2) language, which shapes suggestions; and (3) behaviors in a call for the participant to respond in keeping with the implicit and explicit rules of a top-down constructed context. The definition also correctly notes that relaxation is an element that cuts across many diverse hypnotic inductions and helps to establish the context as "hypnotic."

We suggest that hypnotic responsiveness, including the domain of subjective experiences, is intimately associated with a sensitivity to contextual influences and an ability to experience cognitive-affective-behavioral plasticity in response to top-down generated rules for responding. These top-down rules are engendered by culturally-based associations participants develop apart from (e.g., via the media) and within the immediate context of "hypnosis." Perhaps the most central rule is to behave and experience hypnosis in a way that mirrors expectancies and beliefs about how a good hypnotic subject should respond. Imaginative suggestions, which often are interwoven through the entire hypnotic proceedings, including the induction, provide more specific, often more implicit "rules" (e.g., lift your arm and experience the rising as involuntary in response to a hand levitation suggestion) and vary in terms of their cues and demands that guide what motivated participants experience. Ideally, suggestions evoke stored memories, associations, and mental representations and stimulate experiences consistent with suggested events, which unfold on a more or less automatic basis, as is the case with most everyday actions and cognitive activities. According to the sociocognitive perspective, in the hypnotic context, these events are attributed to the influence of suggestions and "hypnosis" (Kirsch & Lynn, 1999).

According to this view, simply using the word "hypnosis" in the context of what is perceived to be an induction may be sufficient to establish a rule-governed context for responding to imaginative suggestions. Yet, we will argue that what precedes and follows any ritualized induction may be every bit as influential in determining hypnotic responding as the induction itself.

Turning now to the "next" definition of the hypnotic induction, a decade later, the American Psychological Association hypnosis division defined the hypnotic induction this way: "Hypnosis typically involves an introduction to the procedure during which the subject is told that suggestions for imaginative experiences will be presented. The hypnotic induction is an extended initial suggestion for using one's imagination, and may contain further elaborations of the introduction ..." (Green, Barabasz, Barrett, & Montgomery, 2005, p. 262).

One virtue of this definition is that it correctly implies that the hypnotic induction is merely one aspect of the hypnotic proceeding and that the induction often proceeds from the information provided by the hypnotist that precedes the induction. Indeed, perhaps more often than not, there may be no more than a sliver thin dividing line, if any at all, between activities that precede and follow the induction, and no boundary of demarcation between suggestions contained in the induction and those that follow. The definition is also in keeping with the fact that many inductions have in common explicit suggestions to deflect attention from the external environment (other than the hypnotist and suggestions) and narrow and focus attention internally on suggestion-related imaginings and, in so doing, vividly imagine and experience suggested events.

Accordingly, a key point of our thesis is that although hypnosis is typically described as involving two crucial phases or components—the induction and suggestions—these components are actually only two of numerous threads in a much broader "hypnotic" skein. Indeed, it is often imprecise to describe what transpires in terms of clear-cut phases or stages, so that where the "induction" begins and ends is often a strained, arbitrary, and artificial distinction. Rather, the induction is often preceded by an informed consent procedure in research settings; an introduction by the hypnotist, which frames and contextualizes hypnosis; and questions the participant asks about hypnosis followed by the hypnotist's responses. The induction itself is typically comprised of suggestions that often stream unobtrusively into experimental test or clinical suggestions that are targeted to achieve research or clinical objectives. As we will illustrate, all of these components seem to serve a common purpose: (1) to build and validate the top-down constructed cognitive-affective context—loosely speaking the participants' "experiential world"—from which the hypnotic behavior arises, and (2) perhaps to also reduce the impact of bottom-up input (e.g., distracting sensations) on hypnotic responding.

In certain clinical contexts, the lines between the induction and other aspects of hypnosis may be further blurred or eliminated. For example, in the popular Ericksonian tradition the therapist may attempt to induce hypnosis on an entirely informal and conversational basis, integrating suggestions into stories and anecdotes, metaphors, and information derived from the person's past and current everyday experiences in a seamless manner (see Matthews, Lankton, & Lankton, 1993; Yapko, 2012). In research settings, the induction will typically be more standardized and more formally demarcated from other aspects of the induction of hypnosis than in clinical contexts, although this issue has not been explored on an empirical basis.

Unfortunately, researchers have not subjected more informal conversational approaches to hypnosis to scrutiny in a systematic fashion. Nor has the role of sociocognitive variables been studied extensively in Ericksonian-type hypnosis, although the literature we review below on the equivalence of traditional authoritative direct versus indirect and permissive suggestions, which are mainstays of the Ericksonian approach, suggests that there is nothing "special" about the latter type of suggestions in terms of their ability to increase hypnotic responsiveness.

But to return to our point of emphasis, the hypnotic induction and suggestions are often enfolded within a larger framework of events and potentially complex interpersonal transactions (particularly in clinical contexts). Hypnosis unfurls from the inception of the hypnotist-participant contact and extends to suggestions or instructions to terminate hypnosis (i.e., at the count of 5, you will "come out of hypnosis"), which effectively deactivates the top-down constructed context, and the parting interaction of the hypnotist and participant. Moreover, hypnosis—particularly in clinical settings in which suggestions are typically tailored to the individual—often unfolds as a reciprocal process in which the patient's responses influence subsequent hypnotist interventions in a recursive manner on a moment-to-moment basis.

The second definition also hints at the role of imagination as a mechanism in producing hypnotic responses. Indeed, many inductions include suggestions that actively encourage use of the imagination and thinking and imagining along with suggestions, as well as suggestions that imply that suggested events will occur involuntarily or automatically. Nevertheless, the definition does not explain how using one's imagination facilitates responsiveness to suggestions and begs the question of how participants translate what is imagined into felt sensations and involuntary actions consistent with the aim of suggestions. Nor is it always the case that inductions emphasize specifically the use of imagination.

The third and most recent definition of hypnosis (Elkins, Barabasz, Council, & Spiegel, 2015) states that the hypnotic induction is "a procedure designed to induce hypnosis.... The definition is designed such that it does not specify what procedures may be involved or the context in which they occur. This may allow for procedures that involve interaction between a therapist and client, self-hypnosis procedures, or other procedures that may be identified in the future in clinical practice of research (such as through advances in technology" (p. 6).

This definition skirts any attempt to specify attributes of the induction, mechanisms associated with successful responding, and the place of the induction in the broader procedures. This latter definition, in an attempt to be "theoretically neutral," is arguably a step backwards in developing an operational understanding of inductions and arriving at even a rudimentary mechanistic explanation for their role and function (see Lynn, Green, et al., 2015). Generally speaking, the lack of specificity and elaboration in these three definitions reflects the sparse attention in the literature paid to the induction per se.

The Induction of Hypnosis in the Broader Scheme of Hypnosis

To better understand the role of the induction and its place in the overall scheme of hypnosis, we will first examine the typical hypnosis setting and the effects of different inductions on hypnotic responsiveness. We will suggest that the specific nature of the induction appears to play a negligible role in affecting hypnotic responding. In contrast, we will suggest that successful responding depends on a constellation of attitudes, beliefs, understandings, expectancies, motivation, and response sets of participants, and on rapport with the hypnotist in clinical settings, in particular. These variables, clearly identified with the sociocognitive perspective of hypnosis (e.g., Lynn, Laurence, & Kirsch, 2015; Kirsch, 1990; Spanos, 1986), promote cognitive-affective-behavioral plasticity that fosters increased responsiveness to specific suggestions within the broader hypnotic context. This broad context sets new parameters for how "reality" is temporarily experienced and how information is processed. We will further develop this argument in the course of our discussion of commonalities associated with diverse inductions and the broader scheme of hypnosis, research on the hypnotic induction, and empirical efforts to increase hypnotic responsiveness.

The Hypnotic Setting

The setting in which hypnosis is typically conducted crucially marks the situation as "hypnotic." For example, the setting is characteristically designed to enhance physical comfort, relaxation, and quiet to limit distractions. The participant may be seated in a comfortable chair or couch and be encouraged to pay attention to both the hypnotist's voice and to get involved with the suggestions and relax. The lighting may be soft or dimmed. The office or experimental room appointed with paintings or photographs selected to promote a calm and relaxed state of mind (e.g., bucolic or beach scenes, sunsets). Eye closure is often one of the first suggestions or instructions presented, and is geared to at once to direct attention away from the external milieu and to facilitate a more narrow or concerted focus on imagery and internal experiences as they arise. The hypnotist's voice, often presented in a "hypnotic like" pitch and cadence—which mirrors cultural beliefs regarding what is "hypnotic"—also sets the situation apart from the mundane and can act as nonverbal suggestion to "go into hypnosis" (Barber, 1985). Together, the effect of the hypnotist's presentation may be to amplify the effects of suggestions and top-down influences while depreciating the impact of bottom-up input (e.g., distracting sensations, perceptions, affects) that interfere with involvement in suggestions.

Prehypnotic Information

From the first to the last words the hypnotist utters, the intention is to make the experience of hypnosis less foreign and more palatable to participants and to minimize anxiety and oppositional resistance while increasing curiosity about hypnosis and maximizing expectations for positive responding. To facilitate comfort with the idea of "being hypnotized," the preamble may liken hypnosis to familiar scenarios, such as involvement in watching a movie or getting absorbed while driving, or experiencing a beautiful sunset or a visit to a favorite place. This information counters the widely prevailing myth that hypnosis involves going into a "trance" far removed from everyday experience. Alternatively, hypnosis may be presented as involving cooperation, an altered state of consciousness, or a state of dissociation or heightened suggestibility.

Still, in keeping with our earlier discussion, we suspect that the particular way in which hypnosis is described may be less important than casting the situation as "hypnotic," thereby locating hypnosis within a broader cultural frame, with attendant connotations of increased responsiveness and heightened expectations. The single, powerful word "hypnosis," by meaningfully evoking culture-bound associations regarding what it connotes to be hypnotized, may, therefore, account for many of the impressive effects we attribute to the broader, sometimes lengthy and elaborate induction procedure.

An important goal of facilitative prehypnotic information is to counteract misconceptions about hypnosis and negative beliefs and attitudes that may impede optimal responding. These misconceptions include the culturally prevalent ideas that (1) hypnosis robs people of their willpower and they cannot resist or oppose suggestions, and, instead, respond robotically; (2) hypnosis is associated with gullibility, low intelligence, or a lack of willpower; (3) people lose awareness of their surroundings or develop spontaneous amnesia for what occurred during hypnosis; and (4) people will "not be able to come out of hypnosis" (see Green, Page, Rasekhy, Johnson, & Bernhardt, 2006; Lynn, Rhue, & Kirsch, 2010).

Prehypnotic motivational information can further convey the expectation that many people are able to respond to a variety of suggestions, the experience of hypnosis will be enjoyable and relaxing—often directly reinforced with suggestions for relaxation in the induction—and that people respond to suggestions to different degrees, so as to minimize negative expectancies arising from less than "perfect" or sub-optimal responding. Participants may also be instructed to think and imagine along with suggestions and to experience them to the fullest extent possible, thereby motivating goal-directed and active responses to suggestions and minimizing bottom-up influences (Barber & Calverley, 1964; Barber, Spanos, & Chaves, 1972). These efforts are designed to encourage participants to approach the experience with a positive, motivated, cognitively committed set to respond, rather than face the prospect of hypnosis with fear and trepidation or passively wait for a response to "just happen."

To further minimize response-interfering concerns and potential resistance, participants may benefit from a demonstration that they can respond easily to nonhypnotic suggestions, such as an easy to pass suggestion for arm levitation, or head falling, as included in the Harvard Group Scale of Hypnotic Susceptibility: Form A (HGSHS:A; Shor & Orne, 1962). Or to counteract common fears of relinquishing control, the hypnotist may encourage deliberate and active resistance to a suggestion, such as hands moving together (as if pulled by a magnetic force), to "prove to participants and the hypnotist" that they can actively resist (Gfeller, Lynn, & Pribble, 1986). For some participants (typically highly suggestible) who respond—despite instructions to resist the hypnotist (see Lynn, Nash, Rhue, Frauman, & Sweeney, 1984)—the hypnotist can comment on how their strong response suggests that they are excellent hypnotic subjects. The hypnotist might add that if a suggestion were provided to engage in an action that violated their ethics or personal standards or values, they could easily resist (Coe, Kobayashi, & Howard, 1973).

Can the preamble make a difference? Lynn, Vanderhoff, Shindler, and Stafford (2002) compared the impact of prehypnotic instructions that informed participants that the ability to experience hypnosis depended on their ability to achieve an altered state of consciousness or "trance" versus their willingness to cooperate. The latter instructions are included in the Carleton University Scale of Hypnotic Responsiveness (CURSS; Spanos, Radtke, Hodgins, Stam, & Bertrand, 1983). Participants who received the altered state set indicated prior to hypnosis that they would respond to fewer suggestions and later responded to fewer suggestions compared with participants who received the standard instructions that emphasized cooperation. We interpreted these findings as indicating that participants' expectancies about successful responding are dampened by the prospect of entering a trance state that may be perceived to be difficult to achieve, or associated with negative connotations, and that when their experience fails to match their expectations, it diminishes their responsiveness to suggestion (see Lynn, Green, Jaquith, & Gasior, 2003).

In another study, Accardi, Cleere, Lynn, and Kirsch (2013) found no differences in participant responsiveness across rationales that experimenters provided regarding hypnosis when we equated the rationales for induced expectancies about successful responding. More specifically, in one condition we presented hypnosis in keeping with the preamble that accompanies the HGSHS:A (Shor & Orne, 1962), which informs participants that hypnosis is "largely a question of willingness to be receptive and responsive to ideas, and to allow these ideas to act on you without interference." We compared the effects of this rationale with one that indicated that hypnosis could be used as a non-deceptive placebo (Kirsch, 1994). This rationale informed participants, "Hypnosis acts very much like a placebo … in this study, we can use hypnosis as a placebo because hypnosis can be used without any deception at all … and like a placebo, hypnosis seems to work by mobilizing people's positive expectancies" (p. 108).

To control for expectations, in both conditions we told participants that hypnosis works by mobilizing participants' positive expectancies, but no mention of hypnosis being a placebo was presented in the standard condition. We found that participants responded comparably in terms of average hypnotic attitudes, prehypnotic expectances, behavioral responsiveness to suggestions, and hypnotic experiences assayed on a post-hypnotic basis, compared with the standard hypnosis rationale. Unfortunately, research on the effects of the rationale and the provision of prehypnotic information is scant; much more work needs to be done.

Comparing Hypnotic Inductions

Given commonalities we referred to across inductions and other aspects of the hypnotic proceedings, it follows to ask whether the nature of the induction per se has much of a bearing on hypnotic responsiveness. Researchers have discovered that it appears to make no difference in behavioral responding whether the induction is (1) administered in a group or on an individual basis (Bentler & Hilgard, 1963); (2) relatively long or short (Klinger, 1970); (3) administered live or via audio tape (Fassler, Lynn, & Knox, 2008); (4) administered using a traditional eye closure induction or a standardized Chiasson (1973) technique (hand moves toward face and when it reaches the face, the participant experiences a deep state of hypnosis; Page & Handley, 1991); (5) taken from the Carleton University Responsiveness Scale induction or a modified version of the Stanford Hypnotic Susceptibility Scale, Form C; and (6) presented as heterohypnosis or self-hypnosis (Hammond, Haskins-Bartsch, Grant, & McGhee, 1988).

Additionally, researchers have examined the effects of inductions in terms of whether the suggestions contained in them are direct versus indirect. Direct suggestions are statements that are specific, clear, directive, and command like, often delivered in an authoritative manner (O'Hanlon, 1987), such as "Your arm will rise up off the resting surface" and "You are very deeply relaxed." In contrast, indirect suggestions (Matthews et al., 1993; Stone & Lundy, 1985) typically share one or more of the following features. They are permissive, often nonspecific or ambiguous, and allow for choice and a range of appropriate responses, such as "You may experience a light, deep, or medium trance today. I wonder just how deep you will go?"

Researchers have generally found no differences in behavioral responses to direct versus indirect inductions and suggestions (see Lynn, Neufeld, & Mare, 1993). Lynn, Neufeld, and Matyi (1987) is one of the few studies that manipulated the induction wording independent of suggestion wording. The wording of the induction had no effect on subjects' responsivity and their ratings of subjective involvement or suggestion-related involuntariness.

Nevertheless, aside from the induction, some studies (Lynn et al., 1987; Lynn, Weekes, Matyi, & Neufeld, 1988; Matthews, Bennett, Gallagher, & Bean, 1985; Matthews & Mosher, 1988; Weekes & Lynn, 1990) have found that direct suggestions produce greater subjective involvement, feelings of involuntariness, and diminished resistance (Matthews & Mosher, 1988). Yet, when Matthews and Mosher (1988) equated the inductions for length and delivery time, they failed to replicate their earlier findings. And still other research has found no difference between direct and indirect suggestions on measures of involuntariness (Stone & Lundy, 1985) and subjective experience (Matheson & Shue, 1987).

Since Lynn et al.'s (1993) review, the majority of studies have found no differences in behavioral and/or subjective responses between direct suggestions and inductions and their indirect counterparts (Groth-Marnat & Mitchell, 1998; Hawkins, Liossi, Ewart, Hatira, & Kosmidis, 1998; Maurer, Santangelo, & Claiborn, 1993; Pitsch, Sapp, & McNeely, 2001; Szabó, 1993). Although the findings regarding subjective measures are somewhat mixed, there is little ambiguity regarding conclusions that can be drawn with regard to behavioral (i.e., objective) responses: virtually no support exists for the advantage of indirect suggestions over direct suggestions. It appears to be the case that the differences in wording between direct and indirect inductions and suggestions are inconsequential at the level of semantic processing and activation in the hypnotic context.

This lack of difference among inductions does not preclude differences in individual preferences for one induction over another. Spinhoven, Baak, Van Dyck, and Vermeulen (1988) used a version of the Harvard scale adapted with indirect suggestions and found that subjects who received the indirect and direct Harvard scales had identical average hypnotizability scores. Nevertheless, 20 subjects indicated a preference for the Harvard, whereas 15 subjects preferred the indirect scale, and five were neutral in their preference.

Researchers have also compared a traditional induction with a more unconventional and arguably indirect induction. Matthews, Kirsch, and Mosher (1985) tested Bandler and Grinder's (1975) claim that the so-called double induction is superior to traditional hypnosis. Half of the right-handed subjects received the Stanford Hypnotic Susceptibility Scale, Form C (SHSS:C; Weitzenhoffer & Hilgard, 1962) induction, and the other half received a stereo delivery of two simultaneously presented audio tracks. The audio track that was directed to the subjects' dominant hemisphere (left ear) used Erickson's hand levitation induction, while what the researchers referred to as "child-like grammar messages," such as "wondering," "hands lifting," "sleep," and so forth, were delivered to the nondominant (right ear) hemisphere. The following day the order of inductions was reversed. No differences in hypnotizability scores were evidenced following either induction; however, subjects who received the double induction first were later less responsive to suggestions following both inductions than were subjects who received the standard induction first. The findings contradict Bandler and Grinder's (1975) assertion that the double induction is an especially powerful means of inducing hypnosis (… one of the most powerful techniques which we have developed is the double induction…, p. 194).

As many different hypnotic inductions share a common element—they provide suggestions for physical and/or mental relaxation and behavioral stillness—an arguably greater departure from the traditional relaxation-based induction is the so-called active-alert induction. Bányai and Hilgard (1976) compared an active-alert induction, in which participants received suggestions for increased alertness with their eyes open, while riding a bicycle ergometer, with a traditional relaxation induction (i.e., eye fixation with instructions to relax) followed by suggestions from a standardized scale (SHSS:B; Weitzenhoffer & Hilgard, 1959). The researchers found no differences in hypnotic responding between the two inductions in the context of a within-subjects design with randomized alternation between alert-active and traditional inductions. Across both inductions, highly suggestible participants reported that they achieved "altered states." More recently, Wark (2006) summarized the findings across multiple studies (e.g., Cardeña, 2005; Malott, 1984; Miller, Barabasz, & Barabasz, 1991) that substituted an alert or hyper-alert induction for a more traditional relaxation-based induction and concluded that there were practically no significant differences across suggestion types.

Cardeña, Alarcon, Capafons, and Bayot (1998) conducted an interesting study that provided a creative demonstration of the value of induction preparation. The researchers developed a set of energizing exercises to prepare subjects for an "active hand" induction in which participants were invited to recall or imagine experiences intended to increase heartbeat, respiration, and wide visual expansion. The actual induction involved moving the right hand vertically up and down rapidly and then suggesting increased heartbeat, respiration, and alertness. The researchers found that participants were significantly more responsive and more likely to stay in the study compared with Bányai and Hilgard's (1976) bicycle induction.

Increasing Responsiveness to Hypnosis

Our discussion has emphasized the value of considering the induction in terms of the broader events of hypnosis. Cardeña et al.'s study highlights the potential of instructional efforts to increase responsiveness as influential in the induction of hypnosis. Relatedly, Vickery, Kirsch, Council, and Sirkin (1985) provided participants with information and experimenter demonstration regarding imaginative cognitive strategies to respond effectively to suggestions followed by practice in using the cognitive strategies. When this "cognitive skill induction" was preceded by a traditional hypnotic induction, subjective responses to hypnosis were enhanced significantly and objective response was enhanced marginally, compared with the traditional induction. However, when the order was reversed, the inductions did not produce differences in subjective or objective responses. The traditional induction engendered greater alterations in consciousness, prompting the researchers to comment, "… the skill induction teaches subjects cognitive strategies that enhance responsivity to suggestions in subsequent hypnotic experiences independent of the alterations in consciousness elicited by trance induction" (p. 131).

Around the time of this research, Gorassini and Spanos (1986) initiated a line of studies that focused on efforts to systematically enhance hypnotic suggestibility by teaching not only cognitive strategies, but also enhancing response expectancies, minimizing or eliminating negative beliefs about hypnosis, and enhancing rapport and minimizing resistance to responding to suggestions. More specifically, the Carleton Skills Training Program (CSTP) the researchers developed includes the following components: (1) information to instill positive attitudes about hypnosis and motivation to respond; (2) instructions regarding how to use imaginal strategies to promote successful responding and instructions regarding how to interpret suggestions (e.g., enactment instructions that one must actually lift the hand while imagining it is rising by itself); (3) exposure to a video-taped model who enacts successful responses to suggestions and verbalizes imagery-based strategies to facilitate subjective response; and (4) practice in responding to suggestions. The selection of variables to target in this program was inspired by the sociocognitive model of hypnosis (see Kirsch, 1990; Lynn, Laurence, & Kirsch, 2015; Spanos, 1986, 1991), which holds that attitudes, beliefs, expectancies, motivation, responsiveness to nonhypnotic imaginative suggestions, and cognitive strategies are variables key to understanding and potentially facilitating hypnotic responsiveness.

Spanos and his associates (see Gfeller & Gorassini, 2010; Gorassini & Spanos, 1999) have determined that approximately 50% of initially low suggestible subjects who underwent the CSTP scored as high suggestible at post-testing with standardized inductions. Importantly, researchers have documented large magnitude CSTP treatment gains that have persisted for two and a half years (Spanos, Cross, Menary, & Smith, 1988) across studies in Spain (Cangas & Pérez, 1998), Poland (Niedzwienska, 2000), and England (Fellows & Ragg, 1992). Because the CSTP produces increases in both objective and subjective responsiveness to hypnotic suggestions, with gains generalizing to novel test suggestions (Spanos, 1986), it is possible that suggestibility training can increase responsiveness to clinically relevant suggestions related to hypnotic suggestibility, such as for pain control (see Lynn, 2004; Lynn & Sherman, 2000).

Before leaving this topic, it bears mention that rapport is another aspect of the hypnotic situation that is amenable to modification. Lynn et al. (1991) tested high and low suggestible participants in either a high or a low rapport condition. In the high rapport condition, the hypnotist was friendly, smiled, and disclosed to the participant on relatively intimate topics selected from a list ranked in intimacy. In the low rapport condition, the hypnotist was formal in demeanor and disclosed on only the most superficial topics. Initially low responsive participants passed more than 2.5 suggestions and, on average, scored in the medium hypnotizable range after the manipulation of positive rapport, whereas the initially highly suggestible participants were unaffected by the rapport manipulation.

Researchers have also shown that rapport also exerts an effect on the impact of CSTP training. Gfeller et al. (1987) reported that 25% of initially low suggestible participants tested as highly suggestible after training in a relatively "neutral" rapport condition compared with 50% of participants who tested as highly suggestible after training in a condition designed to facilitate rapport with the trainer. Unfortunately, typically little is done to increase rapport, at least in the context of experimental hypnosis, which is perhaps one reason why it seems to matter little whether instructions are provided in a live format or via an audio recording (Fassler et al. 2008), or whether hypnosis is defined as self-hypnosis and participants are trained to administer self-suggestions (Barber, 1985).

The CSTP program has not been without its critics, as justifiable questions linger regarding the extent to which post-training gains reflect instructed versus more spontaneous, ability-related cognitive and experiential processes (see Lynn et al., 2015). Nevertheless, following Gfeller and Gorassini (2010), we suggest that it may be fruitful to include many of the elements associated with the CSTP into relatively brief procedures initiated prior to and during inductions, because research has substantiated the role of elements of the CSTP as accounting for substantial variability in hypnotic responding (see Lynn, Laurence et al., 2015).

As we have indicated, prehypnotic information can be used to bolster positive expectancies, increase motivation, correct misconceptions about hypnosis, and facilitate rapport with participants. It may also be worthwhile to attempt to minimize top down impediments to hypnotic responding in hypnotic suggestibility modification programs and inductions more generally. For example, participants could be instructed to accept that initially distracting thoughts and sensations may arise in the course of events, and "that is perfectly fine, just know that they are natural occurrences and should not get in the way at all with your ability to experience suggestions … you can easily become absorbed in your experiences as you find that these thoughts and sensations recede into the background of your consciousness as you get more deeply involved in your experience of hypnosis."

Methods and suggestions intended to enhance rapport, motivation, and positive expectancies, could be included in hypnotic inductions and conceivably be individualized based on a careful assessment of the person with an eye toward optimizing hypnotic performance. The effects of individualizing inductions and procedures is clearly an understudied area, with only one study to date comparing a standardized hypnotic suggestibility scale, based on a relaxation induction, with an individualized version of the same scale to determine whether individualizing the induction enhances hypnotic responsiveness. In research conducted by Van Der Does, Van Dyck, Spinhoven, and Kloosman (1989), participants were tested twice; once with the standardized Stanford Hypnotic Clinical Scale: Adult (Morgan & Hilgard, 1978) and once with an adapted, individualized version of the same scale in which the hypnotherapists (experienced members of the Netherlands Society of Hypnosis) were "… free to use whatever induction procedures and wording of suggestions seemed appropriate for a particular *S*" (p. 183). The researchers found no differences across the standardized and individualized version of the scale. Nevertheless, the criteria for individualizing the procedures were neither standardized nor theory-based, so much research needs to be done on individualizing suggestions to guide and facilitate clinical work.

A novel way to increase hypnotic suggestibility may be to provide instructions or suggestions to facilitate goal-directed behavior in the hypnotic context. Gollwitzer

(1999) has distinguished between goal setting and implementation intentions. Implementation intentions involve establishing contingent "if-then" relationships to better effect the realization of a particular goal. For example, a generalized goal might be "I would really like to experience hypnosis," whereas an implementation intention is subordinate to the generalized goal and typically better specified. Accordingly, an implementation intention might be "If I think and imagine along with suggestions, then I will get more absorbed in them" or "If I get really absorbed with suggestions, then I will be more responsive to suggestions."

The implementation intention, thus, introduces if-then rule sets, parameters for experience and behavior that could become an integral part of the cognitive-affective-behavioral context, which, we expect, would increase hypnotic responsiveness more efficiently and less ambiguously than generalized goals. In clinical practice and research, such implementation intention instructions could be incorporated into inductions and even framed as suggestions (e.g., "If you think and imagine along with the suggestion for your arm to rise, then you will experience your arm rising), and/or presented in the context of prehypnotic information. To facilitate possibly even deeper cognitive processing, the hypnotist could couch the instructions more in terms of a question along the lines of: "What if you think and imagine along with the suggestion for your arm to rise, and then experience your arm rising?" We are currently investigating whether including information and suggestions to facilitate implementation intentions will facilitate hypnotic responding compared with information and suggestions specifying more generalized goal contemplation. We suggest that when the positive components of hypnotic responsiveness we identified are included in hypnotic procedures, including in the induction per se, participants will respond closer to the limits of their abilities to experience suggestions.

Conclusions, Reflections, and Research Recommendations

In this article, we have taken note of the tremendous variability in hypnotic inductions and procedures that render it difficult to draw unambiguous conclusions and interpretations regarding the nature, role, intended purpose, and impact of inductions on hypnotic responding. We now suggest that the problem of disambiguating the induction from other elements of the broader scheme of hypnosis begins even prior to the hypnotic session. More specifically, it is difficult to disentangle the effects of an induction from information provided prior to even starting the hypnosis session in the informed consent procedures in a research context, or in the earliest informal or nonstandardized comments by the hypnotist in a clinical setting. Indeed, how the session is cast (e.g., what is the nature of hypnosis; why is it being used; what is the probability that it will help in a particular circumstance), as well as information about myths and potential risks, may vary widely among hypnosis sessions and studies and exert important and as yet often under-appreciated effects on hypnotic responding.

We suggest that the impact of formal and informal pre-session information on hypnotic responsiveness should be carefully considered, even when using standardized scales of hypnotizability. Formal inductions, the wording of suggestions, and the amount of time between suggestions delivered are often carefully scripted and well-elucidated. Nevertheless, unscripted or non-standardized information presented before the hypnosis session even begins may be just as important as what transpires after the session starts in determining research or clinical outcomes. Indeed, virtually no attention has been devoted to prehypnosis session information conveyed to participants in informed consent procedures and in the description of the nuts and bolts of the study, which may differ widely across laboratories and clinics and may be presented on a more or less informal basis.

Investigators would well serve the field by summarizing the information they present to participants at all stages of their research in published reports, as such information is all-too-rarely presented in both research and clinical accounts. In fact, with participant consent, it would be valuable to archive in DVD format or on a password protected site on the Internet an entire interaction, from start to finish, with a single participant or group undergoing hypnosis to be made available to researchers interested in acquiring detailed information about the research for purposes of evaluation of the study and/or replication.

An interesting aspect of pre-session information, and actually the conduct of the entire study, is that it may be subject to extra-experimental influences and pressures. For example, some institutional review boards (IRBs) may insist that prospective participants be presented with a list of potential risks that have been reported in the literature previously, such as the possibility of headaches, muscle stiffness, and tiredness, whereas other IRBs may not require such information. Pre-session information may also differ in terms of the extent to which information about participants' ability to resist suggestions, should they choose to do so, is emphasized or ignored. Simply providing a "common example" of a type of suggestion that participants might expect to receive during the procedure proper may serve to shape, strengthen, or alter prehypnosis expectancies and might make findings across studies difficult to compare and interpret to the extent that this information differs or is absent across studies.

In one of the few studies that addressed very "early" information that participants were provided with, Coe, Peterson, and Gwynn (1995) reported that individuals who received brief instructions before hypnosis, which provided very specific warnings of negative aftereffects (i.e., "approximately one half of subjects have reported mild, short-term aftereffects, such as headache") with no positive information about hypnosis, reported more negative aftereffects than did participants in which no mention was made of positive or negative aftereffects, or more balanced information was presented (i.e., "some mildly unpleasant experiences," plus "most persons report their experiences to be pleasurable and interesting"). Page and Handley (1996) later reported significant correlations between hypnotic suggestibility and the report of aftereffects and number of somatic complaints.

The therapist's explanation for why hypnosis is considered to be a useful adjunctive treatment may be critically important in the clinical context. The following variables may further impact how clients respond to and view hypnosis (e.g., as a primary care intervention versus a "last ditch" effort to bring about change): (1) whether the decision to use hypnosis or a particular induction is based on a unilateral therapist decision versus a collaborative one, (2) the timing regarding when to bring hypnosis into treatment, and (3) the decision regarding whether to implement hypnosis in conjunction with other strategies (e.g., acceptance-mindfulness based interventions). Accordingly, research examining the potential effects of these variables on hypnotic responding or clinical outcomes would be welcome.

Participant preference for different hypnotic inductions, which may be especially important in the clinical arena, is also a little studied area, as induction preference may be associated with positive treatment expectancies and may be impactful in terms of subjective, if not objective, response to suggestions and the overall hypnotic procedures. It would be interesting for researchers to examine the effects of preference for inductions in the context of providing individuals with the opportunity to observe models that undergo different inductions and verbalize their responses to the inductions. Such observation might provide participants with valuable information regarding which induction would be most appealing and thereby elicit the most positive response expectancies. There is also a pressing need to examine potential differences between formal/standardized inductions, well-demarcated from other aspects of the procedures, and more free-flowing, informal, and conversational inductions and interventions in keeping with the Ericksonian tradition.

Additionally, we suggest that researchers explore the effects of the mere inclusion of the word or label of "hypnosis" and matching inductions with abilities. If all the induction does is to establish an hypnotic context, and little more, engaging top-down processing, than labeling virtually any activity, ranging from taking a few breaths, to walking, to closing one's eyes, to feeling relaxation in a single body part would be expected to produce outcomes equivalent to a more elaborate and lengthy induction. It would also be interesting to determine whether it would be possible to increase hypnotic responsiveness by matching the nature of induction to participants' abilities. For example, researchers might ask whether highly imaginative people would benefit from inductions that played to their imaginative abilities by emphasizing the use of imagination or by priming imaginative responses prior to hypnosis, relative to participants with less well-developed imaginative abilities.

The fact that an elaborate induction is apparently not necessary in the case of self-hypnosis also bolsters the hypothesis that the formal induction of hypnosis can play a minimal role in engendering and determining responsivity to suggestions. From a socio-cognitive perspective, the same variables that affect so-called hetero-hypnosis, also probably come into play when the methods are defined as self-hypnosis. Merely labeling the procedures as "hypnosis," particularly after the person is first "hypnotized" or participants are told that "all hypnosis is really self-hypnosis," as is often the case, likely activates attitudes, beliefs, and expectancies regarding hypnosis that are deeply rooted in our culture. Still, limited research has directly compared responsiveness to hypnosis when the procedures are defined as self- versus hetero-hypnosis, and research that compares the role of sociocognitive variables across hetero- versus self-hypnosis is certainly warranted.

Clinical practitioners and researchers not infrequently encounter participants who deny the fact that they were "hypnotized" or minimize their responsiveness to hypnotic suggestions, despite the fact that they display a high level of behavioral responsiveness to suggestions. These types of reports have not been studied systematically, and deserve such scrutiny, although they may simply be indicators of mismatches between participants' experience and their expectancies regarding how "good" or "excellent" hypnotic subjects experience hypnosis. For example, if participants do not believe that they achieved the proverbial and poorly defined "trance state," they may report after hypnosis that they were "not hypnotized." In fact, researchers have shown that participants who test at the extremes of hypnotic high suggestibility do not tend to rate their responsiveness in accordance with their actual objective performance, because there are no clear-cut widely accepted subjective criteria that determine whether a person is "hypnotized" or not (Martin & Lynn, 1996).

Clinicians will also encounter individuals who are initially highly skeptical of their ability to experience hypnosis. However, most initial suggestions in research protocols, and many suggestions in psychotherapy contexts, are easy to pass (see Barber, 1985) and, if passed by initially skeptical participants, may provide strong and compelling positive expectations for subsequent successful responding ("Well, here I thought I could not be hypnotized, so I must be more hypnotizable than I thought" or, "Hypnosis must be very powerful if I could respond despite my skepticism") in these individuals. This phenomenon has not been the subject of study in the laboratory. Expectancies arise not only during the induction, but also as a function of participant self-observation of their responsiveness to imaginative suggestions, which generally produce equivalent levels of responsiveness, regardless of whether they are preceded by an induction or not (Meyer & Lynn, 2011). Studies of the link between different types of inductions and changes in expectations over the course of a hypnosis session have not been reported to date.

Note that the sociocognitive perspective does not discount the possibility that researchers will, one day, isolate an as yet unidentified "ability factor" that is reliably and robustly associated with the transformation of verbal suggestions into involuntary experiences. Unfortunately, the search for such ability has not proved to be very rewarding to date. For example, measures of dissociation and absorption account for only a small percent of variability in hypnotic responding, especially when hypnotic suggestibility and measures of these constructs are administered in separate test contexts (see Council, Kirsch, & Grant, 1996; Kirsch & Lynn, 1998). Still, it is worthwhile to continue to search for one or more abilities, in isolation or in combination, which can account for significant variability in hypnotic responding and experience.

The sociocognitive model holds that the experience of suggestion-related involuntariness is related to participants' expectancies, the passive wording of suggestions, the presence of goal-directed fantasies contained in suggestions (i.e., "imagined situations which, if they were to occur, would be expected to lead to the involuntary occurrence of the motor response called for by the suggestion": Spanos, Rivers, & Ross, 1977), and a response set to "let things happen" (see Lynn, Rhue, and Weekes, 1990 for an in-depth examination of this topic). Previous studies have not assessed, in light of the aforementioned variables, the potentially distinct experiences of involuntariness associated with the suggestions in the induction versus those that follow.

In closing, we wish to underscore the point that it is problematic to consider hypnosis narrowly as consisting of only two broad phases: the induction and the suggestions, and to ignore the role of procedures and variables in the broader hypnotic scheme key to account for individual differences in hypnotic responding. Participants probably respond to a broad gestalt of variables and subtle and not so subtle conscious and unconscious influences, many of which, nevertheless, can be identified, isolated, quantified, and studied in a programmatic manner. These variables come together in the language of suggestions before, during, and after the induction that play an instrumental role in constructing the cognitive-affective-behavioral context of hypnosis.

Although our preference is to view a conglomerate of sociocognitive variables as particularly influential, variables from other traditions and perspectives, such as dissociation theories of hypnosis, are also worthy of investigation, and Lynn and Green (2011) have suggested the possibility of rapprochement between sociocognitive and dissociation theories of hypnosis. Acquiring a better understanding of what researchers and clinicians can do to enhance participants' ability to respond to suggestions should also be a priority. Clearly, different inductions, as well as other constituents that shape the totality of experiences that we call "hypnosis," deserve continued and closer scrutiny by researchers and clinicians alike.

References

Accardi, M., Cleere, C., Lynn, S. J., & Kirsch, I. (2013). Placebo versus "standard" hypnosis rationale: Attitudes, expectancies, hypnotic responsiveness, and experiences. *American Journal of Clinical Hypnosis*, *56*, 103–114. doi:10.1080/00029157.2013.769087

Bányai, E. I., & Hilgard, E. R. (1976). A comparison of active-alert hypnotic induction with traditional relaxation induction. *Journal of Abnormal Psychology*, *85*, 218–224. doi:10.1037/0021-843X.85.2.218

Barber, T. X. (1985). Hypnosuggestive procedures as catalysts for psychotherapies. In S. J. Lynn & J. P. Garske (Eds.), *Contemporary psychotherapies: Models and methods* (pp. 333–376). Columbus, OH: Charles E. Merrill.

Barber, T. X., & Calverley, D. S. (1964). An experimental study of "hypnotic" (auditory and visual) hallucinations. *The Journal of Abnormal and Social Psychology*, *68*(1), 13–20. doi:10.1037/h0042175

Barber, T. X., Spanos, N. P., & Chaves, J. F. (1974). *Hypnosis, imagination, and human potentialities* (Vol. 46). Oxford, UK: Pergamon.

Bandler, R., & Grinder, J. (1975). *Patterns of hypnotic techniques of Milton H. Erickson, M.D.* (vol.1., p. 194). Cupertino, CA: Meta Communications.

Bentler, P. M., & Hilgard, E. R. (1963). A comparison of group and individual induction of hypnosis with self-scoring and observer-scoring. *International Journal of Clinical and Experimental Hypnosis*, *11*, 49–54. doi:10.1080/00207146308409227

Cangas, A. J., & Pérez, M. (1998). The effect of two procedures on hypnotic susceptibility modification. *Contemporary Hypnosis & Integrative Therapy*, *15*(4), 212–218. doi:10.1002/(ISSN) 1557-0711

Cardeña, E. (2005). The phenomenology of deep hypnosis: Quiescent and physically active. *International Journal of Clinical and Experimental Hypnosis*, *53*, 37–59. doi:10.1080/00207140490914234

Cardeña, E., Alarcon, A., Capafons, A., & Bayot, A. (1998). Effects on suggestibility of a new method of active-alert hypnosis: Alert hand. *International Journal of Clinical & Experimental Hypnosis*, *46*(3), 280–294. doi:10.1080/00207149808410008

Chiasson, S. (1973). Chiasson's method. *Syllabus on hypnosis and a handbook of therapeutic suggestions*. Bloomingdale, IL: American Society of Clinical Hypnosis Education and Research Foundation.

Coe, W. C., Kobayashi, K., & Howard, M. L. (1973). Experimental and ethical problems of evaluating the influence of hypnosis in antisocial conduct. *Journal of Abnormal Psychology*, *82*(3), 476–482. doi:10.1037/h0035365

Coe, W. C., Peterson, P., & Gwynn, M. (1995). Expectations and sequelae to hypnosis: Initial findings. *American Journal of Clinical Hypnosis*, *38*(1), 3–12.

Council, J. R., Kirsch, I., & Grant, D. L. (1996). *Hypnosis and imagination* (pp. 41–65). R. Kunzendorf, N. Spanos, & B. Wallace (Eds.). Amityville, NY: Baywood Publishing.

Du Maurier, G. (1984/2009). *Trilby*. UK: London, Osgood, Mcilvaine & Company.

Elkins, G. R., Barabasz, A. F., Council, J. R., & Spiegel, D. (2015). Advancing research and practice: The revised APA Division 30 definition of hypnosis. *American Journal of Clinical Hypnosis*, *57*, 378–385. doi:10.1080/00029157.2015.1011465

Fassler, O., Lynn, S. J., & Knox, J. (2008). Is hypnotic suggestibility a stable trait? *Consciousness and Cognition*, *17*, 240–253. doi:10.1016/j.concog.2007.05.004

Fellows, B. J., & Ragg, L. (1992). The carleton skills training program: A preliminary British trial. *Contemporary Hypnosis*, *9*(3), 169–174.

Gfeller, J., & Gorassini, D. R. (2010). Enhancing hypnotizability and treatment response. In S. J. Lynn, J. W. Rhue, & I. Kirsch (Eds.), *Handbook of clinical hypnosis* (pp. 339–356). Washington, DC: American Psychological Association.

Gfeller, J., Lynn, S. J., & Pribble, W. (1987). Enhancing hypnotic susceptibility: Interpersonal and rapport factors. *Journal of Personality and Social Psychology*, *52*, 586–595. doi:10.1037/0022-3514.52.3.586

Gibbons, D. E., & Lynn, S. J. (2010). Hypnotic inductions: A primer. In *Handbook of clinical hypnosis* (2 nd ed., pp. 267–293). Washington, DC: American Psychological Association.

Gollwitzer, P. M. (1999). Implementation intentions: Strong effects of simple plans. *American Psychologist*, *54*(7), 493–503. doi:10.1037/0003-066X.54.7.493

Gorassini, D. R., & Spanos, N. P. (1986). A social-cognitive skills approach to the successful modification of hypnotic susceptibility. *Journal of Personality and Social Psychology*, *50*(5), 1004–1012. doi:10.1037/0022-3514.50.5.1004

Gorassini, D. R., & Spanos, N. P. (1999). The carleton skill training program for modifying hypnotic suggestibility: Original version and variations. In I. Kirsch, A. Capafons, E. Cardeña-Buelna, & S. Amigó (Eds.), *Clinical hypnosis and self-regulation: Cognitive-behavioral perspectives* (pp. 141–177). Washington, DC: American Psychological Association.

Green, J. P., Barabasz, A. F., Barrett, D., & Montgomery, G. H. (2005). Forging ahead: The 2003 APA Division 30 definition of hypnosis. *International Journal of Clinical and Experimental Hypnosis*, *53*, 259–264. doi:10.1080/00207140590961321

Green, J. P., Page, R. A., Rasekhy, R., Johnson, L. K., & Bernhardt, S. E. (2006). Cultural views and attitudes about hypnosis: A survey of college students across four countries. *International Journal of Clinical and Experimental Hypnosis*, *54*, 263–280. doi:10.1080/00207140600689439

Groth-Marnat, G., & Mitchell, K. (1998). Responsiveness to direct versus indirect hypnotic procedures: The role of resistance as a predictor variable. *International Journal of Clinical and Experimental Hypnosis*, *46*, 324–333. doi:10.1080/00207149808410012

Hammond, D. C., Haskins-Bartsch, C., Grant, C. W., & McGhee, M. (1988). Comparison of self-directed and tape-assisted self-hypnosis. *American Journal of Clinical Hypnosis*, *31*, 129–137. doi:10.1080/00029157.1988.10402879

Hawkins, P. J., Liossi, C., Ewart, B. W., Hatira, P., & Kosmidis, V. H. (1998). Hypnosis in the alleviation of procedure related pain and distress in paediatric oncology patients. *Contemporary Hypnosis*, *15*(4), 199–207. doi:10.1002/(ISSN)1557-0711

Kirsch, I. (1990). *Changing expectations: A key to effective psychotherapy.* Pacific Grove, CA: Thomson Brooks/Cole Publishing Co.

Kirsch, I. (1994). Defining hypnosis for the public. *Contemporary Hypnosis*, *11*(3), 142–143.

Kirsch, I., & Lynn, S. J. (1998). Dissociation theories of hypnosis. *Psychological Bulletin*, *123*, 100–115. doi:10.1037/0033-2909.123.1.100

Kirsch, I., & Lynn, S. J. (1999). Automaticity in clinical psychology. *American Psychologist*, *54*(7), 504–515. doi:037/0003-066X.54.7.504

Klinger, B. I. (1970). Effect of peer model reponsiveness and length of induction procedure on hypnotic responsiveness. *Journal of Abnormal Psychology*, *75*, 15–18. doi:10.1037/h0028683

Lynn, S. J. (2004). Enhancing hypnotizability: The effects of compliance versus imagery. *American Journal of Clinical Hypnosis*, *47*, 117–128. doi:10.1080/00029157.2004.10403630

Lynn, S. J., & Green, J. P. (2011). The sociocognitive and dissociation theories of hypnosis: Toward a rapprochement. *International Journal of Clinical and Experimental Hypnosis*, *59*, 277–293. doi:10.1080/00207144.2011.570652

Lynn, S. J., Green, J. P., Jaquith, L., & Gasior, D. (2003). Hypnosis and performance standards. *International Journal of Clinical and Experimental Hypnosis*, *51*(1), 51–65. doi:10.1076/iceh.51.1.51.14062

Lynn, S. J., Green, J. P., Kirsch, I., Capafons, A., Lilienfeld, S. O., Laurence, J.-R., & Montgomery, G. H. (2015). Grounding hypnosis in science: The "new" APA Division 30 definition of hypnosis as a step backwards. *American Journal of Clinical Hypnosis*, *57*(4), 390–401. doi:10.1080/00029157.2015.1011472

Lynn, S. J., Kirsch, I., Knox, J., & Lilienfeld, S. (2006). Hypnosis and neuroscience: Implications for the altered state debate. In G. Jamieson (Ed.), *Hypnosis and conscious states: The cognitive-neuroscience perspective*. New York/UK: Oxford University Press.

Lynn, S. J., Laurence, J.-R., & Kirsch, I. (2015). Hypnosis, suggestion, and suggestibility: An integrative model. *American Journal of Clinical Hypnosis*, *57*(3), 314–329. doi:10.1080/00029157.2014.976783

Lynn, S. J., Nash, M. R., Rhue, J., Frauman, D., & Sweeney, C. (1984). Nonvolition, expectancies, and hypnotic rapport. *Journal of Abnormal Psychology*, *93*, 295–303. doi:10.1037/0021-843X.93.3.295

Lynn, S. J., Neufeld, V. R., & Mare, C. (1993). Direct versus indirect suggestions: A conceptual and methodological review. *International Journal of Clinical and Experimental Hypnosis*, *41*, 124–152. doi:10.1080/00207149308414543

Lynn, S. J., Neufeld, V. R., & Matyi, C. L. (1987). Inductions versus suggestions: Effects of direct and indirect wording on hypnotic responding and experience. *Journal of Abnormal Psychology*, *96*, 76–79. doi:10.1037/0021-843X.96.1.76

Lynn, S. J., Rhue, J. W., & Kirsch, I. (Eds.). (2010). *Handbook of clinical hypnosis* (2nd ed.). Washington, DC: American Psychological Association.

Lynn, S. J., & Sherman, S. J. (2000). The clinical importance of sociocognitive models of hypnosis: Response set theory and Erickson's strategic interventions. *American Journal of Clinical Hypnosis*, *42*, 294–315. doi:10.1080/00029157.2000.10734363

Lynn, S. J., Vanderhoff, H., Shindler, K., & Stafford, J. (2002). Defining hypnosis as a trance vs. cooperation: Hypnotic inductions, suggestibility, and performance standards. *American Journal of Clinical Hypnosis*, *44*, 231–240. doi:10.1080/00029157.2002.10403483

Lynn, S. J., Weekes, J., Brentar, J., Neufeld, V., Zivney, O., & Weiss, F. (1991). Interpersonal climate and hypnotizability level: Effects on hypnotic performance, rapport, and archaic involvement. *Journal of Personality and Social Psychology*, *60*, 739–743. doi:10.1037/0022-3514.60.5.739

Lynn, S. J., Weekes, J. R., Matyi, C. L., & Neufeld, V. (1988). Direct versus indirect suggestions, archaic involvement, and hypnotic experience. *Journal of Abnormal Psychology*, *97*, 296–301. doi:10.1037/0021-843X.97.3.296

Malott, J. M. (1984). Active-alert hypnosis: Replication and extension of previous research. *Journal of Abnormal Psychology*, *93*, 246–249. doi:10.1037/0021-843X.93.2.246

Martin, D., & Lynn, S. J. (1996). The successful discrimination of hypnotizable and simulating participants: The hypnotic simulation index. *International Journal of Clinical and Experimental Hypnosis*, *44*, 338–353. doi:10.1080/00207149608416097

Matheson, G., & Shue, K. L. (1987, March). *"Hypnotic language": A study of the experience of direct vs. indirect suggestions*. Paper presented to the Fourth European Congress of Hypnosis in Psychotherapy and Psychosomatic Medicine, Oxford, UK.

Matthews, W. J., Bennett, H., Gallagher, M., & Bean, W. (1985). Indirect versus direct hypnotic suggestions—An initial investigation: A brief communication. *International Journal of Clinical and Experimental Hypnosis*, *33*, 219–223. doi:10.1080/00207148508406650

Matthews, W. J., Kirsch, I., & Mosher, D. (1985). Double hypnotic induction: An initial empirical test. *Journal of Abnormal Psychology*, *94*, 92–95. doi:10.1037/0021-843X.94.1.92

Matthews, W. J., Lankton, S., & Lankton, C. (1993). An Ericksonian model of hypnotherapy. In J. W. Rhue, S. J. Lynn, & I. Kirsch (Eds.), *Handbook of clinical hypnosis* (pp. 187–214). Washington, DC: American Psychological Association.

Matthews, W. J., & Mosher, D. L. (1988). Direct and indirect hypnotic suggestion in a laboratory setting. *British Journal of Experimental & Clinical Hypnosis*, *5*(2), 63–71.

Maurer, C., Santangelo, M., & Claiborn, C. D. (1993). The effects of direct versus indirect hypnotic suggestion on pain in a cold pressor task. *International Journal of Clinical and Experimental Hypnosis*, *41*, 305–316. doi:10.1080/00207149308414560

Meyer, E., & Lynn, S. J. (2011). Responding to hypnotic and nonhypnotic suggestions: Performance standards, imaginative suggestibility, and response expectancies. *International Journal of Clinical and Experimental Hypnosis*, *59*(3), 327–349. doi:10.1080/00207144.2011.570660

Miller, M. F., Barabasz, A. F., & Barabasz, M. (1991). Effects of active alert and relaxation hypnotic inductions on cold pressor pain. *Journal of Abnormal Psychology*, *100*, 223–226. doi:10.1037/0021-843X.100.2.223

Morgan, A. H., & Hilgard, J. R. (1978). The Stanford hypnotic clinical scale for adults. *American Journal of Clinical Hypnosis*, *21*(2–3), 134–147. doi:10.1080/00029157.1978.10403968

Niedzwienska, A. (2000). Goal-directed fantasy does not explain the training effect of the Carleton skills training package. *International Journal of Clinical and Experimental Hypnosis*, *48*, 404–417.

O'Hanlon, W. H. (1987). *Taproots: Underlying principles of Milton Erickson's therapy and hypnosis*. New York, NY: WW Norton & Co.

Page, R. A., & Handley, G. W. (1991). A comparison of the effects of standardized Chiasson and eye-closure inductions on susceptibility scores. *American Journal of Clinical Hypnosis*, *34*, 46–50. doi:10.1080/00029157.1991.10402959

Page, R. A., & Handley, G. W. (1996). In search of predictors of hypnotic sequelae. *American Journal of Clinical Hypnosis*, *39*(2), 93–96. doi:10.1080/00029157.1996.10403371

Pintar, J., & Lynn, S. J. (2008). *A brief history of hypnosis*. New York, NY: Wiley-Blackwell.

Pitsch, E., Sapp, M., & McNeely, R. L. (2001). Effects of locus of control, hypnotizability, transcript type, and gender on vividness of imagination, hypnotic depth, and inner subjective experiences of automaticity. *Australian Journal of Clinical Hypnotherapy and Hypnosis*, *22*(1), 1–10.

Sheehan, P. W., & Perry, C. W. (1976). *Methodologies of hypnosis (psychology revivals): A critical appraisal of contemporary paradigms of hypnosis*. London, England: Routledge.

Shor, R. E., & Orne, E. C. (1962). *Harvard group scale of hypnotic susceptibility*. Palo Alto, CA: Consulting Psychologists Press, Inc.

Spanos, N. P. (1986). Hypnotic behavior: A social-psychological interpretation of amnesia, analgesia, and "trance logic." *Behavioral and Brain Sciences*, *9*(03), 449–467. doi:10.1017/S0140525X00046537

Spanos, N. P. (1991). A sociocognitive approach to hypnosis. In S. J. Lynn & J. W. Rhue (Eds.), *Theories of hypnosis* (pp. 324–361). New York, NY: Guilford.

Spanos, N. P., Cross, W. F., Menary, E., & Smith, J. (1988). Long term effects of cognitive-skill training for the enhancement of hypnotic susceptibility. *British Journal of Experimental & Clinical Hypnosis*, *5*(2), 73–78.

Spanos, N. P., Radtke, H. L., Hodgins, D. C., Stam, H. J., & Bertrand, L. D. (1983). The Carleton University responsiveness to suggestion scale: Normative data and psychometric properties. *Psychological Reports*, *53*(2), 523–535. doi:10.2466/pr0.1983.53.2.523

Spanos, N. P., Rivers, S. M., & Ross, S. (1977). Experienced involuntariness and response to hypnotic suggestions. *Annals of the New York Academy of Sciences*, *296*(1), 208–221.

Spinhoven, D., Baak, D., Van Dyck, R., & Vermeulen, P. (1988). The effectiveness of an authoritative versus permissive style of hypnotic communication. *International Journal of Clinical and Experimental Hypnosis*, *36*, 182–191. doi:10.1080/00207148808410507

Stone, J. A., & Lundy, R. M. (1985). Behavioral compliance with direct and indirect body movement suggestions. *Journal of Abnormal Psychology*, *94*(3), 256–263. doi:10.1037/0021-843X.94.3.256

Szabó, C. (1993). The phenomenology of the experiences and the depth of hypnosis: Comparison of direct and indirect induction techniques. *International Journal of Clinical and Experimental Hypnosis*, *41*(3), 225–233. doi:10.1080/00207149308414552

Van Der Does, A. J. W., Van Dyck, R., Spinhoven, P., & Kloosman, A. (1989). The effectiveness of standardized versus individualized hypnotic suggestions: A brief communication. *International Journal of Clinical and Experimental Hypnosis*, *37*, 1–5. doi:10.1080/00207148908410528

Vickery, A. R., Kirsch, I., Council, J. R., & Sirkin, M. I. (1985). Cognitive skill and traditional trance hypnotic inductions: A within-subjects comparison. *Journal of Consulting and Clinical Psychology*, *53*(1), 131–133. doi:10.1037/0022-006X.53.1.131

Wark, D. M. (2006). Alert hypnosis: A review and case report. *American Journal of Clinical Hypnosis*, *48*(4), 291–300. doi:10.1080/00029157.2006.10401536

Weekes, J. R., & Lynn, S. J. (1990). Hypnosis suggestion type, and subjective experience—The order-effects hypothesis revisited: A brief communication. *International Journal of Clinical and Experimental Hypnosis*, *38*, 95–100. doi:10.1080/00207149008414504

Weitzenhoffer, A. M., & Hilgard, E. R. (1959). *Stanford hypnotic susceptibility scale, forms A and B*. Palo Alto, CA: Consulting Psychologists Press.

Weitzenhoffer, A. M., & Hilgard, E. R. (1962). *Stanford hypnotic susceptibility scale, form C* (Vol. 27). Palo Alto, CA: Consulting Psychologists Press.

Yapko, M. D. (2012). *Trancework: An introduction to the practice of clinical hypnosis* (4th ed.). London, England: Routledge.

Index

Note: Page numbers in *italics* refer to figures
Page numbers in **bold** refer to tables